Writer's Guide to Fairies, Witches and Spirit Journeys

Ty Hulse

TyHulse.com

Into the Spirit World

A dark storm bears down on the Hungarian village, rumbling with hail. There are dragons in that storm, and with it comes the people's greatest enemy – hunger. Should the storm hit their fields, the people will have another starving winter of stuffing their bellies with inedible leaves to keep the hunger away, another winter where they'll have to decide who has enough to eat and who dies. One young man still recalls the whimpers of his little sister during the last starving winter, when she lay so motionless, he'd thought she'd died. He also recalls the constant funerals and the wails of those so hungry they thought they would be next. He will not allow his village to starve like that again. He lays down as if asleep, and in his trance, his soul flies from his body in the form of a wolf to do battle with the witches, serpents, and dragons of the storm. Victory means that his village will eat this winter, but should he lose, people will starve, and many will die.

Three hundred miles to the southwest, in Italy, armies of shaman-warriors known as benandanti ride animal spirits such as hares to battle against witches who are trying to steal the life of the land. To the north, people send their souls from their bodies in the form of wolves to attack the devil at the gates of hell, before he can escape with the crop seed he has stolen from their village. Further north men send their soul from their body in the form of giant bears to assist their comrades in arms, and to the east, a man's soul battles a giant in order to rescue the spirits who bring the fish up the river or to return rain to the dry fields.

Shamanism is a life and death struggle for the survival of communities which takes place in a world of spirits, for human villages couldn't survive without battling, negotiating with, or seeking aid from powers which most people will never see. Among the most dramatic stories of European shaman's are the shaman-witch battles between different lands or against dark spirits, in which witches known by many different names in many different countries would raid each other's villages for the life of the land, for milk from the cattle, and to stop or cause storms. These same witches would protect their own villages from other witches, and the dark forces which were always seeking to steal life and destroy crops. Equally as dramatic, although less attested to in Europe, are the tales of people

3

entering the other world to rescue a soul in order to bring the dead and dying back to life and health. But, perhaps the most common reason to enter the other world was to take part in the witches Sabbath, which Pocs states was likely a remnant of the witches of old communicating with the spirits of the dead and otherworld. A way to learn magic and negotiate for their village's success. Regardless of the shaman's purpose for entering the spirit world, once there, they had to deal with its strange denizens and navigate its extensive lands. Doing so created many of the epic stories we now call myths and fairy tales.

Witches were Shamans
Europe obviously had many magical traditions, and not all of them were shamanistic in nature. That said, shamanistic traditions at least somewhat inspired the most interesting witches in Europe. Wilby states that;

> Scholars in this field unanimously acknowledge that descriptions of encounters between cunning folk or witches and individual spirit-helpers or familiar spirits are also, like descriptions of Sabbath experiences, likely to have derived from pre-Christian shamanistic visionary traditions.

Shamanism is the use of some form of trance to commune with the other world in one of three ways. The first way of communicating was via spirit journeys in which the shaman's soul leaves their body, the second was via familiar spirits in which the shaman communicates with spirit entities which assist them, and the third was via possession in which spirits possess the shaman in order to speak for them or commune with them. Almost no witches used all three of these methods for communicating with the spirit world, and in Central and Eastern Europe, most only used one.
There were many other magical and magico-religious traditions within Europe of course, such as Necromancers who summoned spirits to them, and prophets which communicated with otherworldly powers without using one of the shamanistic methods, and magicians who would mix herbs and magical formulas. But the shamanistic traditions were perhaps the most common. Such shaman's went by many names; such as cunning, witches, benandanti, talos, etc. I choose the term witch in this book to describe European shamans (despite the fact

4

that it usually only referred to evil shamans in the past with words like cunning folk referring to good users of magic) because it has become the most common term for practitioners of magic using otherworldly power within our culture.

The Spirit World

What happens in the spirit world matters, perhaps more than what happens in the mortal one. Any injury the shaman-witch receives in the spirit world is suffered by their mortal self. Worse still, however, their soul can be in jeopardy in the spirit world. This means that while the witch/shaman's body might be laying in bed, or sitting in meditation, the dangers they faced in the spirit journey were very real. What's more, the stakes were often high. Such stakes could be anything from the life of an individual to the survival of their entire village or nation.

The spirit world in which the witch shaman's journeyed was filled with numerous creatures, strange and beautiful, which could almost all be either enemy or friend. Success in their journey often depended on their ability to negotiate with these creatures, which is why fairy tales are often more about being clever than strong, for there were only a limited number of beings who could ever fight many of the monsters in the other world. Even the gods of Norse and Greek myth would often sneak past, flee from, trick, or be captured by these creatures. Indeed, I would argue that negotiation and trickery were the two most important parts of surviving the European spirit world. In a Russian fairy tale, in which the young protagonist is about to journey to meet the child-eating monster who lives at the edge of the land of the dead known as Baba Yaga, a Russian Grandmother gives her the following advice; "Now listen to me, my darlings, I will give you a hint: Be kind and good to everyone; do not speak ill words to anyone; do not despise helping the weakest, and always hope that for you, too, there will be the needed help."

In the modern day, the film that best depicts a spirit journey is "Spirited Away." As with many such fairy tales, the protagonist in this story is expected to work hard and act polite in order to survive. Yet at the same time, through her kindness, she receives help from a number of spirit creatures, and so is able to accomplish what might otherwise be impossible tasks. Baba Yaga, the aforementioned monster who commonly devoured children, would also require girls who showed up to her home to clean, weave, and perform other choirs or suffer death. Here too the protagonists succeeded not by their own skill, but by their

5

kindness and politeness to the beings of the spirit world. Such stories are common throughout Europe and Asia. The characters in these stories were rarely able to succeed or survive without help from the magical residents of the spirit world, yet these same residents were also the ones who threatened and killed them if they failed. Understanding the residents of the spirit world then is perhaps the most important part to understanding the spirit world itself, and most of these residents fall into one of four types.

First, there are the spirits of the dead or other beings that seem so human it's often hard to tell the difference. These beings farm, herd cattle, and generally live just as humans in the mortal world would, which is why understanding culture is important to understanding the nature of the spirit world. Of course, such people often live in the shadow of dragons, giants, and other magical beings which share their world in a much more obvious way.

Second are the fairy beings and deities who often have the common fairy traits I will discuss in greater detail in the following chapters. These are usually the rulers of the other world, and the controllers of human fate.

Third are familiar spirits or potential familiar spirits. These are often animal spirits that the character encounters and must befriend, but they can also be giants, people, or anything that for whatever reason has a strong desire to provide aid to the mortal traveler through their realm, or a witch seeking to cast spells.

Finally, there are the monsters of the other world. In fairy tales, the other worlds and enchanted lands are often ruled over by dragons, giants, hags, or other beasts which need to be overcome in order for the characters to obtain wealth, or even the right to continue living.

The spirit world in which these characters live is a strange reflection of our own, often so similar that it's hard to tell one from the other. There are differences, however, such as an actual monster in place of the more prosaic human lords who were simply monstrous. Of course, the presence such monstrous beings doesn't necessarily mean that an action is taking place in some other world. After all, people believed that their world could have such creatures, and it wasn't atypical for dragons to be the spirit rulers of a place within the mortal world. By the same token, an actual human ruler could appear in stories with shamanistic themes. In Selkup lore, Icha is a shaman "who rules over mice who lay his bones bare, and after he has taken advantage of his terrifying skeletal appearance and has received a tsar's daughter as his wife, they bring his flesh back to him, and he sticks it back onto his bones... and preforms other shamanic deeds." It's interesting to note in such stories that while the tsar was a real person who ruled over the Selkup, at least from a distance of thousands of miles, he and his children seem to become stand-ins for supernatural beings. This is similar to stories in England where the Queen of the Byzantine Empire might magically appear to a young knight and tell him how to defeat a dragon, just as a fairy or goddess might. This is because distant rulers were constantly being intermingled with the otherworld. Here we see evidence that people believed the other world and the human world were much more permeable than we might think in the modern day. Indeed, in many cases, the beings dwelling in the spirit world were people's neighbors, for they lived within the fireplace, the bathhouse, the backyard, and between the fields. One could, at times, enter the other world simply by walking three times round a hill in the right direction, or stepping off the path, or walking the cross-roads at Christmas. The separation between the human and the fairy world was so permeable that the people of Ireland called the fairies their "good neighbors."

Our Good Neighbors

Fairies – Owners of the Land

A gentle snow falls as you set your fish traps in the river as silently as you can. The bitter pain of hunger has long since been replaced by the raging agony of starvation, by the desperate stuffing of yourself with dirt, inedible leaves, moss, anything to make the pain of slowly starving go away. Even when you slip on the icy mud and crash headlong into the freezing water, you do your best to keep quiet. The spirit who lives in the forest behind you loves the quiet, and swearing would offend the sensitive spirit of the water. What would be worse would be to let the spirit of the cold know that you are suffering, which would serve to incur its wrath. So, without any sign of discomfort, you quietly climb out of the freezing water and finish setting your fish traps. Finally, done, you pour a little gruel, close to the last of your food into the water, and as politely as possible, explain to the spirit of the river that your family is starving and ask it to provide you with fish. As you leave your traps, you hang some fabric from a tree for the spirit within, hoping that it too will improve your luck. For you only have one hope left, that the fairies who own the land around you will take pity and share their bounty with your family.

Many people feel they are out of place, as if they are intruders in this strange world of ours. At one time, people believed that this was because they didn't live in a truly human world. Instead, they believed that our world was ruled by a plethora of magical creatures that could take many forms from dragons to fairy women. Those humans wishing to move to a new home had to fight and make peace with these magical rulers of the land, and often times, the act of making peace with the magical owners of the land could be thought of as leasing a piece of land from them. People would make offerings of food, money, or cloth to the spirits in return for the right to live and prosper in a particular place. Take for example, a story from the Ural Mountains in which some hunters discover a large lake. Upon approaching the lake, the hunters startled some water spirits on the shore. The spirits fled into the water, and the hunters thought of fleeing as well; however, when they saw how many fish were jumping in the lake, they overcome their fear and started to fish. However, try as they might, they had no luck, even with the fish jumping all around them. Eventually, they went to their elders for advice. An old man told them that they must make an offering to the water spirits if they want to fish the lake. Based on the old man's advice the hunters sacrificed a white bull and cooked it. They left some of the meat in the bushes near the lake, and the next day when they returned, they were able to catch a lot of fish. Since that time, the fish were so plentiful that people forgot the times of famine. (M. A. Созина, 2002)

Compare the above tale to a memorate from Buckow, German in which two farmers were fishing when a nix came out of the water and asked them for cloth to make trousers. One farmer refused and the other promised he would bring the cloth the next day. After he kept his word, every net that he threw into the water was filled with fish. The farmer who had refused the nix's request, however, never caught fish again. In the world of fairies, success in life was predicated on maintaining a good relationship with the spirits who controlled the land. Today, these owners of the land are often thought of as "Nature Spirits", but this term only gives a small part of the picture. In truth, the spirit owners of the land are beings, which were attached to a specific location, which doesn't necessarily make them nature spirits in the way we would think of it. As we'll see many of these fairies wanted people to be successful at farmers, manufacturing, hunting, fishing, and herding animals. In Scotland, the Glaistig were spirit owners of the land that sometimes-helped blacksmiths. In other places, they helped farmers, or even lived in people's homes and did chores. Such fairies protected respectful people who lived on their land, and as people moved in, these fairies would on occasion adopt families or even whole cities, and so they can be thought of as the spirits of human civilization and prosperity, even if they were also the spirits of trees.

In ancient Greece, nymphs became the patrons of cities and of civilization. They were the ones who taught humans about morality and civilization, and they expected humans to abide by each of these. In general, land spirits have a strong sense of morality. Thus, those that said swear words, committed crimes, bragged too much, or did unclean things within the fairies' territory were likely to be punished. Therefore, such fairies were not some distant beings, but rather entities that not only lived all around people, but also affected and were affected by human culture. Many of the ideas people retained about what they should do and how they should live were based on ideas about the spirits of the land on which their lives depended. Make no mistake: people once believed that their happiness depended on these spirits, which were often said not only to help them with their profession but to protect them from the power of evil spirits.

An especially interesting case of spirits as guardians of a region are the zmey, sort of dragon like creatures in Bulgaria. Each village in Bulgaria had its own guardian zmey, who would battle against evil lamia and hala to protect the land from drought and hail. If the zmyey was wounded in battle there would be heavy rain and hail and people would need to feed and take care of the wounded zmey, with milk, white bread, and wine. These would fight each other, and each often had hidden treasure. Those women who the zmey fell in love with would pine, suffering a form of mental illness similar in some ways to the shaman's sickness. As to whether this resemblance is superficial or not, I cannot say (MacDermott, 1998). In either case this story also shows that the guardians who protected people could also be feared.

The fact that the fairies were the original owners of the land influenced the way people believed they acted and why they did what they did. For example, in Ireland, the fairies would waltz into any home they wished at night as if they owned the place, which, since the house was on their land, they believed they did, and anyone who stayed up too late, thus preventing the fairies from exercising their right to the kitchens and hearths at night was punished. The fairies in Ireland wanted to kill one woman who was staying up late, but couldn't so long as she was handling flax for spinning thread is a magical act. So, she worked the flax until the morning cock crow banished the fairies back to their underground homes (Yeats and Gregory).

Just as they expected to be able to enter the common areas of the house, the fairies also expected these places to be kept clean. In one story, a vagabond was staying the night in someone's house where the lazy servant didn't clean the common areas properly before going to bed. The vagabond, being knowledgeable, left a little bread out for the fairies. That night, after everyone had gone to sleep:

> "Therein came in three wild-looking women to spend part of the night in comfort; but the turf had been allowed to burn out, and the hearth was unswept and comfortless. Two of them sat down while the third searched the dressed and draws for some food. But nothing was to be found" (Kennedy).

The vagabond awoke to see the fairies complaining about the servant's laziness. The fairies threw a piece of thread at the servant and it stuck inside her leg. The fairies then ate the bread the vagabond had left for them, leaving a few crumbs behind. The next day, the servant's leg had swollen to a terrible size and she was in great pain. Knowing how to cure her pain, the vagabond got her to promise to always cleanup for the fairies, to leave them a bit of bread, and then used the crumbs the fairies had left to make a poultice that allowed the piece of string to be removed from the servant's leg. (Kennedy)

There are, of course, exceptions to every rule, so there are a number of interesting stories about people violating their "probation" against staying up late and joining the fairies in their revels. In the story of Shaun Long, for example, a young worker wakes up to find ladies and gentlemen around the hearth, "discussing the merits of sundry bottles of superior whisky." These night visitors were dressed in splendidly beautiful, albeit old fashioned clothing. Each of these fairies put on a red cap and anointed their foreheads with a potion from a basin, and said:

> *"Pick up Pick up all you crumbs*
> *But touch nothing with your thumbs*
> *Hi over to England"*

They vanished, but Shaun Long managed to get a hold of this potion just before the last fairy vanished, and using his own red cap, tried casting the spell on himself, at which point he found himself in England, joining the fairies in their partying which this time took place in a rich man's house, who's food and drink the fairies stole.

In addition to believing that they had the right to people's houses at night, fairies also believed that they should have the right to a certain amount of food. In Ireland, a person shouldn't pick all the fruit and vegetables, they shouldn't take blackberries after a certain date, nor should they drink every last drop of whisky, wine, or milk – for the last bit of everything should be left for the fairies.

> "Whenever a meal is eaten upon the grass in an open field, and the crumbs are not shaken down upon the spot for their use, there they are sure to leave one of their curses, called the fair gurtha or the hungry grass; for whoever passes over that particular spot for ever afterwards is liable to be struck down with weakness and hunger; unless he can taste a morsel of bread he neither will nor can recover". (Carleton)

So, while the fairies had ultimately accepted the presence of their human neighbors, they still demanded a few things from people in order to allow them to live in peace. There is of course another interpretation to leaving the crumbs for the fairies, which is that people of ancient Greece would often leave the crumbs for the spirits of the dead. Fairies by their nature are confusing beings, and so there will almost always be multiple theories about any given fairy's nature. Regardless, however, the fairies often had certain pieces of land that they believed to be theirs and wouldn't give up, no matter what.

> "Tim Dorney's family lived by the Pooka's marsh for generations. But the man decided to drive the Pooka away and grow hay on the fairies land. In revenge, the Pooka took the form of a horse and snatched Tim up onto his back to take him on a wild ride. The man couldn't jump off the Pooka, for an invisible force held him fast. Later, when the man still wouldn't relent, the Pooka drove the man's cattle off a cliff causing him to become so poor that he lost his farm" (Hardy).

In another story:

> The building of Brelade's Church
> The place people wanted to build St. Brelade's Church was special to the fairies. So, after having dug the foundations, laid the stones, and left their tools for the next day, the workmen went home for the night. When they came back the next day, everything had been moved a mile away. The workmen tried to move everything back, but once more, it was all moved the next day. Realizing that they couldn't get any work done with the fairies working against them, the church was built on the site the fairies had moved everything to.

There are dozens of similar tales of the fairies blocking people from building on certain locations, often until the people paid the fairies for the right to build. Occasionally, this meant human sacrifice. In Germany, for example, some people were trying to build a church, but all their work was undone. So, the people bought a slave boy and buried him in a cavity at the base of the church. More frequently, animal or food sacrifices were provided in return for the right to build in a location. Still, it's obvious that people believed they needed to pay the spirits for the right to live in certain locations. Fairies needed food from humanities' in many of these tales, so it was often in the fairies' best interest to get along with humans to a point. This, in turn, often led to peace between humans and fairies. For example, the hulde of Aurland attacked any building people tried to build on a hill, pulling the buildings down and tormenting animals and people on them. However, they did allow people to grow hay on these hills, as the fairies needed hay for their own cattle, and milk from human cattle (Flom, 1949).

However, people didn't always buy the land from the fairies. Sometimes, they fought them for it. In Japan, for example, some people were being attacked by the Yato-no-kami when they tried to clear some land for rice paddies. In Japanese lore, the Yato-no-Kami appear as serpents with horns on their heads. They could not only kill people; they could curse them so that they would never be able to have children. So, angered by the fact that the Yato-no-kami were preventing people from establishing the farms they needed to survive, a hero named, Matachi, went out and slew the kami of the land, driving them up into the mountains. Above the land where the people were cultivating, he stuck a stick into the ground and declared that the kami could have everything above that, but that everything below it would belong to the humans. After this, he formed a relationship with the kami in which he would offer them rice in return for their help making the fields more fertile.

Something similar happened in Ireland when heroes with magical powers drove the tuatha de danann underground. The tuatha de danann then became sidhe, or fairies and deities. Even though humans and fairies began to act as neighbors after this, and would even make exchanges with each other, there was still some level of animosity between the humans and magical beings of a land that had been conquered. This animosity is often reflected in the stories of peoples' interactions with fairyland in such places.

While it might seem that fairies were automatically in the right in their disagreement with humans over the use of the land, (after all, from the fairies' perspective, humans came in and took what belonged to them), it's important to keep in mind that people once viewed morality very differently. Perhaps more importantly, the people who moved into a new land were often starving, and humans often viewed the right to survive as a moral right. Thus, fairies that prevented people from surviving were often believed to be in the wrong, whether they were protecting their land or not. This led to a number of battles with fairies in places where people normally respected the wilderness. The Mari-El, for example, still go into sacred groves to leave offerings for the spirits that live in and among the trees, including the Keremet. However, there are a few stories of a few times when one of the Keremet didn't reciprocate these offerings.

> For many years, people pleaded with the dark Keremet (named Shaitan) of the grove to be kinder, and to be merciful with them. The trees were lined with coins, hats, and even sacrificed horses. Even storms destroyed their crops and the people's patience turned to anger as hatred boiled in their hearts. The men grabbed up their bows and axes, and rushed into the inky darkness of the forest.
> A great battle raged in the woodland. For many hours, they fought the spirits before sunlight pierced the misty forest. Those who survived surveyed the battle scene and realized to their horror that they had been fighting and killing each other. Shaitan had beguiled them, using illusions so that they had thought friends were foes. After this, tears of sorrow flowed from the women and the earth goddess, Mland Awa. The tears flowed and flowed until a black lake of blood and tears formed which Shaitan disappeared into.

In this story, the Keremet killed the people who had moved into its land despite their best attempts to pay it off with various offerings. People had the presumption that if they made offerings to the spirits, the spirits would automatically reciprocate these offerings. The people of Japan had a similar view of the Yata-no-Kami who refused to allow people to cultivate pieces of the land, and the people of hunting cultures also held similar views. Take the komi tale of a wicked forest spirit for example:

> Once on the River Lupe, there lived a powerful man named Pera. He lived by hunting the wild game of the time, and was so fast and so strong that he could even chase down moose and bears with a spear. Although he had a cabin, he never slept in it for he felt cramped inside. Instead, he slept outside by the fire. In that time, there were many dangerous spirits in the forests, and one particularly dangerous spirit prevented all the people of a village from hunting, and stole their reindeer. So, the

14

people left him fish cakes, eggs, and other foods. They even offered him dogs, for most forest spirits love the taste of dog meat. The spirit ate all their offerings, but continued to attack them.

When he heard about this, Pera was furious, so he put on his skies, took up his bow, and went out into the wicked spirits forest (Limerov, Ulyashev, et al., 2003)

Pera ultimately defeats the forest monster by tricking him into thinking that he was asleep, when he'd really placed a pine covered log under his blanket. When the monster attacked this pine covered log, Pera ambushed the monster.

The stories of dragons as the spirits and rulers of lands and water ways are common, with people often leaving offerings for the dragons in return for the right to live on the land. Often such dragons eventually needed to be expelled in order that people could thrive and build their civilization. In these stories, people had an expectation that if they offered something to the spirits, they should get something in return. At the time that many of these stories took place, humans still lived very much aware that they were at the mercy of nature. So, when nature, or whatever spirits lived around the people weren't merciful, it sparked animosity. Perhaps one way to think of this is the rights of a King vs the rights of the serfs. During the Medieval Era, Kings owned all the land on which peasants lived, but that shouldn't necessarily have given them the right to cause people to starve to death. People fighting a greedy spirit owner of the land can be considered akin to Robin Hood fighting a greedy Lord. The lord of the land, human or fairy, might technically own the land and have a right to tax, but that doesn't mean he can't overdo it. Of course, in Komi lore, and other places such things rarely happened. Typically, the owners of the land were fairly reasonable, and willing to allow those who remain respectful the right to thrive.

Our Good and Caring Neighbors

The fairies that own the land on which people live are also humanities' neighbors, and so have an automatic interest in humanity the way we have an interest in local sports teams and our neighbors. The fairies desire to live in a good community. As such, they rewarded those who followed their social and moral

15

rules and punished those who did not. In his book on Celtic lore, Wentz states that:

> "The *gentry* take a great interest in the affairs of men, and they always stand for justice and right. Any side they favor in our wars, that side wins. They favored the Boers, and the Boers did get their rights. They told me they favored the Japanese and not the Russians, because the Russians are tyrants."

Because fairies were often believed to be responsible for people's success in farming and other endeavors, people would make offerings to the fairies for their help. This s particularly true in Wilstermarsch:

> "Every morning, the housemaids would spill milk for the underground people. Beer and crumbs from the table were also offered to them in a similar way. If the milk wasn't offered, the underground people would steal it. People wanted them happy, for everywhere they went they caused the beer brewed better. In Alversdorf, the underground people would steal pots and kettles, and cause other mischiefs. Yet they also blessed people's cattle to never become sick (remember that cattle were a primary means of wealth, so this mattered a lot). They also left magical pots for people which caused the seeds held in them to grow faster, milk gathered into them to churn richer, and water held in them to make those who drank from them healthier" (Grasse, 1868)

Fairies were constantly watching their human neighbors and thus became emotionally attached to them. There is a story from Brittany about a fairy called a margot that lived below a human's house. At first, she was leery of the people living overhead, but she listened to them talking and heard their child playing every single day for years. So, when the child grew so sick that he was dying, she was the one who provided a magical potion to cure him. In old English pantomimes, which were usually performed around Christmas time, the fairies often played the role of our protectors against evil forces (Gomme, 1890). This isn't to say that fairies were always good neighbors, for indeed, fairies were very often cranky, old neighbors. There are numerous stories about fairies attacking people for whistling when they wanted silence, as well as stories about fairies killing

16

whole families for building their home in the wrong spot, etc. Once, some fairies in Ireland punished a woman with an illness for seven years because her children threw dirty water out at dusk and hit one of the invisible fairies.

The punishment of seven years of illness seems like a bit of overkill for such a simple mistake, and indeed, fairies were often childish and vindictive. Like many cranky neighbors, fairies would seek to impose their moral values on those who lived within their community, i.e., humans. These values tended to be fairly conservative as fairies hated certain types of change and unfamiliar things. Sometimes, new ways of doing things would actually frighten fairies away. For example, in the Alps, a woman brewed beer in an eggshell in front of a fairy that was causing her trouble, and the fairy was so disturbed by the fact that she'd never seen anyone do something like that before that she actually fled.

The idea that fairies both protect us and impose values on us, which we might resent, can make them seem like a secret, invisible police which likely contributed to humanities' ambivalence towards them. Still, the fairies policing behavior is another means by which cultures came to be defined, and the belief that the fairies policed us proved useful for helping society maintain the cohesion necessary to survive. Among other things, people would give to the poor because the fairies demanded it, and act in other socially positive ways. One group of fairies in Ireland even punished a man for beating his wife by storming into the house and beating him.

Regardless, being policed by invisible creatures is probably one of the reasons that people were often afraid of the fairies. In Scotland, people would decorate their houses with holly in order to keep fairies from getting in. In other places, the last handful of corn reaped would be dressed up as a Harvest Maiden and hung up in the farmer's house to aid in keeping them (the fairies) out until next harvest. For the farmer wanted them around during harvest time but worried about the trouble they might cause during other times.

As with all neighbors, fairies and humans could begin to feud with each other, which often lead to some very horrific consequences. In France, the fairies were destroying a man's fields. So, he hid in the apple orchard, and when the fairies came into the orchard, he crept upon one of them with a large stick and killed her.

A farmer in Launenberg named Koch had several horses grow sick and die. Eventually, he discovered that his stable was over a zwerg's home and that the horse's urine was flowing down into the zwerg's home. So, the man moved his stable, and the zwerg rewarded him by giving him an endless spool of string. Often times, however, such feuds ended with the humans driving the fairies away or sending them deeper into hiding. For example, in one German city:

> "Because the young zwerg kept coming into the fields to steal peas and peppers, the Magistrate sent men to drive them away. No one knows if they remain or if they have moved to another land".

Both fairies and humans had to be leery of the other, making their relationship as neighbors tense. Fairies weren't always thrilled about having humans for neighbors, for fairies sometimes considered humans to be untrustworthy, destructive, disrespectful, and dangerous. Even so, it sometimes proved hard for them to keep hating humans regardless of what humans had done to them in the past. Indeed, there are innumerable tales about humans and fairies getting along with each other.

In one German tale, a farmer from Esebeck was plowing his field close to the forest when he smelled someone baking a cake. Feeling hungry, he wished out loud that he could have a piece. Then, much to his surprise when he plowed back to the spot, he found a beautiful cake in a bowl for him. He ate it, thanked the fairies, and continued plowing. This same story can be found in England and France, and while it's not exactly "epic," it does show that fairies and humans could sometimes have fairly normal interactions. Such normal interactions are an important motivator.

In another German fairy tale, a farmer who lived near Elliehausen knew a zwerg who borrowed a pot from him once in a while. One day, he noticed that the zwerg was pregnant and offered to stand as godfather for the baby when it was born - an offer that she took him up on. Again, what makes this story interesting is how normal the interactions between humans and fairies could be.

In Lengden, Westerberge, and other cities, zwergs would sneak into people's homes to bake bread in their ovens. The zwerg would then leave behind one of the loaves of bread as payment for the use of the oven. The notion of fairies sharing human homes was a common one, which we'll frequently visit in this book. Similarly, in Derbyshire, people would clean their homes before they went to bed, for the fairies wouldn't visit a dirty home, and people wanted fairies to visit them here since they brought good things. Some fairies even used human homes for their weddings.

> The wedding of a Puke (Germany)
> A maid had a puk who always kept the house in good order. One day, he asked her to bring a fine lunch for him and a wedding between some fairies that day.
> So, the girl brought the wondrous meal to the Hausgenoffen table, and a long parade of tiny fairies walked into the kitchen (the hauspuks natural residence). The beautifully dressed bride and groom went first, followed by many more pairs.
> At the end of the wedding, the maid's hauspuk friend carried some wood shavings in and gave it to her. The girl wondered at the strange gift but was very happy when she discovered that what she'd kept to start fires with had turned into gold.

Fairies also commonly asked humans to work for them. In France, for example, a fairy known as a margot hired a boy to herd her animals and even asked him to stand as the godfather to one of her children (Sebillot). In Norway, a huldre woman asked a human woman to watch over her cows while the huldre woman went to stand as godmother for one of her grandchildren. As it turned out, the huldre lived right under the human's front porch. The human agreed to help, took good care of the cows, and was rewarded with one of the huldre's cows at the end of the summer (Christianson, 1964).

Fairies would also attend human festivals, for example, water fairies attending human dances. In such cases, the only way to tell that the person you were dancing with was a fairy was by the wet hem of their clothes that would not dry.

Again, if one wishes to understand the fairies in many stories, one has to understand that they were neighbors to humans, so despite other issues they might have had, they often felt a connection with the people who lived near them.

I've included three additional memorates about fairies to further define the relationship between them and people.

> Trold's Cow (Denmark)
> A trold lived in a mound in Horns Field. He owned a black cow which he paid the herd boy who watched the

human farmer's cows to watch while it grazed with the other cows. The trold would leave the herd boy a plate of pancakes and two shillings by the mound. Then, one year, the farmer hired a nasty boy to watch the cows. After eating the pancakes and taking the shilling on the first day of work, he pulled down his pants and did his business on the plate. From that day on, he had to watch the cow without any pancakes or shillings.

.

Since fairies cared about humans as neighbors, they also had a tendency to help humanity. This will be made abundantly clear from many stories of the fairies, and from the fact that fairies would train witches to help the poor and the sick. The following story, however, is a great example of this kindness.

The Fairies Heal a Wounded Soldier – Abridged

Three Tyrolean solders were battling against the French and Bavarians in a mountain pass. Bullets whistled up at them from the massive army below but the Tyrolean men held their ground. A woman brought a pail of milk up to them for their lunch, the bullets still flying wildly about. While she was there the soldier she was in love with was shot in the chest. She grabbed up her jacket and tried to stop his bleeding.

While she was pressing down on his wound enemy stormed up the hill forcing the other two gunmen to fall back. As the enemy rushed past the girl remained hidden with her mortally wounded love.

Once the enemy was gone a Fairy Queen appeared adorned with a golden crown. She comforted the girl and gave her magical herbs to place on the wound. Then came a troop of Erdmännlein (fairies) who lifted the wounded man. They took the girl and soldier to a magnificent hall of crystal.

Here sat the King of the Erdmännlein, he came down to the injured man. He ran his hand over the wound and told the girl to be of good cheer for soon the gunman would be healed. The Queen then gave the girl a potion to give to the man, every now and then for some time which she did until at last he was well again.

She and the soldier that beautiful place until the man was fully healed. They were then given some diamonds from the garden and they departed. Soon after, they celebrated their wedding. (Lyncker, 1854)

Witches and Our Good Neighbors

The fact that fairies were humanities neighbors, and could care deeply about humans given the right circumstances, or could punish humans who angered them played an important part in the nature of witches in Europe. Indeed, in many cases, the witch-shamans were chosen by the fairies to help the people of their community. In Greenland, some Scandinavian settlers were starving due to a poor fishing season, so they invited a spae-queen (a volva or witch shaman figure). Once she'd seated herself in a high place prepared for her, another woman started to sing the traditional songs.

> The spae-queen thanked her for the song. "Many spirits," said she, "have been present under its charm, and were pleased to listen to the song, who before would turn away from us, and grant us no such homage. And now are many things clear to me which before were hidden both from me and others. And I am able this to say, that the dearth will last no longer, the season improving as spring advances. The epidemic of fever which has long oppressed us will disappear quicker than we could have hoped (Stephen, 1880)

Here, the spirits came to listen to the song, which acted as a means to entertain them and soften their disposition towards the people. Thus, the spae-queen was able to communicate and negotiate with them.

In Scotland, a man named Thomas the Rhymer was taken by the fairy queen into the fairy realm, where he was taught the art of divination, for the benefit of humanity. This wasn't unusual. One of the more famous witches of Cornwall, a woman named Anne Jefferies was knitting in the garden in 1645 when six fairies dressed in green came over the garden hedge. These fairies took her soul to fairyland, her body falling into convulsions. When she returns, the fairies have given her the power to heal the sick. Fairies were as anxious to help humanity as they were to obtain help from humans, and witches were a means by which they could do both while retaining their privacy.

21

The witches Sabbat, in which witches would leave their bodies at night in order to take spirit journeys where they would celebrate with fairies, ancestral spirits, and other beings, often took place near their homes. These Sabbats took two forms, those which were held by kindly fairies that wanted to help the humans of the community, and those held by wicked and vindictive beings. Of course, many fairies weren't clear cut but acted both good and bad depending upon their mood at the moment. In either case, the witches would learn magic and obtain magical items from the neighbors of their community in the spirit world. Ultimately, it is the fact that spirits cared about humans, were neighbors with humans, that is the reason we have witches at all, for good or for ill.

Domesticated Fairies

Many fairies went from being neighbors of humanity to living in people's homes and on their farms. Given that even the most wild fairies were attracted to human food, fairies that were once creatures of the forests could become house fairies. In Italy troops of fairies with animal features who normally caused mischief began to change. In one Italian tale a young widow in Casola and her child were starving from a poor harvest and nearly milkless cow.

> One night Joan couldn't sleep so she went to the kitchen, where she heard some strange noises coming from her cupboard. She walked up to it with a light, and found three buffardello inside. The buffardello told her the light hurt their eyes so she moved it away. Then she started to cry and scold them, telling them that if they stole her bread she and her child would starve.
> The beffardelli told her that if she left them alone, they would bring her some more bread, and take care of the cow. The woman did as they asked, and the next day she found a loaf of bread for her and her child. The barn had been cleaned, and the cow had been milked. The next spring her garden produced more vegetables than it ever had before (Musante, 2003)

In this tale, guilt and compassion fueled the beffardelli to become semi-domesticated. It is of course likely that the beffardelli got the bread for the woman by stealing it from someone else, as was

22

common for fairies. Indeed, much of Europe feared their neighbor's fairies, for these were always seeking to steal food and other items from them.

The connection between humans and fairies further meant that humans could sometimes hire fairies. In one tale, a Frisian man named Harro Harrsen was planning on building a home when;

> He saw a hole in a log, he realized that it would make the perfect place for a little Niskepuk to live. So he built a home, and when it was finished he nailed a board as wide as his hand to act as a trim beneath the hole. He put a bowl filled with gruel and plenty of butter on the trim and in a friendly way called, "Come, loving Niskepuk!" He didn't have to wait long for the Niskepuk's came to look over his new home, which they danced through. Only one of them - who was three inces tall - stayed, living in the hole in the pillar in Harro Harrsen's home."
> From then on Harro always made certain that the puk was given a bowl of porridge which had a large piece of butter. From then on his horses and cows were well groomed and cared for. The cows thrived, gave abundant milk and the sheep bore many lambs. All of this made Harro a wealthy man. His servant, however, wasn't as good in dealing with the Niskepuk. On day the servant went into the stable and got slapped across his face.

As this story shows, even when hired fairies were often in danger of becoming dangerous or even wild creatures. Briggs (1957) recounts the tale of one such fairy who had gone wild;

> A girl used to visit some old ladies who lived at Denton Hall near Newcastle. They had a silkie in their house. (a Northumbrian Brownie) The old ladies were very fond of their silkie. It is true that she made it rather difficult to keep servants, but if they were in a strait she would do all sorts of kind things to help them, particularly cleaning the grates and laying fires ready to light... Silkie left bunches of flowers on the staircase...
>
> The next family didn't get on with fairies, they never saw the silkie but the son of the house was so persecuted by intolerable banging's in his room that they did not stay

in the place for long. It is plain that the bronie had become a boggart.

This bond between humans and fairies is one of the most common themes about memorates on them. In the Alps, those who treated the fairies well were said to reasonably expect the fairies to watch over their cattle, protect them from the plague by adding medicinal herbs to their food, keep horses and cattle from growing sick, and more. Kropej states that;

> Like the fairies, the wild ladies and the krivopete were friendly to those who left them food as offering. They protected their homes and children, reaped wheat, and helped in other ways. Sometimes they enticed a person to perform different chores for them but in return they taught them certain skills and revealed secrets. But if people divulged this knowledge to others, upon returning home, they were punished.

Further such fairies would advise people on when to sow their grain and when to reap it. There are numerous tales of such fairies preventing famine with their advice.
Interestingly enough there were some fairies, which were so domesticated, however, that they almost seemed human, MacCulloch (1903) recounts the following.

> Fairies have sometimes been known to enter into the service of mankind, but by what motives they were actuated in so doing is not clear. A certain "Mess" Dumaresq, of "Les Grands Moulins," once engaged as a farm servant a boy who offered himself. No one knew whence he came, nor did he appear to have any relations. He was extremely lively, active, and attentive to his duties, but so small that he acquired and was known by no other name than that of "P'tit Colin." One morning as Dumaresq was returning from St. Saviour's, he was astonished, on passing the haunted hill known as "La Roque où le Coq Chante," to hear himself called by name. He stopped his horse and looked round, but could see no one. Thinking that his imagination must have deceived him, he began to move on, but was again arrested by the voice. A second time he stopped and looked round, but with no more success than the first. Beginning to feel alarmed, he pushed his horse forward,

but was a third time stopped by the voice. He now summoned up all his courage and asked who it was that called, and what was required of him. The voice immediately answered,—

"Go home directly and tell P'tit Colin that Grand Colin is dead."

Wondering what could be the meaning of this, he made the best of his way home, and, on his arrival, sent for Le Petit Colin, to whom he communicated what had befallen him. The boy replied, "What! Is Le Grand Colin dead? Then I must leave you," and immediately turned round to depart.

"Stop," said Mess Dumaresq, "I must pay you your wages."

"Wages!" said Colin, with a laugh, "I am far richer now than you. Goodbye."

Saying this he left the room and was never afterwards seen or heard of.

The person asked to deliver news to a fairy living in his house is a common story which is found from Ireland all the way into Siberia, although sometimes the domestic fairy within it is a cat, or some other being. Often these fairies were banished from the fairy court and couldn't return until a certain death occurred. Fairy justice, wars and intrigues were brutal things and so many fairies ended up needing to find their way into human homes, where they often did their best to help those who were provided them shelter, even if the humans of the home they were hiding in knew nothing of their presence or nature. Not all domesticated fairies are the same, however. As with every group of fairies there is a lot of variation in personality, background, and motivation, even if it isn't always clear from the stories. Take the common theme that domesticated fairies will tend to leave a person's service once they are given clothes. In Germany, for example, a Nörggelein entered the service of a man as a goat herder, demanding only a piece of bread that had been buttered on both sides as payment. The man eventually decided to give his fairy goatherd some clothes, but this made the goatherd so happy, delighted he jumped about with childish glee, and left the house never to return. Other fairies are wild at heart and grow offended when given clothes, still others feel that once they have clothes they are too fancy to continue working, and others have been banished from the fairy courts until such time as they can obtain the gift of clothes for their service to people. Finally, of course there are domesticated fairies who demand clothes and cloth to make clothes as payment for their services.

Such differences come about because each fairy has a different reason for choosing to work for people. Some of them had been banished from the fairy courts and could not return until they labored for humans for a set amount of time, others were the ancestral spirits of a family or a home, still others were the spirits of a place who moved in with people, and of course there were also the wild fairies who came into people's homes seeking food, and others are refugees hiding from wars between fairies. Each of these fairies would have different motivations and personalities.

Culture the Key to Understanding Fairies

The fact that people believed fairies were their neighbors, means that people often believed that fairies shared a similar culture and political structure to their own. Perhaps more importantly fairies are an important part of our cultural heritage and central to many folk religions. This is why understanding a particular fairy requires an understanding of the culture that that believed in it. This is a circular notion, however, for to understand a culture one needs to also understand the fairies they believed in. After all, folk religion is an important part of any cultural identity. Consider Joan of Arc's village, Domremy, a fairly typical village in Medieval France. Like most villages in France, it was near a tree and spring of water where the fairy women were believed to gather.

> "Sometimes she (Joan of Arc) went to take a walk with the other girls and she made near the tree crowns of flowers for the image of Our Lade of Domremy... She saw young girls put garlands on the branches of the tree." (Sullivan, 1999)

These children then danced and sang round this tree for fun. During her witch trial, Joan of Arc claimed that she didn't associate these activities with fairies; however, many other people did. Even the mayor's wife, Aubery, had seen the fairy ladies gathering around the tree where the children played. Thus, the holidays which Joan celebrated as well as the games

26

she played as a child were related to the people's beliefs in the fairies. While the Clerics at Joan of Arcs witch trial made a big deal about her visiting the fairy tree and the activities around it, it wasn't really. Nearly every town and village had similar places. Trees and springs of water which were considered to be a focal point for the fairies dotted the landscape and acted as one of the centers of people's lives. (Sullivan)

While reading mythology, keep in mind that the most important use of mythology was to reinforce morality and social norms. For example, in Medieval England, people were often generous to the poor partially because the fairies and god demanded it. Another example can be found in every hunting culture I've studied, where there were spirits who would punish people who bragged about their success while hunting. This belief in spirits made people humble, which helped to create stronger social cohesion that lead to a better chance of survival for the community as a whole.

The importance of this belief in fairies/spirits to people's cultural survival meant that such beliefs permeated and affected nearly every aspect of people's lives. Often times, fairies were a reflection of people's hopes and fears. So, because of this, one shouldn't simply look at what fairies did in fairy tales; one also has to look at how people acted in response to their belief in fairies. For while many fairy tales take on a darker edge and are even considered horror stories, people didn't necessarily act like they were constantly afraid of fairies. Just like in Joan of Arc's village, people might tell horror stories about fairies, but then seek them out for blessings and healing, for while everyone likely heard fairy tales, such stories were secondary to most people's experience. For most people, fairies were a constant presence. It's not only telling that people celebrated under and around fairy trees, but they would often go to drink from the fairy waters to be cured of illnesses. This tells us that despite many of the horror stories about "wicked" fairies, people perceived their relationship with at least some of them as mostly positive.

What we see from the fairy tree and waters near Joan of Arc's village, the English who would pantomime helpful fairies, and the hunters who would leave gifts for fairies is that there was a separation between the stories people told and the way they believed fairies interacted with them in their daily lives. This is true in the modern day as well. We tell horror stories about, and are afraid of serial killers, but most of us will never encounter

27

one, and will have neighbors who are friendly or at the very least aren't murderers.

Joan of Arc would later express a wish that she could continue to spin wool with her mother, a common activity for girls in France at this time. Based on this, one has to wonder if there were any Holda figures roaming the countryside near her. Holda was a fairy/goddess from the nearby Alps who would reward girls for working hard at their spinning by giving them gifts, much like Santa, while brutally punishing messy and lazy people. It's likely that the people of Joan's village believed that there were fairies similar to the lutins living in barns and houses within her community. These fairies brought luck and punished those who broke social conventions, possibly even those they heard swear. Such fairies also had a huge impact on the way people lived their daily lives. Although it doesn't necessarily relate to fairies, it's also interesting to remember that the idyllic scene of village life that Joan painted was contrasted with the fact that her village was subject to numerous raids by bandits and enemies during the Hundred Years' War. Once, the village of Domrémy-la-Pucelle was even burnt to the ground. With that, we see that people still lived and celebrated their lives even though they were in the midst of one of the most brutal wars of the medieval era.

During Joan of Arc's time and before, people even chose where their villages, homes, and fields would be located based on their belief in fairies. In fact, in the past, people would often look for signs that the fairies who already lived in a particular place would accept them before they moved to a new place or built a new home. Signs that the magical owners of the land approved of them varied from region to region. For example, in some places, people looked for ant mounds while others would camp in a desired location to see if they would be disturbed by spirits during the night. If they didn't sleep well, it was a sign that the spirits didn't want them there. Other times, people would ride horses or bring animals through an area to see how the animals responded to it. What's important to understand is that each place had spirits already living there when people moved in, and people wouldn't build in places where the fairies didn't want them. Ireland, Mari-El, and other places are filled with patches of wilderness in the middle of farms where people believed the fairies didn't want them to plough. Furthermore, the professions people took were often related to their belief in fairies and similar beings. For example, people in far Northeast Asia would sometimes refuse to begin reindeer herding because the spirits there would be offended if they domesticated something which was meant to be wild. To a certain extent, the Irish believed that milk and bread was practically sacred; thus, their farming efforts focused on these until the English killed most of their cattle and forced many of them to shift to farming potatoes. This method of food production had a huge impact on the way the Irish lived.

> The population was scanty and shifting, and settlements were scattered and largely impermanent. The economy was predominantly a pastoral one, with great herds of cattle... wandering over tracts of waste... frequent raids, and petty warfare placed a premium on mobility, and the indifferent quality of much of the land also encouraged Transhumance... the movement of cattle to summer pastures on mountain slopes (Ellis).

While the Irish likely believed in milk-obsessed fairies because of how important cows were to them, rather than choosing to raise cows because of a belief in milk-obsessed fairies, in a fantasy world, fairies very well could have dictated the type of food people would grow/raise. Furthermore, it's possible that their belief system caused them to resist changing the way they lived. In parts of Japan, the women would tell stories and make jokes while planting rice because it would lure the kami out of the mountains whose presence would help the rice to grow. In the stories of some places, these kami enjoyed raunchy humor, while in others, the kami were often easily embarrassed. So, the type of jokes developed and told in each region was partially based on different peoples' ideas about their local kami. Similarly, the people along the Amur River told stories when the men went out to hunt in order to lure woodland spirits into their huts to listen to them so that they wouldn't stop the hunters from being successful.

> Dmitrii Zelenin suggests that folktales were originally a kind of magic, told to entertain and distract forest spirits, so that hunters would be rewarded with game. In certain parts of Russia and Ukraine, telling tales or riddles is prohibited in summer, when sheep bear their young, which Zelinin interprets as the desire to keep potentially harmful spirits away from domesticated animals (Johns, 2010).

There are numerous other examples about how songs, stories, and holidays were important to the relationship between people and fairies. For example, in Ireland, fairies would kill the cattle that stepped onto their hills; however, one man played such beautiful music for the fairies that he earned the right to herd his cattle on the hills (Wentz). Within a fantasy world, we can see how the personality and tastes of local magical creatures would have a huge impact on nearly every aspect of a people's lives.

Nearly every activity that fairies engaged in was viewed through various cultural social lenses. For example, before the invention of matches, it was extremely difficult to light fires under certain circumstances, and because of this, sharing fire was a very common activity. Thus, it was common for fairies to want to sit by and share fires with humans, just as humans did with each other. Fairies would even sneak into people's homes in many countries including Germany, France, Ireland, England, and Russia to sit by the fire. Even in Japan, there are tales of fairies asking to enter peoples' homes to sit by the fires. Elle women from Denmark were typically nervous around people, yet in one tale:

> There was a man burning charcoal in the forest when an elle woman came along and pulled up her dress to warm herself by his fire. He thought he should stoke the fire a bit for her and started poking it with a stick.

The sharing of fires with magical creatures is a common theme in colder climates - so common, in fact, that it sometimes seems like fairies couldn't light fires. Although this is a stretch, given how often mythology indicates that fire was a gift given to humanity, it's possible that people once believed that some fairies didn't have this gift and thus couldn't start fires of their own. Regardless, what's important to understand is that because fire was an important part of people's social lives, it was also an important part of the fairies' interactions with humans, for fairy and human lives were a reflection of each other.

In mythology, human culture often came directly from the fairies. For example, in Greek mythology, it was the nymphs who took humans in and taught us about morals and the difference between right and wrong. Similarly, in British and Irish folk lore, it was the fairies who punished people for being greedy, and in Russia, it was the domovoi (house fairies) who punished people for acting immoral. In all these cases, human morality and cultural protocols were all believed to be based on the desires of fairies. Fairies also taught humans how to make cheese, how to smith, metalwork, and more. Kropej stated that in Slovenia:

> It was believed that fairies gathered at dusk and at nighttime and danced, sang, or strolled through the fields. Wherever they lingered they brought fertility and prosperity. According to some tales, it was the fairies who taught people to sing and dance; this role was assumed also by the Fates. In the vicinity of Varaždin, Matija Valjavec recorded the following story: The Fates were three beautiful, tall, slender, and very strong women. They only seldom appeared at childbirth. Most frequently, they let themselves be seen by girls they had taught to spin and sing, but when the girls started to whistle, the Fates hid from them as well.
> Mankind learned to sing from the mermaids. All the beautiful hymns that are sung in our churches are the work of mermaids who are also responsible for other pretty songs.
> The divja žena (wild lady) taught people how to tie the vine during plowing. Under the rocky mass live the wild women. When they see people are having a hard time they willingly offer their help, and according to some tales, the blacksmiths had learned how to forge from Šembilja.
> The belief that fairies possess special knowledge about the healing powers of plants and objects, in addition to the ability to heal people and animals, is not only widespread in Slovenia, but throughout Europe. (Kropej)

In addition to all the things that fairies have taught us, notice that fairies would also flee from whistling. This could explain why whistling indoors has come to be considered unlucky in many Slavic countries. In any event, if you wish to understand the motivation of a fairy from fairy tales, you should try to understand the culture the story came from.

31

What Are Fairies?

Before digging any deeper into the nature of fairies, let me define what exactly I mean by the word 'fairy'. After all, this word has meant a number of different things to different people. For this book I define the word fairy as a magical being which purposefully manipulates human fate for good or ill, but who do not live in the heavens, hell, or some distant land. Rather, fairies must be humanities neighbors. They must care about what happens to humans, either for good or ill. This does mean that fairies can include a wide range of beings from ancestral spirits to nature spirits and fallen angels. This wide range of possible fairy origins was often discussed by people of various folk religions who saw fairies as each of these beings as well as other creatures. This definition doesn't include devils and angels which live in heavens as well as deities which live in the heavens or underworld, but it can include deities who live alongside humanity within the forest.

It is perhaps worthwhile to add to this definition the common notion that fairies both needed and feared humanity. Fairies might have been incredibly powerful, but so too could humans be. As a result, there is an interesting push and pull between humans and fairies in which they both sought help from and feared the other, they both wanted the other around but wanted the other to leave them alone. This means beings like giants or dragons, who didn't need humans, wouldn't be fairies. Those giants and dragons who did need and fear humans might be, however.

Humans Needed Fairies and Fairies Needed Humans

Beyond just the fact that fairies were humanities neighbors, fairies took an interest in humans because they typically needed humans as much as humans needed them. In other words the relationship between humans and fairies was both symbiotic and antagonistic. For just as humans couldn't survive without fairies, fairies could not survive without humans. Strange as it might seem the fairies needed humans to help them with tasks which we might consider extremely mundane, tasks such as cleaning, herding cattle, and crafting simple objects such as tea kettles and buckets. Menefee (1980) stated that "fairy objects often lack substance, their food can in truth be leaves." What's more, she pointed out, is that fairies often seemed unable to

32

mend their own tools or make things such as ovens or kettles. So, they needed to borrow such tools from humans. This isn't always the case, of course, there are even some places where people would pay fairies with food to mend and build objects for them. Still, there are numerous tales about fairies receiving help from humans with many tasks ranging from midwifery to the use of horses. Briggs (1961) for example, recounts the following story:

> One farmer got on good terms with the pixies. Later, when a church was put in with bells, one of the pixies asked the farmer to borrow his horses to move his family out of range of the sound of the church. The farmer let the horses and the pixies moved to Winsford Hill. The horses were made younger when they were returned.

In other stories, fairies utilized human buildings:

> A woman learned that laumės started frequenting her sauna. "Well, let them do, they are living creatures anyway, so let them bath", she thought. Afterwards, whenever she heated her sauna, she would leave some hot water to laumės. They must have appreciated her goodwill because they rewarded the woman, and each time they would leave her some gifts in the sauna - a nice piece of linen, a towel, or something else – all very skillfully made (Bugiene, 2014)

While in Cornwall, even the wicked spriggans who robbed and killed humans paid a woman with a small coin to use her house as a meeting place and hideout. One night, however, she decided that she could have more. So, while they were dividing up their stolen treasures, she turned her shift inside out, jumped out of bed, and grabbed a gold cup. "Thee shusn't hae one on 'em!" The woman exclaimed, and the spriggans had to flee without their treasure. They did, however, manage to curse the woman so that whenever she put on the shift she would suffer horrible pain (Hunt).

What fairies seemed to crave most of all was human food. This craving was often so strong that it seems that perhaps the fairies couldn't survive without human food. It's also thought that fairy women were often unable to suckle their own children, hence their desire to secure a human wet-nurse (Briggs, 1961).

Even a fairy queen who was sick needed to steal milk from a mortal's cow in order to get better. Wentz stated that:

> The fairy queen was "fretting her life out for want of some milk that has the scent of green grass in it and of the fresh upper air."

Fairy Queens were wealthy. In many stories, they tended to have piles of treasure and magic, yet they could not survive without milk provided by human cows in this memorate. This explains why fairies so often steal from humans or ask for offerings of bread, milk, or other foodstuffs. In fact, whole tribes of fairies would move in order to gain access to human food.

> The Trold Leave Denmark (Denmark)
> East of Hjorring was a mound with trold in it. People would often see these trold dancing at night. However, one of these trold told a man that they were going to move.
> "Why?" The man asked.
> "We can't survive here anymore," the trold told him. "You see the trold have been surviving by stealing food, but people have started putting a cross over everything so we have to move or starve to death."

Without the ability to take human food, the trold in this story were starving to death, indicating how much they needed humanities' food. Because humans were so much more capable of what we would consider mundane tasks it was common in fairy tales for fairies to hire human help, to herd their cattle, to babysit their children, and to clean their homes. It is also common in fairy tales for a creature that is obviously a forest spirit to offer to purchase a person's services with gold or to kidnap people to do work for them.

Finally, it was commonly believed that fairies were diminishing, growing weaker with each generation, and so had trouble having healthy children. This meant that they commonly sought to have children with humans. In the Tyrol Alps there were fairy women who would take attractive looking farmhands in order to have offspring with them (Heyl). This was a common reason for fairies throughout Europe to kidnap humans, as breeding stock in order to have healthier children, for the fairies were dwindling in physical strength.

34

Fairies Feared and Needed Humanity

Beyond just the fact that fairies were humanities neighbors, fairies took an interest in humans because they typically needed humans as much as humans needed them. In other words, the relationship between humans and fairies was both symbiotic and antagonistic. For just as humans couldn't survive without fairies, fairies could not survive without humans. Strange as it might seem, the fairies needed humans to help them with tasks which we might consider extremely mundane, tasks such as cleaning, herding cattle, and crafting simple objects such as tea kettles and buckets. Menefee (1980) stated that "fairy objects often lack substance, their food can in truth be leaves." What's more, she pointed out, is that fairies often seemed unable to mend their own tools or make things such as ovens or kettles. So, they needed to borrow such tools from humans. This isn't always the case, of course, there are even some places where people would pay fairies with food to mend and build objects for them. Still, there are numerous tales about fairies receiving help from humans with many tasks ranging from midwifery to the use of horses. Briggs (1961), for example, recounts the following story:

> One farmer got on good terms with the pixies. Later, when a church was put in with bells, one of the pixies asked the farmer to borrow his horses to move his family out of range of the sound of the church. The farmer let the horses, and the pixies moved to Winsford Hill. The horses were made younger when they were returned.

In other stories, fairies utilized human buildings:

> A woman learned that laumės started frequenting her sauna. "Well, let them do, they are living creatures anyway, so let them bathe," she thought. Afterward, whenever she heated her sauna, she would leave some hot water to laumės. They must have appreciated her goodwill because they rewarded the woman, and each time they would leave her some gifts in the sauna - a nice piece of linen, a towel, or something else – all very skillfully made (Bugiene, 2014).

While in Cornwall, even the wicked spriggans who robbed and killed humans paid a woman with a small coin to use her house as a meeting place and hideout. One night, however, she decided that she could have more. So, while they were dividing up their stolen treasures, she turned her shift inside out, jumped out of bed, and grabbed a gold cup. "Thee shusn't hae one on 'em!" The woman exclaimed, and the spriggans had to flee without their treasure. They did, however, manage to curse the woman so that whenever she put on the shift, she would suffer horrible pain (Hunt).

What fairies seemed to crave most of all was human food. This craving was often so strong that it seems that perhaps the fairies couldn't survive without human food. It's also thought that fairy women were often unable to suckle their own children, hence their desire to secure a human wet-nurse (Briggs, 1961). Even a fairy queen who was sick needed to steal milk from a mortal's cow in order to get better. Wentz stated that:

> The fairy queen was "fretting her life out for want of some milk that has the scent of green grass in it and of the fresh upper air."

Fairy Queens were wealthy. In many stories, they tended to have piles of treasure and magic, yet they could not survive without milk provided by human cows in this memorate. This explains why fairies so often steal from humans or ask for offerings of bread, milk, or other foodstuffs. In fact, whole tribes of fairies would move in order to gain access to human food.

> The Trold Leave Denmark (Denmark)
> East of Hjorring was a mound with trold in it. People would often see these trold dancing at night. However, one of these trold told a man that they were going to move.
> "Why?" The man asked.
> "We can't survive here anymore," the trold told him. "You see the trold have been surviving by stealing food, but people have started putting a cross over everything, so we have to move or starve to death."

Without the ability to take human food, the trold in this story were starving to death, indicating how much they needed humanities' food. Because humans were so much more capable of what we would consider mundane tasks, it was common in fairy tales for fairies to hire human help to herd their cattle, to babysit their children, and to clean their homes. It is also common in fairy tales for a creature that is obviously a forest spirit to offer to purchase a person's services with gold or to kidnap people to do work for them.

Finally, it was commonly believed that fairies were diminishing, growing weaker with each generation, and so had trouble having healthy children. This meant that they commonly sought to have children with humans. In the Tyrol Alps, there were fairy women who would take attractive looking farmhands in order to have offspring with them (Heyl). This was a common reason for fairies throughout Europe to kidnap humans, as breeding stock in order to have healthier children, for the fairies were dwindling in physical strength.

Fairies Feared and Needed Humanity

In much of European lore, the deities rose up and killed the children of the first beings who in turn, had already oftentimes killed their parents as well. With such a violent past, it's no wonder that the deities worried that humans might rise up and kill them. This is why Plato held that Zeus split the originally four-armed and dual-souled humans and made them weaker, out of fear of the humans' strength. Fairies, too, desire to keep secrets from humans. For in the same manner that they will capture us to be their spouses, so will we take them out of greed for their treasure or to fulfill our own lustful desires. Indeed, there was a dwarf who told humans directly that we were mortal and weak due in part to our "faithlessness" (Grimm, 1882). What we see is that fairies believe humans to be their treacherous relatives, so it is possible that the secrets of many forms of magic have been concealed from humans simply to keep us from being even more dangerous. What's more, humans had uncanny magical powers that terrified the fairies.

A trio of fairies had gone down a chimney to enter a house one night, as the fairies normally did. On this night, however, they found that they'd lost their natural power to vanish. All at once, for the first time in their lives, they found themselves trapped. They looked around in horror to find out what was happening and discovered that they were being thwarted by magic greater than their own. It wasn't a wizard, nor a great witch, or warrior. Instead, a little boy was staring at them from the shadows, and so long as he was looking at them, they lost all their magical powers. Imagine how creepy this would be for the fairies to find out that a mere human child had enough power to prevent the fairies from vanishing. This isn't the only story where this happens either. There are numerous tales about humans being able to prevent fairies from vanishing or using magic by staring intently at them. Humans in lore have many natural magical powers, and most of them are designed around battle and thwarting fairy kind.

Briggs indicates that, in many ways, humans are uncanny to fairies; after all, humans can use iron and magical symbols to harm fairies. Sometimes the fairies take advantage of this. The little Wood Wives of Germany, for example, were defenseless against the Wild Huntsman who would chase them down and slaughter them like deer. These Wood Wives would turn to humans for protection, for the humans could make the mark of a cross on the stumps of trees that would keep the Wild Huntsman away from the tree so that the Wood Wives would have a place to hide within (Grimm, 1935).

Humans in lore had many means of driving and keeping fairies away. On entering the forest, Russian peasants would utter a protective prayer to keep the leshii (forest king) away. In ancient Rome, humans could drive away the spirits of nature with a broom, showing the power of civilization over nature. Later this idea would be replaced in part by showing the power of Christianity over nature, but the idea itself remains that civilization could overcome the spirits of nature, that humans had power over something magical.

When one Fairy Queen ordered her servants to kidnap a child and leave a leprechaun in its place, they found that they couldn't lift the baby because of a simple needle in the child's clothes, which to the fairies appeared as heavy as a massive beam of iron. Instead of kidnapping the child, the fairies settled with bestowing gifts on it, making her the grandest lady in the world, the greatest singer, and the best mantle maker. The Fairy Queen, however, promised that if the girl ever left her house, she would turn into a rat. So, although the fairies could still leave a curse, they couldn't move the power of iron.

In Scandinavian lore, the Bäckahästen was a fairy who could spirit away things of value, turn into a pile of sticks, a group of maidens, a pack of dogs, a child, or appear as a horse in order to trick children into riding him so that he could pull them into the water and drown him. However, even a child could thwart this powerful fairy by simply throwing a piece of steel between it at the water (Wigstrom, 1881). In another case, a man blocked the doorway into Fairyland by sticking an iron knife into it so that no fairies or fairy magic could move it (Briggs, 1967), while a shepherd captured three powerful hags from Czechoslovakia known as Yezinkas because they were unable to move when they are struck by a human with brambles (Lawson, 1910).

In addition to iron, magical objects, and symbols, humans have the power of the evil eye; that is, we can cause fairies to lose their powers or to be cursed merely by looking at them. It's not just our ability to use magical items, then, that gives us power. It's also the fact that humans seem to have certain magical powers naturally, even if we're not aware of them. In Scotland, children run around rings but are careful never to run around the same ring nine times in a row as this would give the fairies power over them (Atkinson, 1891). What we see from this is that sometimes humans have a natural protection against the fairies, which can only be surrendered by performing certain acts.

All of these human powers cumulated in a series of wars. When the king of the fairies kidnaped a young man's wife, he had workers dig up the fairy mound, although the fairies kept filling in their work. Eventually, however, it was discovered that putting salt in the hole they had dug would keep the fairies away. "Then the young lord knew he had power over Finvarra," the king of the fairies, and so he and his work crews dug on. Eventually, they could hear fairy music, and they knew they were close. "See now," said one. "Finvarra is sad, for if one of those mortal men strikes a blow on the fairy palace with their spades, it will crumble to dust, and fade away like the mist." It was at this point that the king of the fairies, Finvarra, even with all his powers, had to return the young man's bride (Wilde, 1902).

Jacob Grimm pointed out that, physically, humans lie somewhere between the realms of fairies and giants. While fairies hold power and sway over us, they stand in awe before us (Grimm, 1882). It is relatively common in mythology for humans to capture leprechauns in order to steal their treasure, or to threaten the lives of tree fairies to force them to provide us with fertile fields. Furthermore, some reports also say that fairies abduct humans to strengthen their sickly line (Briggs, 1967). This shows that not only are humans physically stronger than fairies, but also we are close enough to bear children with them. Fairies themselves are not afraid of losing their powers by bringing human blood into their line because humans can gain the powers of fairies as Merlin did, but fairies may always be physically weak and never able to use iron.

Fighting for Fairies

Because of humanities uncanny powers, it was commonly believed throughout Europe that fairies would use them to defend themselves from greater enemies. In Ireland, humans were often recruited to fight for fairy armies against other fairies, for in a fairy war, the side with humans would win if the other didn't have humans with them. In Wales, a human was recruited to slay an enemy which the fairies could not. While in Germany, the medieval book "Heldenbauch" indicates that human heroes were created to protect the dwarves from giants and dragons.

Common Fairy Traits

There are a number of common traits which fairies have in story after story. Of course not all fairies shared all these traits, but most had at least some of them. In order to understand the denizens of the spirit world, it is important to understand these traits.

There are a number of common traits which fairies have in story after story. Of course, not all fairies shared all these traits, but most had at least some of them. In order to understand the denizens of the spirit world, it is important to understand these traits.

Enforcement of Morality

Considering fairies were our neighbors and nosey members of our cultures, it shouldn't be too surprising that they were also enforcers of social norms. In Norway, for example, there was a young man who would constantly go out hunting, instead of working at home like he should. One day he heard two trolls in the hill talking, with one asking to borrow a large cauldron from the other so that she could cook the man who never went home. The troll then chased the young man down the mountainside and back to his home.

This story provides a picture I find amusing, that of two older trolls, sitting together watching their neighborhood go by. Perhaps they have pictures of people they care about up on their equivalent of a fridge. There is another aspect to this story about two old trolls gossiping together about the community around them. That the trolls are watching humans and animals, and care enough about our comings and goings to ensure that we continue to follow social norms. Indeed, fairies seem to have been completely obsessed with morality. In Dartmoor pixies were known to pinch lazy people who didn't get up in time. Further, the pixies hated untidiness with dirt and dust being "abominations" to the pixies, and so people were careful to keep their homes clean in order to avoid punishment and obtain reward from the fairies (Crossing, 1890).

The exact morality of fairies differed from place to place. In one place, it might be that they would punish those who drank, while in another they might punish those who didn't on certain holidays. The fairies would commonly punish loud whistlers and bad singers, or those who threw their water out without warning, for being invisible, they might get hit by this. What's important to understand is that fairies reinforced cultural norms, explaining why they hated cursing. The fairies also demanded hard work but hated greed. Further, the fairies were people's neighbors, so they hated it when people did things that would annoy any neighbor.

Fairies are Childish and Mischievous

> Girl and the Childish Zwerg (Tyrol, Austria)
> A peasant girl was in a church wearing a wild rose behind her ear. A zwerg came along and asked for the flower, but the girl refused the request. Angry, the little man tried to take it by force. He reached for the flower, and the girl slapped his hand away. Furious, the zwerg bit her fingers. The bite bubbled, and the wound didn't heal for a long time. Eventually, a strange node formed on her fingers, which never went away. Indeed when the girl married and had children and grandchildren, they all had the same strange node on their fingers as well.
> (Lyncker, 1854)

Reading fairy tales, one can't help but notice how childish fairies frequently are, almost as if some of them are never truly able to mature. This has something to do with the nature of immortal beings who were born ancient from the beginning and so never truly got to have a childhood. It may also be a result of the fact that so many of them were associated with the spirits of dead children. Percht would lead a troop of fairy-like creatures that lived in the hills. These creatures were in truth the spirits of children who didn't have a name. Such spirits of children craved and sometimes needed to be accepted by humans.

> In Percht and the Cottager, a man went out to search for a godfather for his newborn child. He encountered Percht and her company of children. One of them was wearing nothing but a ragged undergarment. Full of compassion the man said, "oh, you poor Zodawascher."
> Percht responded, "Since you have given the child a name, much good fortune will be yours." Percht vanished, and the man found a rich sponsor. (Smith, 2004)

The immaturity of fairies causes many of them to act in a manner that is almost like a child without parental supervision. The Norggen would in Germany would tease the livestock, mix the peas with the flower, the beans with the barley. When it got dark, he would giggle gleefully as they ran about the houses causing trouble while invisible (Lyncker, 1854). There are numerous other tales, especially from central and southern Europe, about fairies who pull the covers off people's beds, tickle their feet at night, and engage in all sorts of other mischiefs. It is true of course that some of the mischievous fairies may actually be the children of fairies, but it's likely that most of them are fully grown, but are unable to fully mature. Indeed, the stories of fairy mischief are among the most common tales. When the villagers in Germany held festivals and carnivals, the dwarfs would amuse themselves by seeking to outsmart them. When some young men held a grand ball, the dwarfs didn't want to let the opportunity pass without some prank. So three of the dwarfs snuck into the party and pretended to be humans in order to steal the pig that was going to be used for the feast (Jergerlehner, 1907), making the fairies seem like goofy children having a slumber party rivalry.

> Fairy Prank (Germany)
> Two men were walking beside a stream on a gloomy night. Suddenly they heard a voice crying out for help

from the water. So the two men ran to the place where they thought they heard the person drowning, but to their surprise, they heard the voice higher upstream. So they ran upstream a bit more, and the same thing happened. They followed the voice nearly the whole night, all the way up the mountain. Exhausted, they collapsed to rest when they heard a bright laugh. Furious at having been tricked, they stormed back down the mountain.

Part of the reason that fairies might be so mischievous is that much of their magic involves the ability to create illusions and mess with people's minds. In the Shetlands, for example,

> "Tangi had the power of casting a spell over people and animals, which made them insane and led them to drown themselves by jumping over cliffs into the sea. This spell, I have been told, was especially potent if he ran in circles around people."
> One man being attacked in this way struck tangy with an iron knife, breaking the creatures' enchantment. The tangi then ran off in a blue light and disappeared (Teit, 1918).

In Newfoundland, there were people who the fairies caused to hallucinate that they were lost in a vast forest, even as their friends watched them walk around in circles. Fairies didn't just use these powers to torment people. In fact, they sometimes used them to protect their home by making people unable to see the entrance or by causing people to think their own homes were on fire when they were searching for the fairies. Others could use these powers as a form of punishment.

> Once, a person who had lost his way offered him (a Wisp) two silver groschens if he would lead him home safely. The will-o'-the-wisp agreed, and finally, they arrived at the lost man's house. Happy that he was no longer in need of help, he thanked his guide; but instead of the promised payment, he gave him only a small copper coin. The will-o'-the-wisp accepted it, then asked if he could now find his way home by himself.

> He answered, "Yes! I can already see my open front door," but when he stepped toward it, he fell into some

water, for everything he had seen had been only an illusion.

The will-o'-the-wisp takes special delight in tormenting drunks making their way homeward from a fair or an evening of drinking. He leads them astray, and when in their drunkenness they can go no further, preferring instead to sleep off their binge out of doors, then he burns them on the soles of their feet. In some regions the people believe that will-o'-the-wisps are the souls of children who died without being baptized. They are seen especially atop graveyard walls. They disappear when one throws a handful of graveyard soil at them. (Haupt, 1862)

Fairies are Often Shy

Being naturally shy, I almost can't bring myself to clean when there's someone in the room with me. I can't entirely explain the reasons why, but I would rather clean alone than have help. In college, I couldn't clean productively if my roommates were home, so I waited until they were all gone to do it. Such forms of shyness are something that humans often feel, at least to a point. It is also a trait that people believed we shared with the fairies, as shown by the following quotes.

> "Her son is never there when we come around but you see him hiding behind the door or running off into the woods... People say he's a changeling and the fairies took the real one away..." (Rieti, 1991).

> "Near Witzenhausen it was said that the fairies were small, benevolent people. They helped with the reaping of the fields and the threshing of the grain. They also blessed people, but they stopped returning when they realized that people might be spying on them" (Lyncker, 1854).

Such stories about fairies fleeing when they discover they are being spied upon are repeated over and over again in folk tales. These show that fairies were often extremely shy, and such shyness isn't necessarily unknown to people. Many people are more afraid of public speaking than they are of death. To some extent, we all are likely to understand feelings of awkwardness and being judged, as well as the anxiety of being around certain other people. Nearly everyone has felt the desire to hide, to duck away in certain social situations. For fairies, this desire, like almost all their emotions, can become so intense they can hardly stand it. This feeling can be so intense, in fact, that often when these fairies are spied on, they'll sometimes fly into a rage, killing the person who spied on them or fleeing from the place, never to be seen again.

There is some utility to the fairy's shyness, for humans can be dangerous to them. Fairy tales are filled with stories of humans robbing, killing, and kidnapping fairies out of greed, lust, hate, or simply as a means of showing off. Therefore it makes sense for fairies to want to avoid too much contact with people. There is another aspect to the fairies shyness, however, which is the natural desire to keep spiritual and sacred things secret or private. This is especially well documented among the Saami where according to Ørnulv Vorren;

> The second figure shows a fell in Finnmark. It lies near Sieidde-javri and is called Vaddasbakte in the Saami language, in Norwegian Offerberget, —and was reported to be a holy mountain by the missionary Isach Olsen as early as about the year 1700. This mountain, too, has a wide deep crack running across the top of it. Report has it that nobody should say the name of mountain when passing it or else there would soon be bad weather and storms.

When a researcher named Marten asked about a wooden idol he was told that he was "too young and stupid, and it was too important a matter" for him to learn about. While another man suffered a horrible pain in his leg that required long term treatment because he told a researcher where a sacred site was. Such horrible pains in people's legs as punishment by the fairies, probations against saying the name of fairies are common throughout Europe. At least some fairies certainly are remnants of similar deities and ancestral spirits to the ones the Saami worshipped.

British witches too were often forbidden from speaking about their relationship with the fairies. Alison Peirson was told by the fairies that should she speak of them they would kill her. Similarly, another witch named Bessie Dunlop said that her familiar had told her never to speak of him (Wilby). Such strict codes of secretiveness are indicative of the shaman's experience, and so shamans would often have to share their knowledge of the spirit world and the spirits within it through stories, in other words fairy tales.

Wicked Fairies

> "A Fairy appeared before him, and from that moment on, he could not find peace any more. The fairy was following him like a shadow, even when he ate or slept. Neither the priest nor the witch doctor could help him. Totally deranged, he was finally found stabbed in a cave." (Kropej)

Fairies very often represented people's fears. This was truer in some places, such as Newfoundland, where stories of fairy kindness were rare, and tales of people taken or tormented by them were common. Regardless, no fairy is completely good. Recall my mention of Perchta would cut people open to stuff them full of garbage for such minor offenses as not being fast at spinning? Such horrific overkill in their punishments is common place. Take a tale from Connacht, Ireland as an example:

> "To his horror he saw that the fairies were preparing as meat for the feast an old woman, whom they were skinning as she hung from a hook. He was told she was a miser and had a bitter tongue, hence her fate." (Westropp, 1921)

Yes, this sort of story goes along with the fairies' role as enforcers of morality, but the extremity of the punishment, and the horror that the people in these stories feel indicates that people still feared the fairies might go too far. This might explain why other stories portray certain fairies as nothing but wicked.

> "From Islay comes the story of a malevolent fairy. A brother and sister were going along a road by a loch when a little man came running past them and touched the boy as he passed. The boy was paralyzed for the rest of his life. His little sister, who was wearing green was uninjured... strange to find green considered a

46

safeguard. It is usually a dangerous color." (Briggs, 1961)

Worse was a story of fairies from Guensey Island, while lies between Britain and France. This tiny land has some of the most terrifying tales of wicked fairies who sought to kill off the people on the island.

> "Guernsey's alleged witches were accused of communing with the island's pixies and were thought to congregate at prehistoric burial sites. The most notorious pixie was Le Barboue, or Old Bluebeard, said to wheel a barrow of parsnips angrily around the parishes of St Pierre du Bois and Torteval. To appease the pixies, Guernsey folk would leave a bowl of porridge out at night. Mostly, this seems to have worked. Reports of pixie attacks have decreased since the 1600s." (Tunzelmann, 2013)

In another story:

> "They (the fairies) then deputed him to be the bearer of a message to the men of Guernsey, summoning them to give up their wives and daughters, and threatening them with their heaviest displeasure in case of a refusal. Such an exorbitant demand was, of course, with one accord refused, and the Guernseymen prepared to defend their families and drive the bold invaders from their shores. But, alas! what can poor mortals avail against supernatural beings! The fairies drove them eastward with great carnage. The last stand was made near Le Mont Arrivel, but, wearied and dispirited, they fell an easy prey to their merciless enemies, who put every soul to the sword. Their blood flowed down to the shore, and tinged the sea to a considerable distance, and the road where this massacre took place still retains the memory of the deed, and is known to this day by the name of La Rouge Rue. Two men only of St. Andrew's parish are reported to have escaped by hiding in an oven. The fairies then entered into quiet possession of the families and domains of the slain; the widows began to be reconciled to their new masters, the maidens were pleased with their fairy lovers, and the island once more grew prosperous. But this happy state of things could not last forever. The immutable laws of fairyland will not

allow their subjects to sojourn among mortals more than a certain number of years, and at last the dwellers in Sarnia were obliged to bid adieu to the shady valleys, the sunny hills, and flowery plains, which they had delighted to rove amongst and which their skill and industry had materially improved. With heavy hearts they bade adieu to the scene of their fondest recollections, and re-embarked. But, since then, no Guernsey witch has ever needed a broomstick for her nocturnal journeys, having inherited wings from her fairy ancestors, and the old people endeavor to account for the small stature of many families by relating how the fairies once mingled their race with that of mortals." (MacCulloch, 1903)

While it's normal for fairies to attack humans in order to obtain mortal women or men, what's unique about this story is that the fairies actually won this war, compared to most similar stories where it is the humans who win. It's also interesting to note that after this, the humans of Guernsey were part fairy and thus had magical powers. The people of Guernsey were terrified of fairies, causing them to execute over a hundred witches for they believed them to be conspiring with the fairies during the era when Salem, Massachusetts executed less than thirty. Throughout Europe, people avoided places where fairies were reputed to be after dark for fear that the fairies would attack, torment, or kidnap them. A record of deaths from Lamplugh, Cambria between 1656 and 1663 lists four people as having died by being scared to death by the fairies. Exactly what this means isn't clear, but it is clear that people had reason to fear encounters with the good folk.

Inverted

As much as fairies reflect human culture, they also mirror it, in that they will often react or act in exactly the opposite way a mortal would. One fairy women celebrated at a funeral, for she could see that this was the beginning of the deceased's afterlife. Fairies themselves have a strong connection to this afterlife. This is important because the land of the dead in lore was often thought to mirror the mortal world in an inverted, upside down, or poorly reflected way. The fairies were very similar in that their world was backwards. When people wanted to avoid fairy attentions, they would put their shoes on backwards or turn their clothes inside out. According to Monika Kropej;

> Inverted body parts, clothes turned inside out, and branches that have been twisted in the wrong direction are all signs of the fairy world. The Resian kodkodeka, or korkodeka, denoted the wild woman. Kodkodeka was always doing everything differently from others. At the time of acute drought, when everybody yearned for rain, she went to the river to launder her clothes, and loudly begged for the sun to dry the feathers in her pillows. Perpetually on bad terms with everybody else, she finally got tired of everything, set Stolvizza on fire, and left across the Kila mountain. (Kropej, 2014)

The introversion between humans and fairies could explain part of the conflict that people believed we had with each other. Certainly in lore the forests are often depicted as strange and weird places. In Mari-El there are hag figures who sit and clap while laughing, whose feet are turned backwards, who rip the flesh of their bodies to use as weapons. It is further common in Siberia and through into Russia for fairy figures to make things dirtier the harder they clean.

Fairies Need Respect, are Emotionally Sensitive, and Dualistic

Fairies are obsessed with respect, to the point that they will give incredible blessings to those who offer them the least little bit of it. As opposed to this they will curse and sometimes kill those who forget to offer them the proper respect.

> Saami Stuorra-Piera (Big Pete) who lived about the middle of last century; he is reported to have always made a point of sacrificing to the sieidde whenever he passed with his herd in the course of his wanderings. One year he omitted to do so and his herd stampeded and died in a bog. Garra-Rastus (Tough Rasmus) took part of a reindeer horn that lay on the ground and as a result his lead reindeer immediately ran away when it was set out to graze at the next resting place. On another

occasion when some nomad Saamis rested by the
offering stones, one of them spat on the sieidde and then
his best lead reindeer disappeared. It was found again
the following autumn as a pile of bones (Vorren)

A more dramatic story about how violently fairies react to
disrespect comes from Tryol in Southern Austria and Northern
Italy. This story is also a good example of the duality of fairies,
and how when angered they can sometimes turn into monsters
the way a werewolf can. The story is about the Alputz or
Kasermanul who in some stories can appear as a kindly old
man:

Abridged tale of Almputz or Kasermanul and the Lost
Children (Tyrol, Austria).
One icy cold winter's day, a poor mother asked her two
children to gather firewood. While they were at the edge
of the woods, a blizzard swept down from the mountains.
Unable to see through the wind whipped snow, the two
children were soon lost, stumbling through the forest.
Finally, after many hours, they met a friendly little man.
He took them to his home, built a fire for them to warm
themselves, and served them delicious rahmmus* (a hot
cream based desert). At first, the children were afraid of
the strange little man, but by and by, they came to trust
him.
After eating the Rahmmus and some white bread, they
said their prayers and the little man gave them a little
bed where they slept warm until the sun was high in the
sky.
When morning came, they rubbed their eyes and the
little man served them breakfast. They said their
morning prayers and ate the most wonderful white bread
they'd ever eaten. They were so hungry it seemed like
they hadn't eaten in months.
Once they had eaten, the little man gave them some
bread for the road and helped them re-gather their
bundle of wood.
On their way home, the children were surprised to
discover that despite the previous storm the road was
clear of snow. When they got home, their mother turned
pale with fear for she thought that they were ghosts as
they had been gone all winter. It turned out that rather
than just sleeping for one night, the children had slept

50

the whole winter through in the little man's hut. Once the children explained what had happened, however, there was great joy in the house, a joy that became greater when they discovered that the they'd been given bread that had no end. (Heyl, 1897)

In this story, the Almputz was a perfect grandfather figure. However, the truth is that he was more frequently a creature to be feared for rather than appearing as a kindly old man, the Almputz appeared as a wild, black horse with red eyes who would attack and murder those wondering the mountains.

Abridged Tale "Three Hunters and the Almputz"
Many years ago three hunters were caught high in the mountains when night came. They found an empty hut, made a fire and began to make crude jokes. Eventually one of them took a large piece of wood, wrapped it in some dirty rags and called it the Almputz. They put a hat on it and bacon its mouth and started laughing at it. The youngest of the hunters, however, didn't join in. Indeed the others jokes made him uncomfortable for he feared punishment for their arrogance. Finally, after they had used the piece of wood to mock the almputz for a long time they poured some brandy on it.
A loud angry crashing rose up outside, along with the sound of thunder. Terrified the youngest hunter jumped into the haystack. The other two, however, didn't seem to take any notice of the storm outside and continued to mock the wood.
The Almputz stormed into the hut and tore the head off the rudest of the men, then put it on the roof of the cabin as warning. The Almputz spared the youngest for he had done nothing wrong. (Alpenburg, 1857)

There are many similar tales about normally kind fairies turning dangerous as well as fairies who were dangerous turning kind when people show them respect. Indeed, the fairies could often be said to be two creatures at once. Indeed, fairies and deities almost seemed to be their own opposites. This is perhaps best exemplified by Yeat's belief that the cannibalistic far darrigs were leprechauns in a more destructive form. The far darrigs were one of Irelands vampire like monsters who would hypnotize people in order to compel them to aid in capturing and devouring other people. These fairies, who change from a kindly to a monstrous form when upset show that fairies were more than just emotionally sensitive. Their freer nature, their ability to change shape meant that they were dualistic, able to be both monster and kind.

The duality of fairies and supernatural beings is further shown in Hont County, where Kollar reports that children would throw their baby teeth behind the stove and call out, "Jenzibaba, old woman, here is a bone tooth for you, give me an iron one for it." At the same time, however, Jenzibaba would attack and kill people, and would at times devour children. There is a whole host of these hag/fairies that were both dangerous and helpful, and which sometimes even had a beautiful and an ugly form. For example, Perchta would cause healthy births, bring Christmas gifts, take care of the spirits of dead children, and at the same time, kill, blind, or cut people's stomachs open and stuff them with garbage (Johns, 2010).

Similarly the Bean-nighe "portends evil but if anyone who sees her before she sees him gets between her and the water she will grant him three wishes... Anyone bod enough to sees one of her hanging breasts and suck it may claim that he is her foster-child and she will be favorable to him. Of course, her task of washing the clothes of those about to die isn't evil this still shows that a person can easily turn her from this purpose and completely change her nature.

Many deities and fairy creatures are like this, beings with multiple purposes who are mutable. They can be kind and cruel, helpful and harmful, all depending on their mood and how they are treated. This mood shift is often more extreme than that of mortal humans, for the fairies and deities seem to have multiple forms the way a werewolf might. The kind and helpful bwca who aid Welsh people in house, but who can to turn into monsters known as boggarts are most illustrative of this idea. This duality is an important part of shamanism, which I discuss more in the section on hags and deities.

Common Fairy Backgrounds

Briggs (1957) divided English Fairies into six categories: Trooping Fairies, Solitary Fairies, Nature Fairies, Hags, Monsters, and Magicians. To this, I'd like to add Ancestral Spirits, Familiar Spirits, and Forgotten Deities. These aren't the only way to think of fairies, but Briggs has been the foremost expert on British fairies, so it is worth mentioning her ideas.

Trooping Fairies are the fairy courts which have kings, queens, nobility, and, of course, peasantry. Briggs divides this court into the Heroic (the aristocrats) and the Homely (the peasants). Heroic fairies are most often seen hunting, riding, listing to music, dancing and engaging in the other activities of the aristocracy of medieval Europe whereas homely fairies are the ones who, according to Briggs, were interested in agriculture.

Heroic Fairies: The aristocracy of fairyland - the Kings, Queens, and nobility. They hunted, rode in procession, sang, danced, reveled, and listened to music.

Homely Trooping Fairies: The most common in English tradition.
They are agricultural people interested in domestic order. They steal and punish eavesdroppers at times, and are grateful for kindness and cleanliness.

Nature Fairies: The most likely to be owners of wild places. There are not many of these well attested to in England and Ireland as these fairies are better attested in Northern and Eastern Europe. In the lore of the Komi people, their head deity, Jen, divided the world between various masters of the land. These masters of the land had their own hierarchies with a sort of king of a forest or lake, and smaller regions of the forests ruled by lesser lords of the forest. Additionally, there were also rulers of each species of animals. In Eastern European lore, these rulers of the land acted much like feudal lords, waging wars and making treaties with each other. The spirits of the forest would also often wage war on the spirits of the water for these beings hated each other.

Solitary Fairies: Fairies that live alone or in small family units, which haven't been domesticated.

Tutelary Fairies: Fairies which are attached to human families. This simply means that they are house fairies who have either been domesticated nature or solitary fairies, or which are ancestor spirits, such as banshees.

Magicians: Fairies such as Morgan Le Fee which may, in fact, be fallen deities. It's difficult, however, to know exactly how they fit into any existing political system, if they do at all.

Hags/Monsters: Monsters that are similar to solitary fairies or nature spirits. They tend to live alone or in small groups, and exist outside the main law, or under their own law, much like bandits.

Former and Lesser Deities: Our world is filled with deities that people have forgotten. There were deities in Britain who likely got subsumed when the Celts came. Deities who were likely subsumed when the people who built Stonehenge came, and deities who simply lost their place over time. As Odin or Hermes might appear to random people, so too would there likely be stories of some of these deities, stories which could remain even after the belief in them had faded.

Ancestral Spirits: The spirits of the dead. As we've seen, it's difficult in the folklore of most of Europe to separate ancestral spirits from the trooping fairies. It seems likely that in some cases, the ancestral spirits would join with trooping fairies, yet in others, they appear to have their own separate courts from each other.

Even though there are distinctions between different categories of fairies, it's not always clear which fairies belong to what order, or exactly how they are aligned. Lina Bugiene stated in regards to Lithuanian fairies known as laume that:

> "Some time ago, whenever one stepped out at night, one was bound to encounter laumė. There were lots of laumės around! People used to hear them laundering during the warm summer evenings... Sometimes laumės helped the women, who used to work hard in the fields: in the meantime, laumės would come to their homes, bath their children, spin, or weave their linen. But there were also wicked laumės. These would kidnap human children. Laumės also have some trickster features, and human encounters with them can end up both positively or negatively, depending on the capacity of the humans to handle these beings. Laumės are quite akin to the nature spirits of other national traditions, but their

54

precise affiliation is difficult to establish. They are close to forests, waters, and stones; associated both with the earth and the sky." (the rainbow in Lithuanian folklore is called laumėsjuosta' laumė's sash'). (Bugiene, 2015)

The Laumes then have many of the same traits as trooping fairies elsewhere, as well as associations with tutelary fairies and, of course, with nature fairies, though it isn't clear what type of nature fairy they might be. In most cases, it's difficult to state the exact political structure of such fairies, and it's worth bearing in mind that even if the Laumes are all nature spirits, that doesn't mean they agreed with or got along with each other. Among the Slavic, Komi, and others, the primary divide was oftentimes between water and forest spirits who would constantly fight wars with each other. Here too, the forest Kings lived like feudal lords and would make treaties, party, and fight with each other the same way that human feudal lords would. In other words, the same fairy might belong to multiple categories or might be unique enough that it's hard to imagine they belong to any category. Further, there are far more categories that Briggs mentions. These include familiar spirits and former deities.

Familiar Spirits

Shamanism has been a part of humanities' cultures for a long time and was, at one time, the most widespread religious phenomenon outside of the belief in spirits and deities, (Winkelman, 1990). Those people who lived in shamanistic cultures presumed that there were magical creatures who wanted to teach people magic, to work for people, and to guide them. In England, these shamanistic helping spirits are often referred to as familiar spirits and are frequently fairies. Indeed, the fairy-like nature of these helping spirits is common throughout Europe.

> "Cunning Woman, Karin Persdotter... learned sorcery from a male water spirit referred to as 'the man of the stream,' 'the neck,' or 'the river...' nature spirits could be understood as more tangible, more available, and more inclined towards direct intervention in the material world." (Petersen)

Similarly, Thomas the Rhymer of Scotland was taken into elfland, and when he emerged some years later, he had gained the power of prophecy and, interestingly enough, the inability to lie. While in Russia, it was commonly believed that some witches learned magic from the forest King known as the leshii. These people would be taken by the leshii and returning years later with moss in their hair, and nature spirits whispering magical secrets in their ears.

In their roles as helping spirits, fairies could act as both the dreams and fears of the desperate. People could become rich by obtaining a helping spirit; yet, at the same time, obtaining such a spirit often came with great dangers. Further, sometimes, a person might have a spirit attached to them by accident. In Russia, for example, a woman was continuously taken into the woods at night by a leshii after she picked up an object she'd found on the ground which had his spirit connected to it. After that, she was never able to get rid of him regardless of how much she seemingly wanted to. Shamanism and witchcraft are closely associated with the idea of familiar spirits in general.

> Spirit guides are perceived as crucial to the shaman's resolve and power - literal embodiments of his psychic and magical strength. There are two basic types of spirit guide. Firstly, there are spirits which are substantially under the shaman's control and which serve as his familiars. But there are also other spirits - though of more as guardians or helpers - who are available when he needs to call on their aid. These may be minor deities, or the spirits of deceased shamans: entities who maintain a certain independence in their particular realm, and who are not automatically subject to the control of the shaman. Siberian shamans generally have animal helpers like bears, wolves, and hares, or birds like geese, eagles and owls. Yakuts, for example, view bulls, eagles, and bears as their strongest allies, preferring them to wolves or dogs - the spirits of lesser shamans.
>
> Hoppal, :Nature Worship in Siberian Shamanism:

Not all familiar spirits were obtained by shamans and witches, however. In Germany, people often obtained fairy helpers as servants. With one of the most common servants being the puk.

56

Puk typically appeared as little men with pointy red hats who perform choirs, help cattle and farms to thrive, and (at times) steal treasures for the humans they worked with. There were a number of ways of obtaining one of these helping spirits, one of which was to go out on New Year's night and walk the boundaries between seven different fields without looking back or speaking. The owners of the land, which often became house fairies, often lived within these boundaries, which is why building in them was dangerous because by doing so, a person was destroying a fairy home.

Another way to get a puk was to obtain an egg laid by a black hen and keep it from seeing the sun or moon. Then, when the egg hatched, a little man would come out. The newly hatched puk would need to be carried under the armpit of the person seeking its service until it was mature. Thankfully, like most fairies, puks grow up quickly and are often fully developed within a day.

In a tale originating near Prague, a woman had a black hen which laid a black egg with red spots. She threw this into the compost pile, and eventually, a little man known as a Sotek was hatched from it. This man helped her cows thrive so that she became rich. There were many times, however, when a puk would simply show up and demand that a person give them work. The puk could be so obsessed with working for humans that one puk kept tormenting a man for work long after it had made him wealthy. The puk would rush off and finish each job before the man was able to take his next breath, then it was back, violently demanding another job, never giving the man any peace. When the man wasn't fast enough at thinking of another job for the puk to do, it would beat him and drive him into the corner. Soon, the puk had summoned an army of his fellows which all went about violently attacking the man. Despite this, most fairies weren't so violent about demanding work.

Similar to the notion of the puk was that of the Nordic' butter cat.'

> In olden days before this time, there were people who sold themselves or half of their souls to the devil for a considerable sum of money. They made a "butter cat" in order to get more milk. The "butter cat" looked like a ball of yarn. It stole cream and butter from the neighbor. The neighbor could not understand what had become of his butter. But he soon discovered that people who had only

a few cows had a lot of butter. He chased after the "butter cat" and if he could capture it, the person who had sold his soul to the devil would die. (Tartar)

One man, hired to guard a vineyard in Italy summoned, a folletto (a tiny magical person) and offered the folletto some grapes to watch the vineyard for him. The man then went off and went to sleep while the folletto stood watch. Fairies often worked for humans in return for some pay which was usually food, fabric, or money. Just as often, if not more often, however, the witch was believed to work for the fairies, rather than the familiar spirit for the witch. Sami too might obtain the help of a fairy without having to be a witch.

> When the Lapp has reached adolescence and has some task to do in the woods, then the spirit of divination comes to him and makes his appearance, singing a song which the Lapp must remember. The next day the Lapp walks to the same place. If the spirit of divination wants to remain with him, it comes to the same place, makes its appearance again and sings. [...] If the spirit of divination wants to stay with the same Lapp, the Lapp has to sing the same song that he has learned from the spirit of divination. Spirit of divination comes to him whenever he so wishes" (Hultkrantz).

These spirits called sueie are little people, and a Saami could have as many as 4, 5, or 9 helping them. Such guardian spirits are likely connected to many of those who provide aid in fairy tales, such as Puss in Boots.

Others would take control of their fairies through violence or the threat of it. For example, a man named Tohms built a nest in a place that was perfect for a niskepuk. When the niskepuk came to that place and fell asleep, he captured it. He then threatened the nixkepuk with his knife, demanding that it serve him from then on. Despite this rough start, Thoms was careful to always respect the niskepuk from then on, and gave it offerings of food. In return, the niskepuk helped him prosper, and the two of them eventually became close friends.

The close friendship between certain humans and fairies occurs repeatedly in memorates with one of the most interesting being about an old woman and a kobold.

Kobold Gossip

In Bischdorf, there lived a wealthy old woman who had a kobold. They would sit all day near the heath and talk together, and sometimes the neighbors would hear them through the windows. Every once in a while, the kobold would ask the lady if she wanted anything, and she might request a gold chain or a bag of money. A moment later, the kobold would fly up the chimney to retrieve the desired treasure.

Kobolds, in this case, were little men who could turn into dragon-like creatures, and who would often serve people to steal from the neighbors. Others would have some animal that would help them with the same, with a cat or hare being most common.

Among the Skolt Saami each kinship group was accompanied by an animal spirit which was handed down from father to son and mother to daughter. Normally invisible, it could be seen by shamans, but it would protect those it followed regardless of whether they were shamans or not (Hultkrantz). Other Saami believed that there were spirits of sacred mountains which guarded them.

Spirits of the Dead

It is well established that fairies have a strong connection to ancestral spirits, and indeed many fairies are likely to be such. Indeed, people often saw among trooping fairies the faces of people they knew who had died.

> Some European peasants, says Jacob Grimm, believe that the dead "belong to the fairies, and they, therefore, celebrate the death of a person like a festival, with music and dancing. (Spencer, 1917)

Witches who entered fairyland would often encounter the spirits of the dead. One can sight many, many different examples of this idea that the spirits of the dead and fairies were connected. Spencer certainly comes to this conclusion in his book, as does Wentz. Campbell, however, points out that there were numerous stories "which show that according to popular belief, fairies commonly carried off men, women, and children who seemed to die, but really lived underground. In short, that mortals were separated from fairies by a very narrow line."

This line could blur and vanish altogether, especially when it came to the heroic dead. "Shamanistic ideology includes a feature according to which the souls of shamans or worthy persons become, after their death, guardian spirits for those still living, thus acquiring a status different to that of ordinary mortals in the 'other life'" (Bäckman, 1975)

This notion, of great people becoming guardian spirits was common throughout Europe; certainly, the Ancient Greeks and Romans had it. Further, the Russians and Germanic people's had ancestral spirits who lived within their homes and helped to care for the farm. Ancestral spirits such as the tomte who are commonly thought of as fairies today.

Even the trooping fairies, and their kings were strongly associated with the spirits of the ordinary people who had seemingly died.

> A man named Hugh King went with the fairies to a fair on November eve
>
> The fair, which was filled with a crowd of people he had never seen on the island in all his days. And they danced and laughed and drank red wine from little cups. And there were pipers, and harpers, and little cobblers mending shoes, and all the ;most beautiful things in the world to eat and drink, just as if this were in a king's palace...
>
> Then Finvarra showed up and after teasing Hugh a bit some dances came up and began dancing round Hugh, trying to get him to dance with them.
> Finvarra told Hugh to look wel at the people dancing and Hugh realized that these were people he knew who had died before.
> (Wilde)
> Another woman out on November Eve saw a young man named Brien who had drowned the year before. He warned her that the fairies were coming "and amongst them were all the dead who had died as long as she could remember."
> Brien warned her to run for if they drew her into a dance she would never be able to leave...

60

It's important to point out that while some of the fairies were clearly the spirits of the dead, not all of them were. Angels and the spirits of the dead both dwell in heaven, the spirits of the dead, deities, and various other beings dwell within the Greek Underworld. Vallhalla is home to the Asgardians, the Valkaries, and the spirits of the dead at the same time. Thus, it was common in Europe for the spirits of the dead to dwell with many other supernatural beings. Ellis Davidson stated in 'The Lost Beliefs of Northern Europe' that; "There is certainly a link between the Vanir and the land-spirits who dwelt in mound sand hills and in water, supernatural beings who befriended some of the early settlers in Iceland." This last point is important because there were no people, and no spirits of the dead in Iceland when people first showed up, but there were spirits in the mounds and rocks. Later the spirits of the dead would enter these to dwell as well. It is therefore likely that the spirits of the dead dwelt with the Vanir and the spirits of the earth in Nordic lore. What all this means is that it seems likely that people believed that there the spirits of the dead shared their home with other supernatural beings. It is also quite possible that people confounded and mixed up multiple ideas as often happens over time. Certainly, in the modern day we have started to associate with poltergeists what people once associated with angry spirits of the earth and fairies.

Fairies as Deities

In their role as enforcers of morality, as the ones who helped the crops to grow, as those who advised and blessed the heroes of fairytales, it's easy to see fairies as diminished deities. Of course, it's also true that Greek, Roman, and Siberian Pagan societies had both divine and semi-divine beings. That is, in addition to the higher gods, they had nymphs and their ilk. Right up to the modern day, Greece and Italy both believed in creatures very similar to nymphs. These were water women who had been diminished to be dangerous, but which nevertheless are still recognizable as the nymphs. Germany has the Nixie, while Scotland has the glaistig. It is easy, therefore, to imagine that many of the fairies are semi-divine beings, rather than the shadows of full-fledged deities. Yet some of them clearly are deities, or at least have old stories of deities woven into theirs.

Gwyn ap Nudd, the king of the Welsh fairies, is the lord of the underworld, and Briggs states that he "is clearly a Celtic Plato," who in addition to his many jobs was sometimes said to protect humanity from devils which he locked away in the underworld. One should also consider the importance of deities in their lesser forms. Zeus, for example, took the form of a snake to protect people's homes, acting very much like a house fairy might. Similarly, Celander and more recently Eldar Heide have argued that Loki was connected with the fairy-like beings known as Vatten.

> In many parts of Sweeden and Norway, people attributed the crackling or whistling of fire, or the sudden flare of fire from the embers, or the blowing of ash to the Vatten... In Telemark, Norway, as Celander points out, some of these phenomena were attributed to Loke. (Heide, 2011)

In this case, it's conceivable that Loki was always connected with these otherworldly creatures. Certainly, he is stated in mythology to have been born outside the tribe of deities. It's, of course, difficult to reconcile the idea of Loki as a house spirit, and a helper with the best-known myth of him, but keep in mind that a single myth doesn't necessarily indicate what everyone or even the majority of people believed about him. Further, it's important to keep in mind that deities and fairies were dualistic beings. They could be their own opposites, becoming the monster they were meant to protect people against.

Folk Religion, Deities and a Divided Cosmology

Dorcey states that;
> Silvanus emerges as one of the most venerated deities in the Roman Empire... only Jupiter, Hecules, Fortuna, and Mecury eclipse Silvanus in epigraphic terms. Silvanus' known adherents are more numerous than those of Diana, Apollo, Liber Pater, Aesculapius, Venus or Mars.... Yet he Stood completely outside the public cult. He had no state temple, festival or holy day.

> Religious beings like Silvanus are of "little concern to the elite society." Senators and equestrians were not very

interested in him and failed to include him in the state colander. The lettered aristocracy rarely mentioned the god in their writings...

We see this same pattern repeated over and over again. Major belief systems of the lower classes and country people are ignored by those writing about society. Scholars didn't start recording the fairy beliefs of immigrants in America until the twentieth century. Those writing records didn't notice the benandanti until they'd been around for hundreds, possibly thousands of years. Societies have what amounts to two sets of religions, that of the elite and highly educated members of society, and that of the lower classes. This second religion, the folk religion, is the one which believes in fairies and so is the I'm most concerned with. Folk religion is a difficult thing to pin down, in part because a society could have many different folk religions. (Evidence of Shamanism in Russian Folklore Jason Edward Roberts, MA. The University of Texas at Austin, 2011) States that "there were probably as many panthea as there were Slavic Tribes... Slavic shamanism would, however, have a bearing on the way in which indigenous Slavs interacted with their gods. It is perhaps the term "god" itself which most impedes an understanding of ancient Slavic cosmology."

Nilsson in his book on the folk religion of ancient Greece points out that while the cities had come to focus on philosophies and deities such as Zeus "the old faith survived without being disturbed and where the people kept the rustic customs, celebrated the old festivals, and venerated the gods and heroes without doing much thinking about the high gods.... The situation was different elsewhere, especially the cities, where religion had to encounter political life..." In other words, the politics of cities often changed the nature of religion, as did wealth, nobility, and philosophical thinkers. Therefore, what we think of as the ancient Greek religion, was primarily the religion of the cities, with the countryside having a similar but separate belief system.

Accordingly, Roberts argues that one shouldn't look classical era religions of the Greek city and of Rome, which were made for societies with large cities to understand Slavic, Germanic, and Celtic religion. Rather one should look to the Sami and similar shamanistic people and their "shaman pantheons." In looking at shamanistic religions such as the Saami, one finds that the shaman's job is to act as a mediator between the human the spiritual world while the spiritual world's primary purpose was to provide for human's survival.

> The task of the god or seidi was to help the Lapp in the hard struggle for existence; if he was not able to do it, he was worth nothing.... Sacrifices were offered to him according to the principle "do ut des" (I give in order that you may give?

Again, Dorcey points out that "Silvanus was a forest and agricultural deity." When looking around to what deities could do for them, those of cities had little need for the help of such a spirit, while those of the country were dependent upon him, and perhaps saw themselves as living on his land.

This dichotomy of folk religion and state religion is important to understanding the nature of fairies because many fairies are the deities of the folk religion, which have either been retained long after the high deities were forgotten, or are the high deities that have become the localized beings of folk religion.

Loki is a good example of the differences between larger mythology and folk religion in ancient times, and how a belief in a deity could be retained long after his religion had been replaced by another. Heide (2011) points out that;

> It seems there were two Lokis. One was a vatte 'domestic spirit' living under or by the fireplace, helping farmers with the farm work and attracting wealth to the farm. The other, the mythical character, was very different but still derived from the vatte, and many loki myths allude to the vatte.

In essence Heide states that Loki in folklore during the Late Medieval and up into the early modern era was seen as a god of farming and a helper in the house. He was a trickster figure from folklore who helped the deities and humanity come out on top. Yet in the mythology written by a highly educated man who took the stories from the rulers of Iceland, Loki was a treacherous being who would bring about the downfall of the gods. This, of course, is partially due to the ability of deities to be good and wicked at once, but it also seems that the elite of Iceland and the peasants of Scandinavia had some differing views on Loki.

Since many early societies, especially those of hunter-gatherers and small clans had a smaller or even no real elite class, it could be argued that they were all adherents of folk religion. Thus, their pantheon wasn't structured as a noble caste the way that of more stratified societies would be. Perhaps, more interesting for our purposes, I believe that the cosmology which would survive the coming of new religions and the conquest by foreign peoples would be the folk cosmology of the lower classes. After all the conquered people would tend to be in the lower classes, and of course, the lower classes, as Robert so rightly pointed out would still have been concerned with day to day survival, as much if not more than the larger philosophical questions of religion. If they believed that they needed to give bread to the fairy lord of the forest in order to hunt, they would do so. This is borne out by the fact that such rituals continued right up into the modern era. It wasn't until we saw a more extensive system of modern education, more stability, and new ways for the poor to earn a living that we saw rituals designed to appease fairies start to vanish.

This secondary folk religion is where spirit journeys and the ideas of a mediator between the human and spirit world exist. For the upper class, cosmology tended to have priests who only occasionally went on such journeys and interacted with the deities. Further, in folk religions, people often believed that these deities shared the world with them, at least in part. In the stories of folk religions, deities could invisibly share feasts with a village and could live within the mountains, rivers, and the forests. Yes, they might also dwell in heaven and hell, but journeys to encounter and manipulate them could also take place within our own world. There are two spirit journeys about people encountering the spirits of the land which are especially interesting. In the first, Egil placed a curse on the guardian spirits of Iceland so that they would no longer protect his enemies (the king and queen of the nation). To do this, he picked up a hazel branch and put a horse head on it. "I direct this insult against the guardian spirits (known as landvaettir) of this land so that every one of them shall go astray, neither to figure nor find their dwelling places until they have driven King Eirik and Queen Gunnhild from this country."

He then cut his speech in runes within the pole and left it standing in the land. As a result of this spell against the spirits/deities of the nation, the king and queen were indeed soon forced to lead the nation.

In the second story, a man went to spy on Iceland for the King of Denmark. He crossed the ocean in the shape of a whale, and when he came to Iceland he saw all the mountains and hills were full of landvaettir, some big and some small. When he tried to go ashore, a big dragon came down the valley, followed by many serpents, toads, and adders that blew poison against him, forcing him to swim away. The deities of Iceland in this story prevented the man sent to magically spy on it from doing so. To truly understand spirit journeys and folk religion, we must think of everything in our world as inhabited by armies of spirit beings, local deities, which are on some level, in control of each piece of land. This, of course, returns us to the notion that fairies are owners of the land, but it also leads to the question, 'can these owners of the land, in fact, be deities from a shamanistic/folk religious cosmology?' I would argue that they could, what's more, I would argue that the stories of many heroes from places such as Britain and Ireland are in fact stories of deities of the land which are so close to human that it's often hard to tell the two apart. This makes it easy for such deities to have eventually morphed into fairies, for the two fulfilled very similar roles. Thus, folk religions, or at least the shadows of folk religions were far more likely to survive the coming of deities by the conquest of Rome or the later Christianization of Europe. As Lecouteux points out;

> Silvanus followed the Roman army in its conquests, and by virtue of his wild nature, he assimilated the local spirits and even the gods. We know, for example, that he was integrated with Sucellus, the god of the mallet. He did not banish the indigenous deities but coexisted with them, which is often indicated on the label affixed to him and which connects to a specific place.

Folk religions survived because they were both useful and highly adaptable. Among the Saami, we see a ritual sacrifice which was performed by the costal Saami being performed by mountain Saami for a completely different purpose and to different deities. Among both groups of Saami, a boat of birch bark was filled with food as an offering, yet among the coastal Saami, this offering was meant for gods of the sea and wind, while among the mountain Saami, it was meant as an offering to ancestral spirits who lived in the mountains and came out at Christmas time. Such changes to religions and customs were commonplace. As people, transition from fishing and hunting to farming it is likely that they underwent many changes in their system of belief and the uses of their rituals. Tatar indicates that as a likely consequence of being so close to hunting and

66

fishing as their food source, the people of Siberia tended to use rituals similar to those used to increase milk production, except for hunting. In general, the rituals of those close to hunting and gathering were different from those who had been agricultural, pastoral, and industrial for long periods of time. In Europe, magic was most often centered around milk production and the growing of plants, as well as the spinning of thread. While among their Siberian neighbors these same, or similar rituals were used to improve hunting and fishing. The forest spirits to whom people asked for a successful hunt in Siberia, were often asked for help with herding animals in Finland, Russia, and Europe as a whole. Although in some cases, these spirits continued to be the friends of hunters, in places like Scotland, they were generally the enemies of hunters.

Hags and Former Deities

Hags and their kin are perhaps the easiest fairies to recognizes as being the remnants of nearly forgotten deities. Katherine Briggs says that the hag Cailleach Bheur "seems one of the clearest cases of the supernatural creature who was once a primitive goddess, possibly among the ancient Britons before the Celts. There are traces of a very wide cult: Black Annis of the Dane Hills in Leicestershire with her blue face, Gentle Annie of Cromarty Firth, the loathly hag in Chaucer's Wife of Bath's Tale...." Black Annis who's mentioned as an aspect of this goddess was a terrifying monster, who stalk through villages at night, snatching people out of their homes with her clawed hands like an eagle would a mouse. Cailleach herself features as the villain in some Scottish Fairy Tales. Similarly, the stories of ogres likely came from the tales of the Etruscan god Orcus, and the water hags who stalked the English lakes and rivers likely came from nymph like goddesses like those found in Wales, and all across Europe. The nature of these deities wasn't entirely changed by their becoming wicked hags, rather only half of it was remembered. Tymoczko (1985) points out that Celtic deities were a contradiction "represented as attributes with divergent symbolic associations – crow and grain, child and severed head." Tymoczko believes that kindly goddess figures like St. Anne of Ireland and hag monsters such as Dahut who used her powers to bring destruction both came from the same mother goddess, but that the stories of this goddess were split into the nurturing and destructive aspects of her into two beings. "Dahut certainly has features of the Terrible Mother. She is a magician whose supernatural powers and skills bring destruction to her people. Her sexuality is out of control, and she kills the ones she loves. Dahut is associated with images of confinement – she is mistress of a magic wall that holds out the sea..."

This notion that the most famous hags are the darker aspects of dualistic deities makes a lot of sense, for even the Wild Hunter of Germanic lore appears to have been the darkest aspect of Odin. After all, people feared as much as revered their deities all across Eurasia. The goddess of growing plants and spring in Greek lore was also known as Dread Persephone, the queen of the dead who bright plagues on cities, which displeased her. Obviously, chthonic deities such as Hades, and Persephone, the rulers of the realm of the dead, and in the case of Persephone 'an agricultural goddess' weren't hags/fairies by this book's definition. Rather, the ideas and fear people had about them are similar to people's fear of hags and witches. For example, people feared the curses of witches, and in in places like Sicily many of curse tablets written were prayers asking Persephone to cause misery on one's enemies (Cubera). Those who used Persephone to curse others were likely grateful for her help, but always had to worry that someone else might ask Persephone to curse them in similar fashion. Thus, the goddess of spring and plants was also the goddess of the death and evil witchcraft, someone who was both feared and loved.

"The paradox of dualities may have been essential to the mystery instantiated by mythological figures like the goddesses" (Tymoczko, 1985)." As I'll discuss in further detail later on, shamanism has both light and dark, kind and cruel aspects, which means that deities likely had similar aspects to their nature for two reasons. The first is that in order for societies to survive they have to maintain social cohesion. This is done not only through rewards but also through threats. Thus, the motherly nymphs of Greece which, cities believed watched over and protected them, also punished those who broke social prohibitions. They would punish those who swore, who were lazy, dirty, greedy, and unkind. The second reason for this duality is that dualism and liminality where important aspects of the shaman's journey and spiritual ecstasies. For example, cannibalism is a common feature of many shamanistic traditions, or at least it becomes such during times of extreme trouble. There is more to this, however, for shaman's often must suffer to go on their first spirit journey and on their first journeys in the spirit world. This shall be discussed more in the section on "The first Spirit Journey' but it was frequent for those of the spirit world to need to dismember, devour, and torture a person who was to become a shaman. The flesh of a human after all was a weakness, which had to be destroyed in order that the person might be reborn as a more magical being. This was a painful and horrific process. Consider for example the story of the "King of the Golden Mountain" (Golden and Glass mountains being a common location within the spirit world). In this Grimm Brother's fairy tale a man who is given over to the devil but escapes, only to enter the spirit world where he finds a castle on the golden mountain, inside which he finds a snake who says;

> Have you come, oh, my deliverer. I have already waited twelve years for you, this kingdom is bewitched, and you must set it free. How can I do that, he inquired. To-night come twelve black men, covered with chains who will ask what you are doing here, but be silent, give them no answer, and let them do what they will with you, they will torment you, beat you, stab you, let everything pass, only do not speak, at twelve o'clock, they must go away again. On the second night twelve others will come, on the third, four-and-twenty, who will cut off your head, but at twelve o'clock their power will be over, and then if you have endured all, and have not spoken the slightest word, I shall be released. I will come to you, and will have, in a bottle, some of the water of life. I will rub you with that, and then you will come to life again, and be as healthy as before. Then said he, I will gladly set you free. And everything happened just as she had said, the black men could not force a single word from him, and on the third night the snake became a beautiful princess, who came with the water of life and brought him
> back to life again.
> So she threw herself into his arms and kissed him, and there was joy and gladness in the whole castle. After this their marriage was celebrated, and he was king of the golden mountain.

In order to become king of the golden mountain the man in this story needed to suffer great pain. What's more it was often the beings who ate and dismembered the shaman who became their helping spirits, teachers, or the donors who provided them with exactly what they needed to survive. Think, for example, the story of "Hansel and Gretel." In this tale two starving children, abandoned to the forest by their parents to die follow a bird deeper and deeper into the woods, as many esthetics of Europe would follow birds on their spirit journey. Rather than leading them to obvious secrets of divinity, however, this bird leads these two children to a hag known as a Hexe in German. This Hexe is very much like the guardian to the realm of the dead. She cannot see living beings but must rely on scent and touch when dealing with Hansel and Gretel. At the end of the story, Gretel defeats the witch and by doing so is able to obtain the wealth they need to survive the harsh world. This is common of the shaman's journey, that those who experience them must survive being threatened with death, and had to suffer torment in order to obtain what they needed. Many shaman's tortured themselves through cold, starvation, personal lashings, sleep deprivation, and more in order to experience their first spirit journey. It should come as no surprise than that the first spirit journey can be a horrifying experience. It makes sense than that the divine entities, the hags and ogres which people encountered on such a journey would be terrifying as well. Consider also the story of Frau Holle, in which the protagonist on falling into a well finds herself in an other world. Here she lives with Frau Holle, but must work for the old lady in return for a place to stay. Because the protagonist is kind to all within the other world and works hard, she is rewarded. Her stepsister, however, is punished for her unkindness. Both of the girls in this story are threatened with death, and one of them is actually killed – for not working hard enough. Thus Frau Holle, who helped one girl survive, and killed another can be considered both good and bad. Similarly, Frau Holle and her kin care for the spirits of dead and unborn children, making them goddesses of birth and death.

Frau Holle is similar to important Siberian deities such as Ilinta Kota of Selkup mythology is the ancestor of all living beings. She forced the deities of good and evil to stop their war (although the cold war between them continues). She appears as an old women, and when she plucks feathers in the heavens they fall to the ground where they turn into more ducks for people to hunt and live on. On top of this, she cares for the souls of unborn children, sending them to earth on the rays of the morning sun, yet she is also a queen of death. To reach her home one had to travel down a filthy road or other magical paths, deep into the forest. Those who came to her and worked hard would be rewarded with magical scrapers, gall for tanning skin, and sinews for thread. At the same time she punishes those who are lazy and do not work hard. These two figures, Frau Holle and Ilinta Kota, separated by two thousand miles have so much in common about the only thing differing in their nature comes from the fact that Germany viewed their otherworldly figures as bringers of agricultural prosperity which they needed to survive, while the Selkup needing hunting, fishing, and gathering to survive. Further, while Ilinta was a sky deity, the location of Frau Holle's home is often underground with many of the other spirits of agriculture. In each of these characters life and death, the power of cradle and coffin are contained in the same being. What's more, each of these beings would cause suffering or blessings in those who visited them. The duality of deities was an important aspect of their character, and just as many shamans were held to a different moral standard than the normal human, so too were many deities. Zeus, for example, broke with nearly every Greek social more, as did Odin, who on mythology was even banished for a time because of his failure to adhere to Germanic morality. As such, when deities lost their status, and stories about them were told less and less frequently what often remained were the horror stories. For such horror, stories were difficult to forget. Which is why I believe what fascinates people most about hags is the sense that they do stem from something ancient. That they are a part of long forgotten beliefs, from a time when people revered and feared their gods in very personal ways.

Trooping Fairies, Homely Fairies, and Fairy Courts

According to Henderson (2007):

> "The social and political infrastructures of Fairyland were parallel to those of their human counterparts... they were organized into tribes and orders and held children, nurses, marriages, deaths, and burials. They lived under "aristocratic rulers and laws..."

Such ideas are repeated by Campbell (1900)"

> "The fairies... are counterparts of mankind. There are

71

children and old people among them; they practice all kinds of trades and handicrafts; they possess cattle, dogs, arms; they require food, clothing, sleep; they are liable to disease and can be killed. They work similar jobs that mankind works".

Fairies often pursued occupations much like those of humans such as mining for treasures, forging weapons, farming, herding animals, making shoes, and more. These fairy kingdoms were not in some distant land. Rather, they were all around humans in the sky, in mounds, in forests, in magical spaces made larger on the inside than the outside through the fairies' power. When these fairy kingdoms were left undisturbed, they acted peacefully towards humans, and would sometimes even trade bread, cakes, and more with the people who lived near them. They would also utilize human midwives to help them bear their children, while also borrowing human halls for certain celebrations.

While most fairies lived seemingly ordinary lives, all be it in a magical world and with magical powers, there were castles and noble courts among the fairies. Indeed, some fairies lived in courts so wealthy and opulent that it would make the wealthiest human kings and tsars cry tears of jealousy. The dwarfs, for example, have a court in which they are able to compete directly with the deities themselves, thanks to their supernatural ability to craft items of great magic. When the fairy court showed up to serve at King Herla's wedding:

> "Everything that Herla had prepared was left untouched. His servants sat in idleness, for they were not called upon and hence rendered no service. The pygmies were everywhere, winning everybody's thanks, aflame with the glory of their garments and gems, like the sun and moon before other stars, a burden to no one in word or deed, never in the way and never out of the way" (Barber, 1999).

Many people who have seen the fairy courts have been so overcome by the opulence and beauty of them that, after leaving, they long to return so much that they pine away and die. So, the fairies that choose to live in and/or are raised in the fairy court live in a world of extreme opulence, of constant parties, and never-ending dancing. I discuss this further in the section, "The Other World as Heaven".

Moreover, fairies likely lived in smaller villages, or towns,

72

with fantastic country fairs and magical gifts to be sure but otherwise, very much like most humans of their time lived. The seven dwarfs that Snow White encountered, for example, chose to live in a small cottage out in the forest. They were still social and friendly, but they still chose to live a much more isolated and quieter life than their peers.

Many nixies of German lore choose to live in small societies, alongside humans; even going to the human market to do their shopping. Although their great beauty and the fact that the hems of their garments are always wet, occasionally betray their nature. Similarly, the knockers, who dwell in the mines of Cornwall, work alongside humans and seem to live in smaller groups. Those fairies that choose to live apart from the fairy court are much like we would expect humans of the same area to be; except that they tend to remain hidden, have magical powers, and are more obsessed with hard work. This isn't to say that the knockers don't celebrate or dance; rather, it's just to say that this doesn't seem to be the focus of their lives the way it is for some other fairies.

The Politics of Fairyland
Politics plays an important part in the lives of trooping fairies, just as it would in the lives of humans. And as with human politics, the politics of fairyland can be convoluted, with enemies acting as friends and friends acting as enemies within the same court. Take for, for example, the two eventual fairy lords, Gwyn son of Nudd and Gwythyr son of Greidol, both worked for and advices Arthur (Green, 2007). While these two kings of fairyland both worked for Arthur they were still enemies who fought many wars with each other. Gwyn was the king of the tylwyth teg, or the fairies of Wales, and the ruler of Annwn, the otherworld. He had also fought an intense war with Gwythyr over Creiddylad, the daughter of Lludd Silver Hand. This fight was so brutal that during the course of it, Gwynn was said to:

> "Slew Nwython and took his heart, and compelled
> Cyledyr to eat his father's heart; and because of this
> Cyledyr went mad".

Eventually, Arthur stepped in and forced a sort of peace between these two waring deities/fairy kings, one in which they were only allowed to fight a battle with each other once every May. It's been speculated that this represents the battle between winter – lead by Gwyn, and summer – lead by Gwythyr. Yet, despite their ongoing war with each other, they still served King Arthur. This makes sense in the context of ancient politics in which the nobility of a land were free to feud with each other and have their own armies while still serving an emperor or king. In modern fantasy terms, Fairyland seems to be more like "Game of Thrones" than "Star Wars". That is, there are multiple entities, each vying for power, and each with their own interests. Fairy politics can, perhaps, be most closely compared to the medieval politics of the mortal world. In medieval Scotland for example, clans might have united to fight off the English, but they would, at the same time fight each other. Young men would frequently raid their Scottish neighbors to take cattle, even within the same larger clan/nation. While at the same time, some of the Scottish people were engaged in the crusades, and so were fighting alongside the English, then return home and go to war against their former comrades. Given how complex the human world can be, one would expect stories of the fairy realm to be equally as complex. In Ireland, for example, each county had its own fairy court, which were frequently waging war on each other to help their homeland, often by attacking other counties. Thus, each land could be said to have its own fairy guardians who battled the fairies from other lands in order to protect not only themselves, but the people of their lands. According to Wentz:

> "The invisible Irish races have always had a very distinct social organization, so distinct in fact that Ireland can be divided according to its fairy kings and fairy queens and their territories even now; and no doubt that we see in this how the ancient Irish anthropomorphically projected into an animistic belief of their own
> social conditions and racial characteristics. And this social organization and territorial division ought to be understood before we discuss the social troubles and consequent wars of the Sidhe-folk. For example, in Munster, Bodb was king and his enchanted palace was called the Síd of the Men of Femen; and we already know about the over-king Dagda and his Boyne palace near Tara. In more modern times, especially in popular fairy-traditions, Eevil or Eevinn (Aoibhill or Aolbhinn) of the Craig Liath or Grey Rock is a queen of the Munster fairies; and Finvara is king of the Connaught fairies.

There are also the Irish fairy-queens Cleeona (Cliodhna), or in an earlier form Clidna, and Aine".

Kohl (1844) states that:

> "It is quite characteristic of the Irish that their fairies should be divided like the island itself, into counties. You hear of Limerick fairies, and the Donegal Fairies, and the Tipperary fairies, and the fairies of two adjoining counties have their faction fights, just like the inhabitants themselves. In Tipperary, however, is a place in which all the fairies of Ireland are said to hold their meetings".

In other words, Ireland had multiple fairy kings whose territories, more or less, mirrored that of different human counties. In Yeats's "Fairy and Folk Tales of the Irish Peasantry," a man named "McAnally tells how once a peasant saw a battle between the green jacket fairies and the red. When the green jackets began to win, so delighted was he to see the green above the red that he gave a great shout. In a moment, all vanished and he was flung into the ditch".

Humans were very much involved in the politics of the fairy realm, perhaps much like we are involved in rooting for our own local sports teams. There is, however, one difference: when the fairies of one land defeated those of another, they would steal the fertility from the other land. Therefore, the winners of these wars would have a good harvest, while the losers would have a poor one. We perhaps see remnants of this idea in the rituals of the benandanti of Northern Italy and other Alpine traditions. Here, Perchta or some other fairy queen would lead human/shaman figures and fairy like beings to do battle with witches who sought to steal the fertility of the land. Such witches were usually from neighboring villages. It makes sense to presume that such battles might have once been between rival villages for the fertility of the land, to insure that they, not their enemies had a rich harvest. There was in Ireland, among other places, an idea that there was only so much fertility and success to go around. Because of this, spells were performed not simply to insure one's own success, but to steal success from another. So, just as people would go on cattle raids to steal cattle from their neighbors, fairies and witches may have gone to steal success from their neighbors.

Dual Fairy Courts – Seelie vs Unseelie – Good vs Evil

While many, if not most of the wars fought between fairy clans, were between two clans of similar philosophy, just as most of the wars between medieval human nations where, there was an undercurrent of good vs evil in many of Europe's cosmologies. Scotland is famous for having the good Seelie court of fairies as well as the wicked Unseelie court of fairies. This idea of dividing fairies into "good" and "evil" courts isn't necessarily the norm, but it isn't entirely uncommon either. Wentz stated that in Brittany:

> "Souvestre records a story showing how the lutins can assume any animal form, but that their natural form is that of a little man dressed in green; and that the corrigans have declared war on them for being too friendly to men".

There are numerous stories about divisions broken down as kind and wicked, or good and evil fairies from Germany as well. As previously mentioned, however, the most famous good and evil courts of fairies comes from Scotland, where there were two classes of fairies, the good Seelie Court, and the wicked Unseelie Court. According to the Edinburgh Magazine from 1819, the Seelie court of fairies was made up primarily of:

> "...infants, whose parents or guardians were harsh and cruel, by such as fell insensate through wounds, but not dead, in the day of just battle, by persons otherwise worthy, who sometimes repined at the hardness of their lot, and, in short, by such whose lives were in general good, but in a moment of unguardedness, fell into deep sin, and especially allowed themselves peevishly to repine against the just awards of Providence".

That means that good people who weren't quite good enough to get into heaven joined the Seelie Court. This is a very possibly way to explain why people didn't go to heaven in Christian Europe. I presume that originally any good person in Scotland would join something similar to the Seelie Court.
The Unseelie Court, however, was made up of the unclean dead. Unbaptized children (or children who died without a name or outside of the community), those who died in wicked wars,

unmarried people who died in childbirth, and generally anyone who would have been considered wicked by Scottish society. It is further stated that:

> "Nothing gave the fairies and evil spirits such power over the inhabitants of Middle Earth, as the indulgence of peevish repinings. If a parent or guardian, in a fit of spleen against his child or infant ward, cursed it, wishing it dead, or off this earth, it was, except the curser immediately repented, and prayed God to forgive his sin and protect the child, suddenly snatched to Fairy Land. If the child was baptized then it became a member of the Seelie Court, and still had a chance of salvation".

According to this report, the Seelie and Unseelie Courts were spirits of the dead, which would make them different from the owners of the land, and many of the trooping fairies in Scotland. This might explain why only some few of the stories in Scotland mention their existence. This doesn't mean that these fairies were always or only the spirits of the dead, however. Many nature spirits, such as nymphs in Greece were later believed to be the spirits of the dead. It does however seem like there was more division than just Seelie and Unseelie within Scotland. It's likely that they too had many clans of fairies, that would wage war on each other, just as the Seelie and Unseelie Courts did. Regarding whether all these clans were united with either the Seelie or Unseelie Court isn't stated. The Seelie Court, might be like Arthur's Court, in which the King of Summer and King of Winter would work together to battle a greater evil, but would still battle each other.

The dualistic nature of fairy courts isn't as well attested too in other Celtic and Germanic countries, but it still exists. Enough that Briggs stated that "there is a definite folk tradition of benevolent and malevolent fairies... the pretty bright fairies were always draped in white, with wands in their hands and flowers in their hair." The Manx Scrapbook states that:

> Manx fairies were of two kinds; the playful and benignant, the sullen and vindictive. The former were gay and beautiful, but shy; the second kind dwelt apart form the others and from men, in clouds, on mountains, in fogs, on hideous precipice, or in the caverns on the seashore...

While the book "Manx Fairy Tales" says;

> Far uglier than the Fynoderee, are the Bugganes, who
> are horrible and cruel creatures. They can appear in any
> shape they please – as ogres with huge heads and great
> fiery eyes, or without any heads at all.

In addition, there are stories of people hearing the good fairies
punish wicked bogles. Scandinavia had light elves and dark
elves. In Wales, the following tale is recounted:

> "There is a tradition among the Glamorgan peasantry of
> a fairy battle fought on the mountain between Merthyr
> and Aberdare in which the pigmy combatants were on
> horseback. There appeared to be two armies, one of
> which was mounted on milk-white steeds, and the other
> on horses of jet-black. They rode at each other with the
> utmost fury, and their swords could be seen flashing in
> the air like so many penknife blades. The army on the
> white horses won the day, and drove the black-mounted
> force from the field. The whole scene then disappeared in
> a light mist."

This story, with its black and white fairies in battle with one
another, seems to indicate that Wales too had some version of
the Seelie and Unseelie Court. England also has something,
which resembles duel courts with things like festivals in which
people asking good fairies to protect them from bad fairies. That
said, even good fairies weren't pure good, and could become
dangerous quickly. The Fynoderee of Manx, a fairy which was
banished from the fairy court for loving a human, who was
normally helpful, attempted to kidnap one man who sought help
from him, and in the end settled for stealing his cow.
Cosmology in general is frequently divided between good and
evil. Eva Pocs points out that this duality, the competition
between good and evil forces is common in Indo-European lore.
The witches of Eastern Europe were often divided into two
systems, the good and the wicked. Those of heaven and those of
hell. The evil witch shamans would work with snakes and
attempt to steal crops, while the heavenly witch shamans would
oppose them. In Britain and Ireland one of the primary jobs of
the witches was to help the fairies cure those who had been
harmed by other fairies, which also seems to indicate that there
were two forces working against each other.

The Demon Familiars and Forest Devils

In the fairy tale "The Smith and the Devil," the smith loses everything he has and in his depression is about to kill himself when a devil steps out from behind a tree and offers to make the man rich for ten years, if the man agrees to be his thereafter. () believes that his research shows that this and similar stories are roughly 6000 years old. Although there is a debate on the exact age, the story does seem to be far older than Christianity. This leads to the obvious question – who is the devil in the story, or at least who was he before Christianity?

There were numerous beings who opposed the gods in Indo-European lore. The Jotun who would bring about the end of the world in Norse mythology, the Giants and Titans of Greek mythology, and the Fomorians of Irish mythology all attempted to kill off the deities. In all these places then there were kingdoms of powerful beings which acted in opposition to the divine will that guided humanity. Such beings could be seen as devilish, and so it would be easy to imagine these beings as being somewhat akin to demons. This would certainly explain why trolls in the Nordic countries were often said to be involved with witches, while at the same time they often feared thunder, for this reminded them of their greatest enemy – Thor.

The Selkup of Siberia believed in a supreme evil being, as did many of the Siberian and Steppes people. In their case, this being was known as Kysy and is the brother of the good being Icha. They fought epic battles with neither able to live when the Old Mother Woman (a heavenly mother goddess, who is also a goddess of household choirs and birds that come from the heavens to be hunted) came down from the sky and pulled them apart. She ordered Icha to stay in the sky, where he would use lighting to destroy the evil spirits who worked for his brother. These evil spirits include the Cuyil Loz which dwell with their family's underground, and which are always seeking to harm people. They can possess objects, people, and trees, thus the reason these are sometimes struck by lightning.

Kysy was ordered to live in the realm between the sky and the earth, where he devours people's souls. The Old Mother must reserve a portion of people for him, which she records in a book of death. The brothers still struggle and battle, although usually through proxy. Kysy dwells in the sea of the dead, beyond which is the city of the dead. These are located far to the north, where the sky meets the earth. In this case, one of the primary duties of the shaman is to rescue the souls of the dead and sick taken by Kysy and his servants.

Similarly, Scotland, with its divided cosmology of kind Seelie fairies and wicked Unseelie fairies had some of the worst witch hunts in Europe, executing roughly five times as many people per capita as the average. Here, people feared that the wicked fairies might take them into the air and force them to kill their neighbors. It makes sense then that much of what was later thought of as devils and demons in fairy tales were remnants of those beings which opposed the deities in the pre-Christian beliefs.

Yet the devil in the story of "The Devil and the Smith" likely wasn't one of these tribes of beings that opposed the will of the deities. Rather it seems most likely that the devil in this fairy tales was some form of fairy which could act both good and bad. When thinking about the devils and demons that witches interacted with, there are four important things to keep in mind. First, fairies needed human workers and to get them they would often kidnap people, but they might also bargain with people for their help, as happened in the story of "The Devil and the Smith." Second, there were wicked and evil fairies or fairies that acted ambiguously. Some of these fairies were even bloodthirsty and cannibalistic. Such fairy-like beings may have included remnant ideas of the beings who had previously opposed the will of the deities, such as trolls and the Unseelie court. Others included the far darrig who would force people to again murder their neighbors so the far darrig could eat them. One could easily see how such creatures could have wanted witches to work with and for them, and how they could later have been diabolified into being devils and demons.

Third, the fairies themselves often conspired against humans, for the humans had driven them underground or the fairies wanted to kidnap additional humans to work for them. This point is important given that the place with perhaps the highest number of witch trials per capita was Guernsey Island, which feared the witches were conspiring with the fairies in order to kill the people and conquer the island as they had done once before in a bloody battle which had left all the men dead. In this case, the fairies and wanted to kidnap all the women of the island and to establish rule over it. Similarly, in Irish and Tyrol lore people fought battles with fairies over the women they had kidnapped, while in other places the fairies would kill the people of a region with curses and disease.

Fourthly, foreign fairies, even from one county over, were often said to be conspiring against the people of a land. Thus, there were foreign witches who were also conspiring against the people. This later point is especially seen in the witch hunts of Rome which often focused on foreign religious ideas. In 186 B.C. the Roman senate passed laws restricting Bacchanalia, that is the celebrations in honor of Dionysus, because they were believed to engage in wicked practices, which would seem very much like what the Roman's later accused the Christians of doing, and the Christians would later accuse the witches of. These celebrations seem very much like the later witch sabbaths. During these festivals it was believed that there were massive orgies and drunken celebrations, that people were violently abused but their screams were drowned by loud drums. They were also accused of murdering those who violated their rules. The Roman's disliked Dionysus in part because he was an outside god from Greece, who wasn't entirely a part of the Roman structure. So the accusations leveled against Dionysus's followers may have been as false as the accusations later leveled against the Christians for orgies and cannibalistic celebrations with a donkey-headed deity. Thousands of Dionysus's followers were put to death in one of the largest most concentrated witch hunts in European history. These events point to the fact that people did fear the existence of demonic deities and devilish witch sabbaths for at least a few hundred years before Christianity. Meaning that the evil witch sabbaths, like the kindly visits to fairyland, have long-standing traditions. So while as Ivanits points out;

> It is possible that the church also played a role in the diabatization of the spirits because of the mix-up of the Christian idea of the devil and the popular ideas of the forest, water and house spirits.

This mix up likely occurred because there were similarities between many nature spirits and the devils which Christians feared.

Finally, it is important to recall that fairies and ancient deities were dualistic figures. It was after all Persephone, the goddess of spring who was invoked in curses. Thus, even good fairies and deities could act in a wicked manner for a variety of reasons. This last point makes sense for certain types of witches, given that these witches would learn magic from the fairies in order to undo the very curses the fairies had placed on people and seemed to regret having done so (although this might be because of opposing tribes of fairies).

Given that there were wicked fairies and deities in early lore, as well as demons and devils in later lore, it is worth discussing the nature of the witch's relationship with the diabolic familiars and their devilish masters. For this purpose, I refer to all the dark beings, whether a devil who seems to have an interest in the forest, a fairy, a foreign deity, a jotun, etc. as "forest devils" and "demonic familiars." This is because it is difficult, if not impossible, to sort one of the many wicked beings from another. In many cases, the demonic familiar and the witch became friends, if not allies. The witches had been marginalized by society, or were suffering under desperate poverty, or were greedy enough that they jumped at the chance to work with darker powers to obtain more power and wealth. Just as the fairies weren't purely evil, many of these witches and their demonic familiars weren't either, or at the very least they were good at putting on a good face. There are stories of those who spread disease and curse others also healing the sick and providing for the poor, after all.

The witches who served the forest devils would attend multiple witch sabbaths, which involved wild parties, good food, and of course orgies and cannibalism. At these celebrations, the devil would often give the witches potions to use on their neighbors, to help further the spread of suffering. There are many reasons for the forest devil to have desired to cause this suffering. In addition to those already mentioned (opposing the deities, from a foreign land, wishing to overthrow humanity) there is also the general desire and hunger for blood which many supernatural beings had. This goes back to the notion of dark shamanism. Around the world, dark gods would ask shamans to find them human flesh to eat. As Wilby puts it, "there are prediation-cosmologies, in which there are spirits which feed on humans. In such cases, the shaman will negotiate with these beings, allying with them in order to help control their apatite. To do this, the shaman must devour people as well." Wilby continues that there are similar structures to these predation cosmologies in Europe. Of course, foremost of the monsters the witch shamans interacted with in this way was the devil himself. There are, however, many other predatory beings in European mythology. These include a variety of hags, vampires, fairies, lamia, mora demons, trolls, ogres, and more. Fairytales are rife with cannibalism, with nearly every story by Perrault featuring this. Witches of lore participated in these acts of cannibalism and like the shamans elsewhere learned magical secrets while doing so. Often these compulsions to kill and devour weren't under the witches control. Fabia Campaigne wrote that "the Spanish witch is the victim of a tragic destiny from which it is impossible to escape (Wilby)."

It is this latter point, the lack of control which wicked witches had that is one of the most important when discussing the nature of these witches. Many of them, like werewolves, were drawn into their hunger by the powers that had forced them into service or by their own nature. Such people could be horrified by what they had done and would at times wonder why god would allow such a thing, or would call on god to deliver them. Such tortured people didn't always have the greatest relationship with their demon familiars or the forest devil. This latter point wasn't always the case, however. Dark shamans in South America had to form a close working relationship, even a friendship with the cannibal gods in order to stop them from devouring the whole of the world, and in order to use these deities magic to heal as many as they could. The witches too might have needed to form a friendship with the evil beings to stop an even greater evil.

Not all people who became wicked witches were unwilling, however. There were greedy people who would call dark powers in order to obtain wealth. Such people included nobles who would eat human flesh and drink human blood.

The other fear was the marginalized people, people who suffered at the hands of their neighbors and sought revenge, and or the ability to raise their station with the help of dark powers. Most of the people in this latter category were likely falsely accused. Yet there were some who clearly did at least attempt to consort with dark powers for revenge. Purkiss states of two witches

> It is significant that both Anne Bodenham and Anne Jefferies began as servants, members of households from whose wealth and status they were excluded. Perhaps the position of servant gave both women material for their fantasies, a goal to aspire to, while at the same time generating anger and resentment.

Anne Jefferies was also unique among witches in that her story begins with her going out into the wilderness and calling to the fairies to come to her. In both of these cases, the witches became healers, rather than wicked witches. However, if Purkiss is correct in asserting that the supernatural was for many the only means of removing class boundaries and achieving their dreams, one could imagine any number of people choosing to work with any number of beings, no matter how dark. Certainly (), who sparked the witch hunt in () did turn herself in for having used a spirit in dog form to place a curse on someone she'd felt wronged her, after which she was guilt-ridden by the fact that the man had a stroke.

Along with the typical cavalcade of dark spirits, one should also recall that the spirit owners of the land could often act in a way that people would consider devilish. Indeed, fairy tales like "The Devil and the Farmer" in Germany are called the "Farmer and the bogle" in England and "The Farmer and the Bear" in Russia, indicating that the devil in this story was, in fact, an owner of the land. Further, recall that some of these spirit owners of the land would become bloodthirsty, and attack people no matter what the people did. Still, others would take revenge against people for breaking moral prohibitions, in other words, sinning. These owners of the land, or at least beings who seem to be very much like them, would also bargain for people's souls. Bearskin is the story of a soldier who made a deal with a green-coated man with a cloven hoof, who offers him great wealth if he will wear a bearskin cloak, and not bathe, clip his nails, or hair for seven years. This sounds very much like a shaman's esthetic journey, although the payment at the end is money rather than magical powers. Other than the devil's bargain, what's interesting here is the fact that the "devil" in this case offers the man a way out of the deal. Every story of a forest devil making a bargain involves such a loophole to allow clever people the opportunity to escape the bargain they've just made. The most famous example of this would be Rumpelstiltskin allowing the woman he'd made a bargain with the opportunity to guess his name, when most faeries simply take babies from their cribs without giving anything in return. In "The Dragon and the Soldiers," one of these forest devils rescues some humans and makes them wealthy in exchange for the promise that they work for him later, yet he too gives them a way out of their contract. Magical black cats in France would give starving people food and wealth in return for their service later, and then at the last minute, they would give these people a clever way out. There is no clear reason for this, and that is perhaps the biggest challenge to understanding the devilish nature of fairies and ancient deities. There often isn't a clear reason for the things they do.

The following is a Mari-El tale translated from Russian about a man who kills and robs a forest spirit/devil.

The Devils Clothes Mari-el Fairy Tale

Once there was a man who went hunting in the woods alone but accidently forgot his bread at his winter hut. He wandered deep into the woods, but try as he might he couldn't catching anything so he returned to his winter hut at night to find that the devil had broken into his house and was eating his bread. So the man shot the devil with his gun. The devil fell and crawled out of the man's winter hut. Then screaming and crying in pain the devil crawls into the forest.

Scared the man flees into his winter hut and spends the whole night laying in fear. When day comes at last he gets up and sees that the devils blood has coagulated on the floor. He follows the devils bloody tracks into the forest. The man finds the devil lying on a log overthrown and dead. The man comes closer, takes off the clothes of the devil and carries them back home. When he gets home he puts on the devils clothes and then walks inside his house, but his family doesn't notice him because they can't see him.

He takes off the devils clothes and hangs them on the stairs and his wife and children start shouting and crying: "Why has our room disappeared?"

In their eyes the room has turned invisible. The man then puts on the clothes again, the room is visible, but the man himself is invisible again.

"These are the Devil's clothes," the man tells his wife. "When I wear them I become invisible in your eyes."

Later he puts on the clothes again so no man can see him. He goes to the market and steals everything he wants: goods, other things and also money. He kept stealing and stealing and soon became very rich.

After the man and his family had become wealthy one of their neighbors paid them a visit when the husband was away and asked: "How have you become extremely rich?"

"We had been working hard and became this rich," the man's wife replied.

"It's impossible to become so rich even if you work really hard" the neighbor shook her head.

"We found devil's clothes, that's why we are so rich," the man's wife confessed.

"Please give it to us so that we also can go to the market once or twice," the neighbor asked.

"No, I can't give it to you, my husband will be angry," the man's wife disagreed.

"Your husband will not notice anything, I will bring it back quickly," the neighbor pressed.

So the man's wife gave the clothes to the neighbor. The neighbor stole and stole and became rich, but never gave the clothes back. The house of the man who found the clothes was burnt down to the ground by the revengeful devil. They had nothing left, but the neighbor became very rich.

Solitary Fairies

Other fairies choose to live a solitary life, away from humans and even their own kind. In general, I would argue that such solitary fairies are generally individual owners of the land, former deities, and similar such beings. These fairies tend to be far more feral, far more dangerous than others. The dwarfs that choose to live alone, for example, are often cruel and twisted, incapable of gratitude. In "Snow White and Rose Red," the heroines help a dwarf escape the clutches of an eagle and he curses them for it. Another solitary fairy, the Vodianoi of Russia, tends to be a loner, who acts very much like a serial killer. Other fairies choose to be solitary, not necessarily because they are overtly cruel, but because they prefer the company of animals. The Leshii, for example, were the kings of the forest. Semi-solitary fairies that tended to live like bachelors or hermits, they traveled the woods with animals (mostly wolves and bears, but all animals of the forest were under their command) and rarely with anyone else. They tended to live as the ultimate bachelors, gambling, drinking, and throwing wild parties that leveled trees. They were often grouchy and typically rowdy, even when they married and raised children. The solitary nature of this creature also begs the question "what it would be like to be the child of the king of the forest, the child of a creature that only likes to keep company with animals (or the occasional fling, which they might sleep with)?"

The Brown Man of the Muirs is another fairy who is the ruler of the animals, but he will never taste meat, instead choosing to live on nuts and berries. He grows furious with humans who hunt on his land, berating them, challenging them to fights, and ultimately cursing them to grow ill and die (Briggs, 1976).

Cultural Elements and Historical Speculations

Understanding Fairyland Using Cultural Elements

I've already pointed out that human and fairy cultures often reflected each other, such that a man could stumble upon a troll farm that was so much like human farms he couldn't tell the difference until he encountered the inhabitants. Indeed, we often see in stories about people who find their way into the spirit world / fairyland who don't even realize they have crossed over because the two worlds are so similar, until magical things start happening. Forest lords lived like regular hermits in the middle of forests, huldre would herd cattle in the mountains as people did, and others would live in villages ruled over by dragons as if they were serfs. In one fairy story a boy lost his way and fell asleep, he awoke with a tame bear beside him, which he followed. The bear led him to a hut. "A little woman opened the door to him and invited him kindly into the house. There was another little woman sitting by the fire. They gave him something to eat and drink and said he would have to share their bed because there was no other (Briggs)." Later that night he saw them fly away by means of a white cap, and the boy followed them. They went down chimneys and got wine from a cellar.

What intrigues me about this story is how normal the two fairy women seem. There were likely many poor human women who lived so similarly to them that the boy doesn't seem to suspect that they are anything other than human – although perhaps the bear leading him to the women's house should have made him leery. In addition to living very much like certain human women, the fairy women in this story, like many fairies fly off to steal from humans in order to survive, thus their economy and survival is tied to humanity.

Further evidence of the similarity between human and fairy cultures comes from multiple stories in which humans would ask fairies to stand as godmother or father for their child, and fairies would ask humans to do the same. These latter stories, where a human stands godparent for a fairy child are interesting because this means that the fairies were choosing a human to help mentor their child, and perhaps raise them should anything happen. It also means that just as humans had a godparental system, so too did the fairies.

This isn't to say that the fairies culture was an exact reflection of our own, it's merely to point out that they were similar enough that we can use culture as well as fairy tales and myths to speculate on the nature of the fairy and spirit worlds by understanding human cultures. One wonderful example of this is Katheryn Briggs's article "The Fairy Economy" in which she discusses the social structure and economy of fairyland based on tales of fairy weddings and markets. Such speculations using folklore can lead us down a number of interesting paths, and teach us a lot about our own history and society.

Using the History of Folklore to Speculate on Fairy History

A large part of the way any culture or group thinks comes from their history. This would be especially true of fairies who are immortal, or very nearly so. Thus, there would still be fairies today who would remember when Rome invaded Britain, so this event would inform their thinking a lot more than it even would our own. In addition, folklore itself changed over time. These changes can be used to think about the history of the fairies themselves. For example, fairy tales about the German zwerg, (often translated as dwarfs, such as in "Snow White and the Seven Dwarfs.") went through a number of transitions from the early Medieval to the Industrial Revolution.

The Zwerg

An angelic sounding yodel greets the people as they bring their cattle into the spring mountains to graze in Alpine meadows. The people yodel back to the zwerg, the fairies with whom they share their homeland, but rarely ever see anymore. The zwerg for their part can no longer trust humans, yet the memory still lingers of when they lived side by side with people. When their kingdoms were united to battle other threats.

88

Germany during the beginnings of the industrial revolution offers us an interesting picture of fairy tales well beyond the ones that the Grimm brothers collected. In this land, humans and fairies often lived in a sort of uneasy alliance where they would frequently cause trouble for one another, and help each other at the same time.

The zwerg are challenging to understand in large part because the word is a stand in for many fairies from multiple traditions. They include the Celtic fairies which lived in Germany before the Germanic people's came south bringing their dwarves with them, which are also called zwerg. They can also mean the Germanic creatures who competed with and manufactured items for the gods of Germanic Mythology. Then, there are potentially dozens of other fairies from many other traditions which might be called zwerg. This meant that far from being a united kingdom, the zwerg were made up of successive waves of invading fairies who formed into different tribes (Pre-Celtic, Celtic, Germanic, and possibly Roman as well as Slavic) that would occasionally fight battles with each other, and humans. So, if we were to create a history of them, we could begin by saying that they were once fairies from multiple peoples which were each conquered in turn as new fairies moved in. Ultimately, however, they formed a single set of kingdoms that lived alongside the human ones.

In Medieval Lore, the zwerg and the humans got along fairly well. The Epics of this era talk of the zwerg as being angelically beautiful, of dwelling in beautiful halls filled with treasure and magical miracles. These zwerg were master craftsmen appointed by god in the stories of this time to make items for the other beings, including humans, with the giants assigned to protect them from dragons and other foul monsters. However, the giants betrayed them, so, it fell to the human knights to protect them. This early period is interesting because while the zwerg have powerful magical items such as belts that give them great strength and hats which can make them invisible, they weren't able to defend themselves against the giants and dragons as effectively as humans can. Instead, they use their great knowledge of natural magic to help humans by telling the future, offering advice, and gifting them with magical items. Eventually, humans betrayed the zwerg as well.

There were occasional battles between the humans and zwerg, who would fight with each other over the fact that they would steal from each other, and the zwerg would occasionally seduce or even kidnap human women. Despite this, they were allied with humans against their real enemies. Yet, things began to change rather quickly as exemplified by the stories of Goldemar. In the epics of the High Middle Ages, Goldemar was a great king of the zwerg who was still able to call the giants of the Trumunt Forest to help him in battle. Yet, by the 17th century the story of the zwerg with this name had changed to that of a house fairy, as told by Keightly.

> Another celebrated House-spirit was King Goldemar who lived in great intimacy with Neveling von Hardenberg, on the Hardenstein at the Rühr, and often slept in the same bed with him. He played most beautifully on the harp, and he was in the habit of staking great sums of money at dice. He used to call Neveling brother-in-law, and often gave him warning of various things. He talked with all kinds of people, and used to make the clergy blush by discovering their secret transgressions. His hands were thin like those of a frog, cold and soft to feel; he let himself be felt, but no one could see him. After remaining there for three years, he went away without offending anyone. Some call him King Vollmar, and the chamber in which he lived is still said to be called Vollmar's Chamber. He insisted on having a place at the table for himself, and a stall in the stable for his horse; the food, the hay, and the oats were consumed, but of man or horse, nothing more than the shadow ever was seen. When one time a curious person had strewed ashes and tares in his way to make him fall that his foot-prints might be seen, he came behind him as he was lighting the fire and hewed him to pieces, which he put on the spit and roasted, and he began to boil the head and legs. As soon as the meat was ready, it was brought to Vollmar's chamber, and people heard great cries of joy as it was consumed. After this, there was no trace of King Voilmar; but over the door of his chamber was found written, that in future the house would be as unfortunate as it had hitherto been fortunate; the scattered property would not be brought together again till the time when three Hardenbergs of Hardenstein should be living at the same time. The spit and the roasted meat were preserved for a long time; but they disappeared in the Lorrain war in 1651. The pot still remains built into the wall of the kitchen.

Although, this story may or may not have been inspired by the earlier tales of King Goldemar, it does show how much people's thoughts about the zwerg had changed. This begs the question, what happened? In lore, it was commonly believed that humanities relationship with the otherworld had changed. Like the giants before them, humans betrayed the relationship with the otherworld, leaving many of its inhabitants essentially defenseless, and with a new enemy to worry about. This is why German fairies called people faithless and stated that the fairies would not share magical secrets with most people. This is also why so few humans are privy to the magical world. Some fairies, however, still did approach people for help. In one story, a wood wife asked a woodsman to help her by drawing a magical symbol on a tree so that the Wild Huntsman wouldn't be able to get into it and kill her. Humans seem to have some magical power which allows them to keep fairies away, and at times destroy their magic which they could use to protect weaker fairies from the stronger ones. Although, now, since we hardly ever see them, we don't really realize it.

Goldemar's situation also, likely has something to do with his relationship with his zwerg court as well. Another being named Hinzelmann from the Bohemian Forest had been banished by his companions, and so had sought refuge in the castle of Hudemuhlen. Like the zwerg of old, he was able to see the future to an extent and used this to warn the people he'd come to live with of misfortune. Such stories of fairies being banished from fairyland, and needing to live with humans are fairly common, so, this could also explain why Goldemar is living in a human home. However, this situation wasn't unique.

By the industrial revolution, there were still some wealthy zwerg, yet most of the stories about the zwerg depicted them as poor, at times even starving and desperate. Worse, they'd grown weaker and into the ugly twisted creatures we most often associate them with today. This was likely the result of their difficult relationship with humanity and the rest of the magical world which humans had once protected them from. This is also why they'd mostly gone into hiding by then, with only a few exceptions. Yet, they remained clustered around human cities and villages for a while longer, for they still needed humans, and would make exchanges with them. Keightley recounts that;

> Kohmann's grandfather was working in his ground
> which lay in the neighborhood of the place called the
> Dwarfs' hole, and his wife had brought out to the field to

91

him for his breakfast some fresh baked bread, and had laid it, tied up in a napkin at the end of the field, there came up soon after a little Dwarf-woman who spoke to him about his bread, saying, that her own was in the oven, and that her children were hungry and could not wait for it, but that if he would give her his, she would be certain to replace it by noon. The man consented, and at noon she returned, spread out a very white little cloth, and laid on it a smoking hot loaf, and with many thanks and entreaties told him he might eat the bread without any apprehension, and that she would return for the cloth. He did as she desired, and when she returned she told him that there had been so many forges erected that she was quite annoyed, and would be obliged to depart and abandon her favorite dwelling. She also said that the shocking cursing and swearing of the people drove her away, as also the profanation of Sunday, as the country people, instead of going to church, used to go look at their fields which was altogether sinful.

In the folklore of the 18th and 19th centuries, the zwerg were just barely clinging on. The sinfulness of men, a few additional wars with people, and the fact that humans would sometimes steal from them was driving them away. At the same time, they needed humans for more than protection. Humans provided them with food, ovens, teakettles, pots, and other tools. Furthermore, the zwerg women didn't seem to be able to give birth without a human midwife or doctor. Perhaps, they even find some few humans who they feel that they can trust and provide them with magical knowledge and gifts so they can continue to protect them from the dragons, monsters, and giants. After all, these enemies hadn't necessarily gone away. Imagine these zwerg, living as essentially refugees, needing the humans they fear, so, they are forced to cling to the outskirts of villages even as they do their best to remain hidden, except for a few occasional encounters. Out beyond the human villages, the other world is filled with dragons, the unclean dead, giants, and more, all seeking to rob them, all seeking to devour and enslave them. Within the human villages, the population of people is growing ever more disrespectful, and ever worse. In many ways, one can see in this situation what happened to people who lived in nice middle class neighborhoods that were taken over by gangs. Frustration and resentment would occasionally spill over into the zwerg's use of their magic to put curses on people.

This isn't to say that all happiness had left the zwerg. As with Joan of Arc's village, many of them still gambled about, singing, dancing, and having fun. To many of the peasants whose lives were very hard, some of the zwerg's lives seemed wonderful when compared to the work they had to do. Nevertheless, folk tales depict the zwerg as going deeper and deeper into hiding until they weren't seen any more at all. However, one could imagine, that they still recruit a few people to train in magic and help protect them from their enemies.

As you can see, German folklore and history provide an interesting way to think about the history of the zwerg, and how their lives changed over time. Such a history can also provide a catalyst for stories. The English water fairies went from being beings like the Lady of the Lake which helped Arthur bring peace to his kingdom to ugly hags which would drown people, steal chickens, and devour children. The Tengu of Japan went from being wild beings that occasional brought wisdom, to being monsters that attacked people, to gentler philosophers and teachers again. The nymphs of Greece went from being figures of worship who aided shaman figures to spreaders of curses and disease long before Christianity. This likely occurred because stratified societies tend to demonize beings like nymphs which can potentially bring about revolution by declaring the leaders and wealthy of a nation wicked. Of course, one could easily argue that like the Rusalka of Russia who eventually fled in folk tales because they couldn't stand what humanity had become, one could imagine the nymphs growing angry as human society became more immoral to their way of thinking. What's interesting, however, is that in many cases, mythological history follows a few similar themes.

1 – First, humans either conquer the land from the magical beings, make an agreement to essentially rent the land, or the deities tame a wild and dangerous realm so the humans can live there.

2 – Eventually, the humans and fairies settle in and become neighbors, at which point, their relationship while mixed at times, is fairly positive. Typically, during this time, humans encounter fairies fairly regularly because the fairies need humans to help them fight wars, give birth, watch their cattle, clean, etc.

3 - The humans begin to betray the fairies trust, so, while the fairies still need humans, they start to hide from most of them. At this time, the fairies take in just a few witches to teach magic to. Whether these witches are good or evil, or ambiguous depends on the fairies who took them in.

(While many people think this step happened in Europe because of Christianity, it happened in pre-Christian Greece and Rome. It also happened in Japan and Korea. It seems likely that people started to take a negative view of fairies as they became more stratified. That is, the country began to develop a strong noble class. This may be because the fairies could call into question the integrity of the leadership of a country, and so, the leaders would demonize them).

4 - Humans begin to view the fairies in more romantic light. During this later stage, people began to view the fairies as being the paragons of their cultural values. The cities of Ancient Greece, The Grimm Brothers, Yeats, and even the scholars of China and Japan began to view the spirits of the wild as important parts of their national identities. Of course, in the case of places like Ancient Greece the reset button was hit as they were invaded repeatedly. Places like Germany and Ireland eventually lost most of their fairy belief (as did Greece in the modern day).

This progression of fairy lore wasn't exactly the same in each country. More important, the specifics of each stage are different from one culture to another, depending on their history. In addition to digging into the progression of fairy lore, it's also possible to gain insights into fairy beliefs by digging into the history of a people that moved to a region, especially if we were to presume that the certain fairies moved with them.

Marblehead, Massachusetts and the Merging of Fairyland

Although all the Europeans who migrated to America brought their beliefs about the other world and fairies with them, most of these faded quickly as they did in the more populated and educated parts of England, as well as Germany's lowlands. Yet many of these stories of fairies remained in Marblehead Massachusetts where they appear to have intermingled with each other and with the native beliefs of the Naumkeags tribe.

Marblehead divided its fairy realm between good fairies, and wicked pixies. In their folklore fairies were always good-natured little creatures that lived in underground places of gold and silver, with pearls and precious stones. They would dance in the moonlight. If they were caught out in the sun, they had to hide in the shade of flowers and sleep. Children would search for them, for whoever spotted one would have a lucky life. Although Marblehead is predominantly English, these fairies seem a lot sweeter than most of the fairies from English folklore. It's true that the Midlands of England do have fairies which are nice more often than not, but they still tend to have a dark side. This kinder, gentler fairy is especially interesting given that many places in the America's ended up focusing on the fairy's negative traits. Encounters with Newfoundland fairies, for example, almost always end badly, for Newfoundland's fairies were often darker than those in Europe.

Marblehead does have wicked magical creatures, which they call pixies. In Marblehead pixies delighted in causing trouble for people. They especially loved to bewilder people; a person who was " pixilated," as they called it, would wander about for hours. The only remedy for such afflicted persons was to turn their garments. This sounds very much like pixies, but while we think of pixies as mischievous, in Southwest England and Cornwall they were also helpful beings. In Dartmoor pixies would often help the farmers work their fields, and would give coins to good people like a sort of Santa. Therefore, while they caused trouble they were also kind. Not so in Marblehead, however. So why were their pixies mean and their fairies kind? While its impossible to know for certain, history does give us some interesting clues.

The word pixie is used in Cornwall and Southwest England, Devon, and New Forest in Hampshire and Wiltshire. This was an area of conflict for much of England's history, with borders constantly fluctuating. Mrs. Bray, in her book "A Peep at the Pixies: or Legends of the West" talks about a war between the pixies and the fairies, when the fairies invaded Devon. So the idea of separate tribes of pixies and English fairies being in conflict was likely already present in Marblehead, to a point. The first Europeans into Marblehead were Puritans, most of which were likely from the Midlands of England with a smattering of people from Cornwall. Most people from Cornwall were Royalists, whom the Puritans considered their enemies, and a civil war in England would even be fought between these two groups. As time went on more and more fishermen from

95

Cornwall and the Channel Islands migrated to Marblehead. This had to create tension between the people Marblehead, and this was likely reflected, as it often was, in the stories of their fairies. Of course, it would also make sense that the English Fairies and Cornish Pixies would feel tension with each other as well. After all they engaged in war in England.

During this time, the Channel Islands were also home to mass witch trials. Guernsey Island alone found over 103 people guilty of Witchcraft, more than four times as many as Salem later would. They believed that these witches were secretly conspiring with the islands fairies, who had at one time been believed to have slaughtered all the men of their island. Thus, the people of the Channel Islands may have contributed to the idea of a divide between good and wicked fairies.

At this point we see three separate groups of fairies that came from Europe, the kinder fairies of the Midlands which often thrived in moonlight in stories, just as the fairies of Marblehead often did. The pixies which loved to lead people astray, just as the pixies of Marblehead did. And the dangerous, often wicked fairies of the Channel Islands. There is, however, one more piece to this puzzle, and it may be the most important. For European's obviously weren't the first people in Marblehead, the first people were the Naumkeags.

When the Puritans arrived in Marblehead the Naumkeags had been devastated by the Tarrantine, a Mi'kmaq tribe. They were further devastated by plagues which the European's had brought with them. Between the war with the Tarrantine and the diseases brought by the European's perhaps, more than 90% of the Naumkeags population was wiped out. This was one of the most horrific genocides in history. What little of the Naumkeags remained married into other tribes, and with the European's, to the point that there is no one we can point today and say with certainty that they are descended from the Naumkeags.

Yet, the Naumkeags stories seem to remain. The people's who the Naumkeags are related to believe in two tribes of little people. The Mikommo and the Pukwudgie. The Mikommo were benevolent little people who brought good fortune. They would gather under the moon to sing, feast, and dance. They provided food and clothing to the poor, and brought luck to people, although they were rarely ever seen. Pukwudgie were little people that were enemies of the people's cultural hero, and ultimately caused his death. As with the pixies, they could confuse people and cause them to get lost.

It's interesting how much the fairies of the Naumkeags, and European belief resembled each other, so much that its arguable that the two tribes of European and two tribes of Naumkeags fairies merged together to create the folklore of Marblehead. It's difficult to say how often this happened. For one thing, there isn't a lot of information on fairy belief in America. As with Western England and the lowlands of Germany, such belief faded quickly. For another, where these beliefs are present it can be difficult to sort which ideas came from where. After all, America includes many European people, and many native people, each with their own stories, that are often similar to each other.

From folklore we know that European fairies were often fleeing Europe as refugees, so it would make sense for them to have come to America where they might have joined up or entered into conflict with the local fairies. In the case of Marblehead it would seem that they would have joined one of two tribes, continuing their conflicts from Europe in conjunction with the Mikommo and the Pukwudgie here.

The Men in Black and Fairies

In the 19th century stories began to grow of the fairies fleeing their homes in Ireland, England, Russia and Germany for other parts of the world. In many cases the fairies had been driven out by humans who had united with other fairy tribes, or had begun acting against the fairies. Such conflicts with humans were in story often why fairies had gone into hiding in the first place yet having failed to remain hidden they started to flee. The number of these stories of fairies fleeing their homes increased, which shouldn't be too surprising. After all, humans were fleeing Europe in ever greater numbers, and these people brought their fairy stories to America, as they always had. Yet, while we find evidence of this belief in fairies in Newfoundland, Marblehead, the Appellations, Ohio, and a few other places, it mostly faded from people's minds fairly quickly. Within a fantasy world, this forgetfulness might be attributable to the men in black.

The men in black first appear in the written record as typical fairy stories within Dubuque, Ohio in the 1880s. The following quote is from the "Plain Dealer" from that decade.

Some years ago he had a daughter, the sole remaining member of his family living at home. The girl, just approaching womanhood, was afflicted with a strange malady that baffled the skill of physicians....

the girl told her father that all that was done for her by Father Bernard would not help her in the least and that she would go away in a year from that time to live with the fairies.....

In just a year from her disappearance she returned home and related a wonderful tale regarding her absence. She said she had been off with the fairies, with whom she had lived in the most splendid style. They had everything that heart could desire, and spent most of their time in traveling incog. over the country. She had traveled with them and rode in the cars, invisible to mortal eyes....

On the third day after coming to Dubuque she came down stairs and informed Mrs. Hayes that she had to go, that two of the fairies had come for her and that they were now upstairs waiting for her. Mrs. Hayes followed the girl upstairs, and there, to her amazement, she saw two queer-looking beings resembling men dressed in antiquated black costumes, and with them the girl left the house. Mrs. Hayes followed them to the door and watched them go up the street, when, after going half a block, all three suddenly disappeared in the air, since which nothing has ever been heard of the missing girl....

This newspaper article is expanded upon by Iowa's "The Des Moines Register," which gives us the name of the girl taken by the fairies as Miss Kittie. In their story: "Miss Kittie stayed away from the fairies. On the third day, she told her married sister that she had to go again, that the fairies could do without her no longer."

There is so much to unpack in this little story that it's hard to know where to begin, but since this is our first introduction to the now famous Men in Black, it is perhaps best to begin there. There are three important characteristics about fairies and similar beings from folklore that are important to this discussion. The first is that fairies dislike change, and can at times even fear it, to the point that new ideas, tastes, and smells

98

can actually cause them to flee. Witches and fairies both wore pointy hats hundreds of years after these had gone out of style. So the idea that fairies wore antiqued clothing is fairly standard. Second, fairies dislike humans talking too much about them and would often punish and threaten those who did.

Now consider that the next time the men in black appear in the record, they too are trying to keep people from talking about strange events. In the 1940s Harold Dahl spotted some round objects flying in the sky, the next day a man in a black suit took him to a dinner and warned him not to speak of the event. These men in black which have now been connected with stories of aliens repeatedly are also known to frequently wear "old fashioned" clothing. Obviously, from a folkloric perspective there may be no connection between these two stories, other than people having similar thoughts about otherworldly encounters. From the perspective of an urban fantasy, however, it should be clear that the men in black have gone from simply recruiting the people that the fairies need for survival, to trying to keep the activities of the fairies a secret.

The final aspect of this story that is of extreme interest is the fact that Miss Kittie stated that "the fairies could do without her no longer." Fairies, as I've pointed out repeatedly in my books needed humans. Humans seem to have a magical ability to make objects that fairies struggle with such as; fire, buckets, ovens, kettles, and more. Human prepared food helps the fairies heal. Humans can provide fairies with medical aid or help them win wars. The fairies dependence on humans for their own economic wellbeing means that they are constantly trying to improve the economy of some humans, while hurting it among others. This leads to another interesting aspect of fairy, and alien encounters – that of the shaman's esthetic journey.

Steampunk and Modern Fairies

The man screams and tries to back pedal away from the oncoming train, his mind is overwhelmed with fear. Even through closed eyes, he can see the bright light rushing towards him, then, Bam! Something small hits him. He falls to the ground in shock, barely able to process the sound of a laughing kitsune (fox) darting off into the bushes.

The train had been nothing more than an illusion.

Fairies and magical creatures found new ways to take advantage of the rapidly changing world of the Victorian Era (Meiji Era in Japan). In France lutins stole and crashed cars, the fairies of Ireland attacked these cars, in Italy fairies teased road construction crews. Most of the stories we have of fairies adjusting to the new world, however, come from Japan. Here Tenuki (dogs which look like raccoons) took human form to get drunk in bars, foxes began pretending to be trains and cars in order to work their mischief, and kami took on new roles to help people adjust to their new lives.

> When discussing ijirait (fairy like spirits in Inuit lore) Nutaraaluk said:
> They can wear the same clothes that you and I wear. They can go to the store, but no matter how many times they shop the stock never depletes. Over time they can buy snowmobiles just like we do. When we had dogteams, they had dogteams. When we no longer used dogteams and we used snowmobiles, they used snowmobiles. I told you earlier that I had seen this snowmobile light and when I went to check it out there was nothing there because it had belonged to an ijiraq. I knew if it had been human I should have been able to see a person there. I was trying to find the tracks everywhere but I couldn't find any. I knew there was an ijiraq that was trying to communicate with me.
> Interviewing Inuit Elders Edited by Bernard Saladin d' Anglure

One woman traveled on an invisible train car with the fairies, and in Russia, Japan, and other places people would occasionally see ghostly trains and cars.

> One year, toward the end of the holidays, my brother and I had a strange experience, the mystery of which was never solved. We were leaving by the midnight train from Moscow to St. Petersburg. After dinner we said good-bye to our parents and entered the sleigh which was to take us to Moscow. Our road led through a forest called the Silver Forest which stretched for miles without a single dwelling or sign of human life. It was a clear, lovely moonlight night. Suddenly in the heart of the forest, the horses reared, and to our stupefaction we saw

a train pass silently between the trees. The coaches were brilliantly lit and we could distinguish the people seated in them. Our servants crossed themselves, and one of them exclaimed under his breath: "The powers of evil!" Nicholas and I were dumbfounded; no railroad crossed the forest and yet we had all seen the mysterious train glide by (Prince Felix Youssupov).

Again, given that fairies were often the ones who taught humans about technology and human and fairy culture often reflected each other it shouldn't be surprising that there was some notion that fairies also developed technology. Think of the Glaistig in Scotland, which was responsible for nearly any skill people had. They made people good blacksmiths, good tailors, ship builders, etc. It's not a stretch to imagine that they would also make people skilled engineers and airship builders as well. This was also true of Nymphs / Muses in Greece which granted people their skills.

Perhaps the most interesting transition from the past to the modern era is to be found in Japan. Here deities of the mountains and rice growing such as Inari Okami became the kami of modern business as well. Kitsune who had previously helped with growing crops helped to forge magical weapons. Anything which was important to human life could have spirits which people would perform rituals for:

> There are another cases of performing a rite to console the spirits of some tools which were made and utilized by men in everyday life such as needles, knives,shoes; or to purify buildings before inaugurating them including even nuclear power stations or factories of computer machines, wishing that all the labour works and productions involved in there would be done properly and safely.

http://www.socsci.uci.edu/~rgarfias/aris/courses/japan/kami

The fairies didn't always make this transition, however. The changes in cities during the Victorian Era weren't always so prevalent in the countryside, however. For even as the world's cities went through a series of shocking changes the countryside remained isolated for a long time. With no railroads, no electricity it existed apart from the rest of the world, retaining many of their old traditions and ideas about the magical world in which they lived.

For those of you who want to tell the story of steampunk fairies or fairies in a Victorian era world it's easy to imagine a countryside still living what amounts to a Medieval lifestyle, while occasionally viewing airships flying overhead. Certainly, there were villages in Japan that continued to live and work as they always had right up until the early 1960s. The English countryside was filled with places where Cunning (good witches) were still the most important people in some communities right up through WWI.

Indeed, the vast majority of the stories about fairies were collected after people began using steam power fairly frequently. Even so, with the growth of the cities, a number of things happened. First people in the country without work began, for the first time, to move in mass into the cities to work in factories. The number of people living in the country decreased, the number of farmers decreased. Rather than try to struggle through family farms closed up. This in turn transformed the dynamic of the countryside, and worried the fairies who didn't like to see these changes. Thus in Wales and Cornwall there are stories of fairies aiding people who are about to loose their farms and homes, doing some of their work for them at night so that they won't have to close up and move away.

We see similar stories in tales like "The Elves and the Shoe Maker." In this story, which was prevalent throughout Europe some fairies help a Shoemaker who was likely struggling because the industrial revolution and it's use of machines to make clothes and destroyed his business.

This leads to a second important change in the countryside. While the decreasing cost of clothes and shoes greatly helped the poorest of families (shoes had been so expensive children often went barefoot even on frozen ground) it greatly changed the dynamic of the countryside. Once traveling tailors had carried stories and ideas of folk religion from village to village in places like Scotland, but these began to decrease as their jobs were replaced by factories.

Despite the fact that fairies push many of the changes that occur in human society, there are many fairies which are adverse to change. Stories abound of fairies growing angry at people for putting new spices in their food, such as wood wife in Germany who was furious that someone had backed cumin into their bread. They missed the old foods, the old traditions, the old families that they had been neighbors with for generations that had been forced to move on.

In addition houses and farms in the countryside could become abandoned, leaving the family fairies who had lived in these lands for generations alone, without a purpose. In such cases the countryside could quickly become overrun with mischievous boggarts without a home.

Still, despite such changes, life went on much as it always had in the countryside. People retained their old relationship to the fairy world, and even reapplied it in interesting new ways. When the people of Mari-El (in Russia) for example, were called to war in distant lands they would pray and leave offerings to their local Keremet who would in return keep them safe. In one case a Keremet even brought a soldier home for his brothers wedding, before returning him once more to the battlefield. The Japanese had many similar experiences in which local Kami kept them safe during the wars during the Victorian era and helped them defeat Russia during one of the biggest wars of the era.

So for many, the relationship with the spirit world was only enhanced by the changes in the Victorian world. For when people's children were taken to war in distant lands they'd never heard of, or were used to maintain their countries interests in far away colonies which had once seemed like the 'other world' people needed to turn somewhere. This meant that the role of the tutelary spirits which people had once turned to for help with farming had to expand and change rapidly.

There was one more change which occurred during the Victorian era that transformed not only the countryside but all of human society. People in the cities began to think about the country and fairies of their nations with a sense of Romanticism. From the Grimm Brothers to Yeats, people began to believe that the countryside and it's fairies was what truly defined their culture. Fairies became a human symbol of nationalism, a point of pride for the Celts, among others. In a steampunk fantasy world this would have changed our relationship with the fairies. So in a steampunk world many leaders and philosophers would be scrambling for the approval of the fairies. Wars would be between not only two human nations, but fairy nations united with human nations. As more and more people sought to imitate the fairies of their land.

Speculating on Elements of Fairy Culture

Just as Katherine Briggs used folklore to speculate on the nature of the fairies economy, so too can we use folklore to gain a better understanding of many of the elements of fairy culture, and in so doing gain a better understanding of the politics of the spirit world. There are numerous cultural elements, many of which have already been discussed to a point, such as politics. In addition, I would like to discuss economy, technology, integration, and norms of behavior. Each of these cultural elements is different enough from that of humans as to alter the way fairies would think about the world. What's more, we have enough information on each of these to discuss them.

1 – The Economy of Fairyland

Survival, desire, and pleasure are the great motivators, and all three are wrapped up in economics. For the longest time most of humanities economy centered around the obtainment of food, whether this was through agriculture, pastoralism, or hunting and fishing. Fairies too would farm, fish, raise, cattle, make shoes, and have similar sorts of jobs. Yet fairies were often dependent on humans for at least a portion of their food. Many fairies also had trouble creating mundane items such as ovens, pots, or even fire. Yet at the same time fairies were magical and so could help crops grow, create illusions, etc. In other words, the wealth of the fairies depended in large part on the success of the humans economy, which the fairies could influence. Fairy magic and fairy need meant that fairies could be at once wealthy and poor. In a Scottish story, a fairy woman begs a human for food, but when told by the poor human that there is none to give, the fairy drinks the dye the woman is making from heather.

Briggs (1959) states that clean water and bread are often left out for fairies at night.

> Then the fairy ladies would come and wash their babies in the water set ready for them, warm themselves by the fire and eat the bread milk left for them. Then the house would be lucky, and the neat obliging maid would find sixpence in the pail or in her shoe. But if the house was left in disarray, pinching was the best that the maid could expect. Sometimes she might be cursed with lameness.

These fairies needed clean water, a fire, and food from a human, but they had silver in abundance. For silver has magic in it. "Silver bullets and silver knives are efficacious against witches, who are in that respect different from fairies, whose traffic is

104

silver." This, however, didn't make all, or even most fairies wealthy. For fairies frequently, used illusions to make cheap food appear good, and dank caves appear like beautiful palaces. Such fairies were often poor, but they wished to appear rich. As such, one of their most frequent means of obtaining goods was through theft. In some cases, however, they would repay those they stole from with luck, making people who the fairies stole from prosper more than they otherwise would have.

Fairies would visit human markets in disguise in German, Britain, and other places, often to steal what they needed.

> "Strange were the doings of little folk in Ambleside fair and market. Dressed as common folk, they would mingle with the marketing folk, and then by blowing at women at the market stalls, they became invisible, and were enabled to steal things from the stalls."
> Newman, L., & Wilson, E. (1952). Folklore Survivals in the Southern "Lake Counties" and in Essex: A Comparison and Contrast. *Folklore, 63*(2), 91-104. Retrieved from http://www.jstor.org/stable/1257718

Others would disguise themselves and purchase what they needed fairly. There was a nixie in Germany who bought potatoes from a farmer, and brought the farmer to his underwater realm to deliver them, then paid the farmer far more than what was owed. This was typical of the fairies who almost always pay far more than what they owe, and extract more retribution from those who anger them than perhaps they should. Thys Celtic Folklore
Plant Rhys Dwfn visited markets in Cardigan and Fishguard and paid so much they cleared the market and raised the price of grain.

There are a few tales of fairies hosting their own market; however, these are most commonly found in Somerset. Mostly the markets would vanish before people could reach them. A few people who entered them became paralyzed. One man did manage to purchase a mug from one of the fairytales and received leaves for his change. In the morning, his mug had turned to silver, and his leaves to gold. It's possible that that the market wasn't equipped to deal with money, as there are reports that fairies didn't exchange money at these, such as the description of a market from Cornwall:

Still, a great part of the small folks diverted themselves in parading up and down, on the green, between the standings and dancing-ground, examining the pretty things displayed. They didn't seem to have any money amongst them to buy anything, yet they often bartered their trinkets and changed them from stall to stall.

Fairies also bartered for their needs with their human neighbors. Antiquities and Folklore of Worcestershire – Man mends a fairy's three-legged stool. (419)
Campbell Tales of the Western Ighlands II – Fairy Kettle tale.
A woman of Peace would often borrow a wife's kettle: when she lent it she would say;

> A smith is able to make Cold iron hot with coal, The due of a kettle is bones, and to bring back the kettle whole. When she said that the Woman of Peace always brought the kettle back with plenty of bones to make soup. However, her husband being afraid of the woman of peace upset her, so she didn't return the kettle one day. The human woman went and stole the kettle back, and the dogs of peace chased her, She threw meat for them to slow them until her own human dogs came out and drove them back. The woman of peace never came to borrow her kettle again.

Leather says in Herfordshire Folklore
> One day, a man was working in the fields when he heard the fairies talking over their baking; they said they had no peel. He said, "I'll find a peel." He made one and left it out in the field where they could easily see it. Next day it was gone, and in its place, the fairies had given him a batch of delicious cakes.

What the fairies magic and dependence on humans means is that in addition to the typical jobs of raising their own food and making their own items, there were four additional which fairies focused on. The first of these was banditry, for having magical powers which allowed fairies to sneak and create illusions meant that they could steal what they needed. Fairies often lived under people's hearths so that they could lift one of the heath stones and snatch down the freshly baked bread. Other fairies would sneak into people's homes at night or mug them on the roads. There were risks in this, however, as there are numerous tales of humans killing and driving away fairies who steal from them.

The second job fairies commonly had was helping humans create objects and grow crops grow, thus;

> In Scotland and England, their (the fairies) skill seems to be chiefly in agriculture, for Brownies, pisgies and trooping fairies all help with threshing, reaping and mowing. Spinning and weaving seem to be principle skills with them everywhere, and in the Highlands of Scotland, they are sometimes spoken of as skilled smiths, though in most places the fairies cannot touch iron or steel. Medicine and the knowledge of herbs is an almost universal skill; but above all, they are masters of glamour and shapeshifting so they can appear large or small, hideous or beautiful, animal or human at will. They can also control the weather, foresee the future, and are very powerful in blessing and banning (Briggs, 1959)

This means that while fairies can be kind, some of them only act that way out of utility need. Even nature spirits in Europe seemed to desire food and cloth from humans, and so would allow hunters and fishers to take animals in return for such offerings. In addition, fairies helped one man become a master carpenter so that he would be better at making ships and another back become a master blacksmith. Indeed, it seems as though it was commonly believed that human mastery of nearly any craft could have been granted by the fairies. Thus, while fairies may not always have been skilled at building an economy of their own, they could use magic to aid humans in doing this.

Thirdly, fairies would trade with humans or borrow from them. Such activities, however, required humans to be aware of their presence and so this job seems to have decreased over time. There are, however, some stories of nixies, and the like directly purchasing food from farmers.

Fourthly, fairies could hire or kidnap humans to work for them, providing them with what they needed.

Emotional Goods
It should be noted that while food and mundane goods are the biggest part of an economy, emotional goods such as stories, music, and the like are also important pieces of the puzzle.

Fairies delighted in music, dance, and similar things. Aristocratic fairies especially spent most of their time engaged in these activities, and would even hire or kidnap humans who could perform music. Fairies of the land would often go to listen to humans joke and tell stories, so even here, humans were an important part of the fairy economy. Yet despite their importance to the fairies' economy, fairies sought to remain hidden from humanity.

Internal fairy economy
Of course, the fairy's dependence on humans is only part of the story, as already mentioned in the section on trooping fairies, fairies could provide some of their own food and goods, in much the same way humans did. That is, the primary fairy economy reflected that of the human economy. Thus, they would herd cattle, fish, hunt, farm, make shoes, and perform any number of mundane tasks.

Fairy Technology
There were also many tools that were believed to have specific effects on the magico-religious world. Bells could drive fairies away, certain types of windows could let the spirits of the dead leave a house, and more. In Newfoundland, it was often believed that technology such as cars and trains were responsible for driving the fairies further underground, while in places like Japan and Western Alaska, it was believed that the magical world interacted more positively with the new technologies. In most cases, however, it does seem that fairies tend to have similar technology to humans, even if they can't always make it themselves and so must get it from humans. Indeed, it may be that fairies couldn't start fires themselves, given how often they must warm themselves by human fires. Fairies do have one interesting piece of technology – magic. While magic might not be a traditionally human tech, it is one which allows the fairies the chance to survive despite weaknesses in other areas.

Illusions - Much of fairy magic comes from their ability to create illusions or essentially hypnotize people into thinking they are seeing something that isn't there. In Newfoundland, a person caught in the fairy's magic might wander in circles, thinking that they've become lost in a vast forest, while those around them watched as they walked in a small circle around a treeless berry patch. In Norway, a huldra made a man think he was inside a nice house when he was in fact in a little pond, and would have drowned if it weren't for some iron, she had which broke the enchantment he was under. Others have seen the fairies hold wondrous banquets where the food turned out to be nothing more than leaves or sour berries. So, when creating a fairy culture, one has to wonder how being able to use illusions akin to virtual reality might alter a society.

It's also interesting to note that while fairies can turn invisible, they almost never attack someone physically while invisible. Instead, their arrows and other attacks make a person sick, cause strokes, etc. This could indicate an important weakness that the fairies can't immediately harm someone while they are hiding behind their illusions. This would explain why they aren't able to defeat humans in a direct war because, in order to fight people directly, they must be visible and therefore susceptible to the dangers of human strength, iron, symbols, and the evil eye.

Flight and Chants - Through certain chants, fairies could cause objects to fly, or perform other acts of magic. Their power was limited, but as a united group, it could be great. For example, in one story; dozens of fairies were able to chant around the house of a man which had angered them, causing it to float into the sky and to a new location.

Potions and Herbs - A lot of the fairies' magic comes from their knowledge of herbs. In many stories, they live long lives because they know how to get a hold of some magical herb or potion that makes them live longer. They are able to see the fairy realm with the help of some ointment that is put in their children's eyes; however, if a human gets this in their eyes, they can see the fairy realm as well. When fairies help a witch cure illness, cause love, etc., they teach the witch how to mix a potion or give them a potion which they can use. One important point to keep in mind in this is that many of the magical herbs, trees, and plants grow in forests or wild moors without which the fairies would lose access to many of their spells.

Magical Items - Some of the greatest powers come from magical items. The merrow (Irish mermaids) couldn't breathe in the water without red hats. Similarly, the zwerg used red hats to turn invisible and belts in order to grow stronger. Other items such as the spear of lugh were much rarer such that only one fairy was believed to have them.

Nature - Fairies had some control over nature, though how much control they have varied from fairy to fairy. Irish fairies could control the wind to a point. They could buffet a house with gusts of wind, rattling it so that the people inside couldn't sleep, but they didn't seem to be able to blow it over very easily. They could, however, blight someone's crops, or make them prosper. Many fairies, such as the huldra of Norway and the leshii of Russia controlled the forest animals, and so could send bears and wolves to attack a person's animals. Many water spirits could make water toxic when angered, poisoning anyone who drank it. In addition, almost all fairies had the power to cause illness in people and animals.

Integration

How new members of a society are made to respect its ideas and values to the point that they become full members of that society. Certainly, one can imagine the fairies having difficulty raising young fairies in a world where they must keep the fact that they are magical a secret. Especially given the propensity for young fairies to show off. In one story from Northumberland, a fairy girl flies down a chimney and begins to play with the human boy there:

> She certainly showed him some fine games. She made animals out of the ashes that looked and moved like life; and trees with green leaves waving over tiny houses, with men and women an inch high in them, who, when she breathed on them, fell to walking and talking quite properly.

In Wales, there were stories of a boy who encountered and befriended a group of fairies who they didn't even realize were fairy children.

> Once, at the end of the day, on coming back home from the hills, the boy met some lovely children. They were dressed in very fine clothes and had elegant manners. They came up, smiled, and invited him to play with

110

them. He joined in their sports and was too much interested to take note of time. He kept on playing with them until it was pitch dark. Among other games, which he enjoyed, had been that of "The King in his counting house, counting out his money," and "The Queen in her kitchen, eating bread and honey," and "The Girl hanging out the clothes," and "The Saucy Blackbird that snipped off her nose." In playing these, the children had aprons full of what seemed to be real coins, the size of crowns, or five-shilling pieces, each worth a dollar. These had "head and tail," beside letters on them and the boy supposed they were real.

The boy's mother, however, realized at once that these were faires and forbade her child from playing with them, he didn't listen. Unlike most such fairy tales, the boy was better off for his disobedience as the fairies gave the family treasure in their time of need.

Oftentimes such interactions didn't end well for the fairy or human children. Fairy children, after all, were lovers of mischief and their access to magic and treasure made them potential targets for people. In Tyrol, zwerg children were known to sneak into people's farms to steal peas, which lead to humans attacking and driving the fairies away. This latter vent shows why it is dangerous for young fairies to show themselves to humans as they can be kidnapped, killed, or taken hostage. This means fairy parents must be cautious with what few children they have.

In many cases, fairy children are said to be rare, with few fairies actually able to have them with any frequency. Fairies live a long time, potentially thousands of years, or forever. Further, fairies were often believed to be disturbed by new ideas. In many stories, people could get ancient fairies to reveal themselves by making a brewery of eggshells, at which point the fairies would act surprised despite themselves, in Germany this brewing in eggshells is done in order to drive fairies away who aren't changelings while other fairies will scream and run away when people use new spices. Finally, it is notable that fairies still wear pointed hats, long after these have gone out of style. As Wilby puts it, Fairies "wore clothes (adopting local fashions, often quaintly out-of-date)." Their politics too seemed to be out of date and from an older age. Given the fairies age, it perhaps makes sense that they would be disturbed by what is new, that they would be old fashioned.

Imagine then a world where the majority of the population was hundreds of years old, and have a tendency towards being old fashioned. Now imagine children being raised by these old fashioned beings who outnumber them hundreds to one. Keep in mind that even old fairies tend towards childishness, that they enjoy playing with children. One Nis who would steal from the neighbors took a human child with him on his little adventures. In this sense, the ancient fairies would be the younger fairies' peers and playmates to a certain extent. Given this, we can perhaps imagine younger fairies to become much more old fashioned in their thinking than human children would be.

There is more to integration than just how a fairy should raise its own children, for fairies must integrate witches and changelings into their society as well. Recall that () of Iowa lived with the fairies, as do many mortals they take into their world out of necessity. A girl in the Shetlands received many gifts form the fairies because they took her mother into their realm. Musicians and especially beautiful men and women would often be taken into fairyland to marry.

> Woman Marries a Zwerg (Germany)
> A young woman in Braderup had a very hard job like most women on the Frisian Islands. She felt unhappy and envied the zwerg who were always happy and had to do very little work. Once, she went with her neighbor over the hill to where the Önnerersken were dancing. "Oh," she cried. "I would love to marry one of them, wouldn't you?"
> Her friend replied that she would.
> A zwerg heard this, came, and wooed the girl the next day. Soon, the two of them were married, and she went to live with him in his mountain where they had several children.

Other memorates involve people getting gifts from those who've married into fairyland. To a certain extent, integration may have been fairly simple when the humans and fairies cultures were already similar. That said, the fairies do live in both a hidden world and a world of magic. What's more, humans weren't always given happy positions in the fairy world. Indeed, many humans appear to have become slaves within fairyland. A man named Mr. Noy encountered a group of fairies who invited them to eat with each other, but a human girl who had been in love with him warned him not to eat anything, for doing so is how she was trapped among the fairies. She brought them their drinks and acted in the role of a servant, but could not leave on her own. Exactly how the fairies control these people isn't clear, but typically after a person eats certain fairy foods – but not all fairy foods – the person is trapped in the fairy's service.

Witches and other people whom the fairies needed were typically integrated into fairyland through celebrations such as witches Sabbaths. Such celebrations involved food that was safe for people to eat, dances, music, the sharing of magical items, etc. Other witches, however, weren't integrated into fairy society so pleasantly, some were assaulted, tortured, and beaten into doing what the fairies wanted.

Social Interactions, Values, Norms of Behavior

Fairies were often the ones who determined what was moral within any given community by rewarding those who followed their code of behavior and punishing those who broke it. One could presume then that fairies moral code was similar to that of humans. There are some exceptions to this, however.

Honesty
It is difficult to find a story where a fairy or any similar being out and out lies to people. Briggs quotes Eldurus as saying that "the fairies were great lovers and respecters of the truth, and indeed it was not wise to attempt to deceive them, nor will they ever tell a direct lie or break a direct promise, though they may often distort it."

Of course, the fairies rarely ever needed to go out and outspeak a lie. Their power to create illusions meant that they could create an entire false world. Making garbage appear as food, making caves appear as beautiful castles and leaves as gold. People believed the false circumstances the fairies set up. For a fairy could appear as a person's love, or make the land under a haystack appear as a vast dance hall filled with a person's friends. They could use illusions to entice or scare people into automagically doing what they wanted:

113

Some five miles southward of Sligo is a gloomy and tree-bordered pond, a great gathering-place of water-fowl, called, because of its form, the Heart Lake. It is haunted by stranger things than heron, snipe, or wild duck. Out of this lake, as from the white square stone in Ben Bulben, issues an unearthly troop. Once men began to drain it; suddenly, one of them raised a cry that he saw his house in flames. They turned around, and every man there saw his own cottage burning. They hurried home to find it was faery glamour (Yeats "The Celtic Twilight").

What's more, fairies spoke as if their illusions were real. At least people seem to have believed that fairies disguised as a person could lie about being that person, for they wouldn't simply trust someone who said they weren't a fairy. Fairies would call their illusions of food an actual food as well. In essence, the fairies seem to have been willing to speak of the illusionary world they created as if it were the real one, which is essentially a lie. Presuming fairies couldn't lie, except where their illusions were concerned, one must understand that this doesn't mean someone can ever get the perfect truth out of them. This is because fairies wouldn't necessarily make full statements about anything. Human cultures that take the truth so seriously that even accidental lying is to be avoided are frustrating to those from cultures where accidental lying is acceptable. Ask a child from such a culture if their parent is home and they will say, "maybe?" – because their parent might have crawled out or in the window while they weren't looking. Ask them how to do something, and they'll say, "anyway you want," ask them where they are going, and they'll say "over there" with a general nod. Even when a straight answer might benefit them, they often don't give one, meaning it's impossible to tell when they are being evasive on purpose. This is important to keep in mind, because in many books which depict fairies as unable to lie, one can tell when they are being evasive. In reality, someone who couldn't lie likely would always be evasive, even when they want to tell the truth and are doing so.

Charity and Hard Work
Fairies had an obsession with charity and hard work, and would constantly seek to punish those who were lazy and greedy. Often, their punishments for those who didn't work hard and acted in a greedy manner would be overkill by our considerations, for they often killed such people by cutting them

into pieces, tormenting them with diseases, or crushing them under avalanches.

Tranquility
Fairies were obsessed with tranquility, drunks who sang, people who hurt their wives without cause, and those who whistled at night were all likely to be punished by the fairies.

Celebration
Fairies were obsessed with people celebrating holidays in a traditional manner and would punish those who worked on holidays or didn't celebrate properly. On the Isle of Man, we know that at least one fairy was banished from the fairy court because they didn't show up to one of the fairies celebrations.

Sexually Open
Perhaps the biggest difference between mortal morality and that of fairies was that fairies tended to be far more sexually open than humans. This has been true from Russia and Ancient Greece to Ireland. That said fairies could also be sexually jealous and punish those they felt were cheating on them, or banish fairies from fairyland who were rivals for the affection of their love.

Spirit Journeys

Many people have experienced moments of spiritual clarity. Moments in which they connect with an overwhelming universe, in which they realize that there are powers to which they would willingly devote their lives. Such experiences provide people with bigger questions about the world and the nature of reality than – where will my next meal come from?
People have long believed that humanity is not alone, for the mythological cosmology of multiple planes is populated by powerful supernatural beings. It is by traveling through this cosmos that we can truly come to understand the nature of the universe, of humanity, of magic, and the divine. Yet it is only

given to a very few to have the ability to travel the cosmos at will. There are those who will do so accidentally or will be dragged into it against their will, but the witch shaman does so frequently and with specific purposes. Sometimes this purpose can be as simple as the need to commune with the higher powers, to feel connected with the universe, to gain metaphysical enlightenment. Often the shaman journeyed to the otherworld with a specific question, on which the lives of people depended.

The cosmology of ancient people is a difficult thing to break down. Certainly, aspects of it are simple enough. The idea that there are heavens and underworlds in which deities and other supernatural entities dwell is common. Often such planes are connected via a tree or mountain. This isn't the whole story, however, for the fairies and nymphs rarely dwell in the divine realms, neither in the heavens nor the underworld. Rather they existed in a separate realm altogether. We must then discuss cosmology as having four parts.

The Middle Earth

This is our world, within which magical creatures can dwell and hide. Within our world fairies can live under our homes, within trees, in little holes in the wall, etc. Within this world, the fairies can dwell as if they were the borrowers from the famous book or smurfs in secret villages. That is with their own hidden world, but still essentially part of our own. To further confuse things, parts of our world exist in a liminal, semi-divine state. In ancient Greece, the lower parts of mountains lay between the divine and the human world. Caves too could exist between the mortal world and the underworld. In addition, Europeans tended to treat cross-roads, deep forests, the edges of fields, and certain times of the day or year as liminal places, where a person might encounter magical creatures.

Georgia has a dark, but interesting take on the parts of our world which belong to the spirits.

> According to the words of our respondent, 80-year-old Salome Imedadze, these creatures live in deep forests and thickets, termed as "wrong places." They offered their love to all good-looking males and wrestled with the human beings. Tkashmapa wrestled with Salome's brother, Gerasime, who returned home with his clothes torn over and a specific smell of a siren. The man, who entered in an intimate relationship with Tkashmapa, was

116

termed as "enslaved," they returned home speechless and needed special prayers to get back to their normal state. According to the legends, The Lady of Forests was scared of fire, so a person walking in the vicinity of a "wrong place," usually took a torch (zhinzhgili-in Imeretian dialect) with him, to safeguard himself against the siren (Khachapuridze, 2015).

Horror stories are often of magical creatures that are a part of, but separate from our world. Of course, as already mentioned, many, if not most encounters with the spiritual places ended well for people. Thus, the reason people would seek out sacred groves, trees, and fountains. Still, its good to keep in mind that our world was believed to be haunted by forces beyond our control.

The Neighboring Spirit World

Alongside our world are pocket realms in which fairies can live. A girl can be taken by the spirit of a bathhouse in Russian lore, known as a bunnik, and spend her entire life growing up in the home of the bunnik, which is within the bathhouse itself. Yet no one ever sees her or suspects that she or the place she lives is within the small space of a peasant steam bath. This is because parts of fairyland existed seemingly as pocket dimensions within our world. They couldn't be entered into or seen by an ordinary person, except by the occasional accident or with the help of a fairy. Further, they were much larger than the space in the mortal world would indicate. People in Britain and Newfoundland would accidentally stumble into vast forests where there were none, or see vast fairy cities and castles in small gardens.

> He told me that one time he had gone into the gardens, and as he was crossing a path that he usually crossed, he saw trees that were never there before. The trees were about fifty or sixty feet high. He went down the road and then went back again. He did this three times, and the third time he went back, everything was back to normal. He told me that the "Little Johns" must have been there.' (Rieti)

Stories such as this one are common in Western Europe but occur on occasion in Eastern and Northern Europe as well.

117

Such encounters with the otherworld might simply be illusions of course, but they can also include meetings with fairies within their homes. Further, nymphs, rusalka, and their kin often seemed to dwell within such a world, for they lived small patches of beautiful nature, yet in tales had larger homes, homes which ordinary people seemed unable to see. The same appears to have been true of many fairies, whose homes ordinary people didn't see, or were unable to touch unless the fairies allowed them to. This seems to be more than simply invisible homes, however, for the homes and forests of these fairies were larger than the area in which they existed. Such regions were both a part of our world and a part of the spirit world. One could think of them as the border between the two. Consider for example the story of the "Pied Piper" which takes place on the Isle of Wight

> He laid his pipe to his lips afresh, but now there came forth no shrill notes, as it were, of scraping and gnawing, and squeaking and scurrying, but the tune was joyous and resonant, full of happy laughter and merry play. And as he paced down the streets, the elders mocked, but from school-room and play-room, from nursery and workshop, not a child but ran out with eager glee and shouted following gaily at the Piper's call. Dancing, laughing, joining hands and tripping feet, the bright throng moved along up Gold Street and down Silver Street, and beyond Silver Street lay the cool green forest full of old oaks and wide-spreading beeches. In and out among the oak-trees you might catch glimpses of the Piper's many-coloured coat. You might hear the laughter of the children break and fade and die away as deeper and deeper into the lone green wood, the stranger went, and the children followed.

> All the while, the elders watched and waited. They mocked no longer now. And watch and wait as they might, never did they set their eyes again upon the Piper in his partly-coloured coat. Never were their hearts gladdened by the song and dance of the children issuing forth from amongst the ancient oaks of the forest.

The children in this story were simply led to the forest, and their parents could still hear their children within the forest, they couldn't see them or bring them home. In the story of the

118

Habetrot dancing a; "bride led her husband the next day to the flowery knoll, and bade him look through the self-bored stone. Great was his surprise to behold Habetrot dancing and jumping over her rock, singing all the time this ditty to her sisterhood, while they kept time with their spindles:—"

> "We who live in dreary den,
> Are both rank and foul to see?
> Hidden from the glorious sun,
> That teems the fair earth's canopie:
> Ever must our evenings lone
> Be spent on the colludie stone.

> "Cheerless is the evening grey
> When Causleen hath died away,
> But ever bright and ever fair
> Are they who breathe this evening air,
> And lean upon the self-bored stone
> Unseen by all but me alone."

The song ended, Scantlie Mab asked Habetrot what she meant by the last line, "Unseen by all but we alone."

"There is one," replied Habetrot, "whom I bid to come here at this hour, and he has heard my song through the self-bored stone." So saying she rose, opened another door, which was concealed by the roots of an old tree, and invited the pair to come in and see her family.

This nearer otherworld might simply be a trick of illusions, except for the change in the size of the forests people must walk through when introduced to them. Perhaps most telling of all are the notions of fairy paths.

Fairy Paths

Fairies have certain paths which they can use to traverse between their various otherworldly homes. Through these, the fairies living within a tree could travel between their homes in the neighboring spirit worlds, and without needing to expose themselves to the dangers of the mortal world. Yet humans can still obstruct these by building buildings or fences in the middle of them. When a human does this, the fairies grow angry and send storms, act as poltergeists, and occasionally curse the people until a hole is made in the home or fence for them, or the people abandon the home.

> When several of a family have, either owing to hereditary taint, or the unhealthiness of the situation, or other circumstances, been carried off in succession by consumption, or some other lingering complaint, it is attributed to the fact that the house in which they have died having been unluckily built upon the fairy path. This is generally discovered by means of a "traveling women," a sort of sculer,
> The Dublin University Magazine: A Literary and Political Journal, Volume 33

There are numerous mentions of this idea. The Kalasha people of the Hindukush mountains have a very similar notion, and so were historically careful not to build their homes within a fairy path. Again, a Newfoundland story provides a very interesting example of a fairy trapped when human's blocked their path;

> It seems that he had put his house on fairies' path. One night when Jack was at a dance, his mother heard a young child walking back and forth along the front of the house crying. The child stayed there crying all night, and when Jack got home, she told him. Later, Jack heard the crying himself while in the stable. He eventually moved his house again and had no more trouble from the fairies (Rieti)."

What this and similar stories show us is that fairyland could be at once connected and disconnected from the mortal world.

The Deep Spirit Realm
There are parts of the spirit world which are far more difficult to enter. These lay in hills for which a person needs a specific magical key, such as a primrose or a four-leaf clover. These entrances to the otherworld might still lay close at hand, but the otherworld beyond was vast. One of the best places to see this is Wales, where locations such as the Vale of Neath, in Glamorganshire was famous as a center of the fairyland. Here, a

steep, rugged crag called "Craig y Ddinas, was believed to be a stronghold of the fairy tribes.

> Its caves and crevices have been their favorite haunt for many centuries, and upon this rock was held the court of the last fairies who have ever appeared in Wales. Needless to say, there are men still living who remember the visits of the fairies to Craig y Ddinas (Sikes, 1880).

Hades in Greek mythology too was sometimes reachable through caves.
Similarly, other parts of the spirit world required a person to travel for many days through the wilderness, until the mortal wilderness gives way to a vast wilderness of the otherworld.

The Vast Wilderness
The exact cosmological nature of the vast wilderness isn't always clear from fairy tales, but within mythology and fairy tales, in order to travel to nearly any location in the otherworld, or to reach the underworld or heavens, one must travel through a vast – often empty – wilderness. In the tale the "The Three Citrons and the Glass Mountain" a prince is seeking the glass mountain, wondering for a long time over wooded mountains and deserts. When he sits to rest, he startles twelve ravens who fly off.

> The prince jumped to his feet. "Those are the first living creatures I have seen for many a day. I'll go in the direction they have taken," he said to himself, "and perhaps I'll have better luck."
> So he traveled on and after three days and three nights a high castle came in view.
> "Thank God!" he exclaimed, pushing joyfully ahead. "I shall soon have human companionship once more."

The glass mountain itself is an otherworldly location. A fact which is reinforced by the prince having not seen another living creature for days, potentially months of, not even birds. In this case the castle the Raven's lead him to was home to Yezibaba, an old witch and her man eating son. She was friendly to the prince and surprised when she saw him, exclaiming.

121

"Yi, yi, my boy, how did you get here? Why, not even a little bird or a tiny butterfly comes here, much less a human being! You'd better escape if life is dear to you, or my son, when he comes home, will eat you!"

Here again is evidence for the strange emptiness of the vast wilderness of the other world. The emptiness of parts of the spirit world are mentioned in spells to banish evil spirits as well. In these spells the other world was described as being barren and lifeless. Healers in Macedonia would attempt to banish evil spirits;

> "to spaces which were believed to be alien to man. They were spaces that were not culturally conquered and thus outside the village community..... The verbal declarations clearly show that the disease is cast off into a world where humans are not present. Most frequently these unhealthy, lifeless communities are described as villages without roosters, where no dogs bark, no cats, meow, literary, villages which have been abandoned..... They were places where no one could travel and from which there was no return. Places such as Moan Forest and Neverland, for example, are locations where there are no attributes of human culture or symbols of a healthy community bustling with life. and the human body is a widely known practice.... On occasion, the other world is described as better than the one the ill person occupies and the illness is urged to go to this more attractive realm." (Macidonia healers)

Similarly possessing and dangerous spirits in Finland are often banished to strange lands as well;

> "The evil beings I send away, the kehno I incite away, destructive beings I force away, malicious beings I drag away, to sproutless clearings run to waste, to lands unploughed, to swampy dells, to untraversed swamps in which frogs spawn, where muck-worms crawl, to a nameless meadow, unknown by name, where from the earth no herbage sprouts, from the sward no grass exalts itself. If there thou findest not a place, thee I conjure away to the head of the waters of Sumukse, to dark Sariola, to the mist of the sea, to the haze of the lower

air, to the feather-tip of a swan, right under the tongue of a pintail duck." (John Abercromby [1898])

Of course, in most similar stories the emptiness of the vast wilderness area between locations in the other world isn't explicitly mentioned, but the incredible length of the journey is. In Norse mythology the god Hermódr rode from Asgard to Hel to bring Baldr back from the land of the dead.

> "Now this is to be told concerning Hermódr, that he rode nine nights through dark dales and deep, so that he saw not before he was come to the river Gjöll and rode onto the Gjöll-Bridge; which bridge is thatched with glittering gold. Módgudr is the maiden called who guards the bridge; she asked him his name and race, saying that the day before there had ridden over the bridge five companies of dead men; but the bridge thunders no less under thee alone, and thou hast not the color of dead men. Why ridest thou hither on Hel-way?' He answered: 'I am appointed to ride to Hel to seek out Baldr. Hast thou perchance seen Baldr on Hel-way?' She said that Baldr had ridden there over Gjöll's Bridge,--'but down and north lieth Hel-way.'
> 'Then Hermódr rode on till he came to Hel-gate; he dismounted from his steed and made his girths fast, mounted and pricked him with his spurs; and the steed leaped so hard over the gate that he came nowise near to it. Then Hermódr rode home to the hall and dismounted from his steed, went into the hall, and saw sitting there in the high-seat Baldr, his brother; and Hermódr tarried there overnight. At morn Hermódr prayed Hel that Baldr might ride home with him, and told her how great weeping was among the Æsir. But Hel said that in this wise it should be put to the test, whether Baldr were so all-beloved as had been said: 'If all things in the world, quick and dead, weep for him, then he shall go back to the Æsir; but he shall remain with Hel if any gainsay it or will not weep.' Then Hermódr arose; but Baldr led him out of the hall, and took the ring Draupnir and sent it to Odin for a remembrance. And Nanna sent Frigg a linen smock, and yet more gifts, and to Fulla a golden finger-ring.

This story, and others like it demonstrate that the realms in the sky and the underworld realms could be reached by shamanistic figures and their mounts who traveled through the wilderness. We know that Hel was in the underworld and Aesir dwelt in the heavens, and yet Hermódr was able to ride between the two. This is a common notion in mythology and fairy tales, that if one travels far enough through the wilderness they can seemingly reach anywhere. Similarly, the Celtic otherworld could be reached both by traveling underground, but also by sailing far enough west into the sea. Of course, sometimes the otherworld could come to a person as well. In this way they could find themselves in the other world at any moment. When King Arthur wanted to raid the City of Glass and the lands of the dead he sailed to them in a magical white boat. Of course, the other world reached via boat might have been different otherworld reached through caves, for it is difficult to tell which otherworld is being discussed.

It is worth noting that in Germanic lore the guardian to the realm of the dead, as well as the Queen of the Hel were both women. This gives additional credence to the notion that the Russian hag Baba Yaga could have been a guardian to the realm of the dead. It is frequently noted that like many beings in the realm of the dead she often couldn't see living people, but could smell them. What's more a person often couldn't simply walk up to the door of her house, but had to ask the house (which was on chicken legs) to turn the door towards them so they could reach it.

Interestingly enough, this vast wilderness often doesn't seem difficult at all for people to enter. Rather, it is more difficult to navigate and eventually leave. In Selkup lore;

> It is much more difficult for a lay person to leave the unreal world than to get there: "The road was there, the road was, and then it disappeared. (She) looks back, needs to climb up the cedar. She had claws. She climbed up and up. The claws are rubbing away. Then she turned into a squirrel, climbed up and up. The claws are rubbing away again. Then (she) turned into a snake, climbed up and up again. (She) got here. (She) got (here) and found the way again. (She) came home" (the Parabel'). For lay people travelling into the unreal world seems to be a difficult and a distressful ordeal. For example, it is necessary to cross the river source to free oneself from the power of the spirit and to break off

124

wandering and come back home; or to feed the wood-spirit by putting out bread crumbs or a piece of a flat cake, or libating some water at a hillock or the root of a tree (the Ob': Ivankino). The otherworld inhabitants can move in space and time in the form of a whirlwind (Tuchkova, Kuznetsova, Kazakevich, Kim-Maloni, Glushkov, Baidak 2007)

The movement through the shallow underworld was also commonly done in the form of wind. Fairies in Newfoundland and Ireland were especially thought to be able to travel on the wind. It should also be noted that often those entering the spirit world in Europe also had to cross a river, at least sometimes.

The Tree Pathway

In Selkup lore the shaman's staff symbolized the world tree, which did more than simply connect the different layers of the heavens with the earth and the underworld. It was a symbol of the universe itself. Thus, the staff, and the sacred trees connected people to every other part and thing within the universe. In addition to their staff each shaman had a sacred tree, often near their home. Damage to this tree would harm the shaman, and potentially kill them. (Selkup Mythology). In Selkup and likely Germanic as well as Celtic lore, sacrifices made at a tree connected to the world tree would travel up the tree to the deities. This is perhaps why, in Celtic and Germanic lore, the heads of animals were hung from trees. The Mari-El also made sacrifices at the base of trees in order for the spirits and deities to share in the food. Of course, in their case the spirits and deities might actually be hiding within the tree itself. Still, the notion that certain trees could be a pathway to the heavens is an important one.

The Higher Cosmology
Finally, there was the higher cosmology. In early Christian mythology this included seven heavens, nine hells, limbo, etc. In Greek lore this included Hades and the deeper realms as well as the heavenly Olympus. In Nordic mythology this included Helheim and Asgaurd. I could go through one by one and break down dozens of different Eurasian cosmologies, which could have multiple underworlds and multiple heavens. Most often

these cosmologies are divided into two parts – the underworlds and the sky realms. It's important to keep in mind that the underworlds weren't always bad, and indeed the human heavens were often located within them. Nor were the sky realms always good, for giants and other monsters were often located within these. Traveling the higher cosmology could be done by traveling to the different levels of vast wildernesses, across magical oceans or rivers, or by climbing a world pillar, mountain, or tree.

Beings of the spirit worlds
The first three worlds, The Middle Earth, The Neighboring Realm, and the Deeper Spirit World were all populated with fairies, spirits of the dead, giants, dragons, and at times deities so similar to fairies it could be debated whether there was any real difference at all. Deities like Pan for example spent so much time in the mortal realm, and perhaps the other two it does seem that he lived among us, or at least within the neighboring realms. Yet at the same time he wasn't that different from fairies.

The witch shamans of European lore traveled to these first three realms most often. Indeed, it was incredibly rare for there to be stories of people able to travel into the deeper cosmology in European lore. This isn't to say that such journeys didn't happen, simply that they were secondary to most people. Fairyland and the sabbaths in the forests and churches were far more important for most people who went on spirit journeys, and to the daily lives of the peasants. This is why understanding the personalities of the fairies is so important to understanding witch shamans and the spirit journeys they undertook, for these fairies were the inhabitants of the spirit worlds most often visited, and they were the ones who trained, worked with, and for hum the witches worked. It was they who most often dictated the success of a witch's spirit journey and they who essentially determined why the witch was undertaking such a journey.

Entering the spirit world

There were numerous methods for interacting with the spirit world. Across Siberia and in Africa, dancing and singing were common means of calling the spirit world to oneself, or of sending one's soul out into the spirit world. Other people's used masks, idols, drugs, drums, meditation, or a variety of other methods. The three most important methods for entering the spirit world, that is the fairy realm, in Europe were what I term as the dream trance, the near-death experience, and through liminal places and states of being.

Dream Trance and Near Death

Many projected their souls, their subtle self, from their bodies while they slept so that no one would know that they were out battling evil spirits, attending a witch's sabbath, or journeying to speak with gods. Those who were connected to the spirit world could enter this state more or less at will. Witch shamans would frequently lay down when they wanted to project their subtle self from their body. While the subtle self was traveling the witch shaman would typically be so still, they could be mistaken for dead, and indeed if their body were moved or sometimes if someone tried talking to them, they might not be able to return to their body and so would die. I liken this experience to a near-death experience, except that while in a trance, the witch shaman was in control of their spirit journey, those who were dying didn't control where they went. In either case, the advantage of this method was that the witch shaman could travel far away and to distant realms quickly. They could spend days in the spirit world but only have a few moments pass in the mortal one, allowing them to learn or accomplish a lot quickly.

The Subtle Body
Each witch shaman, vampire, and werewolf were believed to have a subtle body, that is a spiritual body which is somewhat akin to that of a ghost. This body was freer than the human body, for it could transform into different animals, sometimes fly (often with the help of magical objects or spirit animals), it could slip through tiny cracks (but not through walls), and travel quickly to distant lands. What's more that sometimes the subtle body could cause mortals to grow tired and fall into a slumber. One can't completely think of this body as ghost-like, however. There is a story of a man who captures a German witch known

as a mora who has been causing him nightmares. This is done by blocking off the whole she used to enter his home, a hole which she must travel through to return home. At this point, finding her beautiful, he marries her. She lives with him for some time, until she can finally convince him to unplug the hole so that she can pass through it and return to her body.

While in subtle form witches are very much like fairies, they can be kept at bay or trapped by humans in similar ways. Further, their bodies are essentially solid. When another mora accidentally wakes up her target, she hides by changing into an apple, which he takes a bite out of, thus killing her. Other subtle bodies are threatened by swords, fire, and grabbed just as if their physical body were present. What's more, their body is often – though not always – visible. It's difficult to say exactly when the subtle body is visible and when it isn't, but it does seem that when they choose to interact with someone in any way, by causing nightmares, by placing a curse, they become visible. What's more, just as with fairies, they can't become invisible again so long as someone is looking at them. Finally, anything that happens to their subtle body happens to their regular body. If their subtle body's foot is shot, their real body suffers the gunshot wound.

Subtle Trance

A skilled shaman can enter a trance while walking around, dancing, or doing pretty much anything. Some of them can do so without anyone even noticing that they have entered this trance-like state. This allows the witch shaman to see the fairies and spirit world around them. Thus, the witch shaman could speak with the fairies that have been summoned that no one else can see, they can walk through the neighboring fairy realm or find the openings to the deeper spirit world. The advantage to this is that unlike the dream trance, their subtle soul never actually leaves its body, so they aren't as vulnerable. That said they aren't able to travel quickly, change form as easily, or enter the most distant realms in the cosmos.

Liminal State

The border between the mortal and spirit worlds is thin in liminal spaces i.e., the boundary between places, times, events, and ideas. Some people would end up in the spirit world because they stepped off the path, found themselves at the crossroads at sunset, or walked three times around a church in the direction the sun travels. There are so many times and places people accidentally found themselves in fairyland; it wouldn't be worth listing them all. What's important to understand is that boundaries were permeable, as were places that were important to nature. Thus, the borders between farms and villages, crossroads, deep forests, under lakes, the tops of mountains, or particularly beautiful pieces of nature could all exist near the spirit world.

Another important aspect of the liminal entry into the spirit world was the fact that certain witches would physically transform and fly in order to interact with the spirit world. The clothes of witches who turned into hares might be found laying in the forest, or the clothes of werewolves might be found in a circle.

Journeys through the spirit world
The journeys into the spirit world could take many forms and have many purposes. The most common forms of spirit journeys in Europe included; spirit battles, wild hunts, Sabbats, fairy tale adventures, and philosophical journeys. With the most common purposes being to defend against spiritual enemies, to steal something spiritual, to rescue someone, or to learn magic and negotiate with otherworldly beings.

Those who traveled the spirit world would do so in human form, but would also transform into animals such as hares, dogs, whales, walrus, swans, and more. Further, many would ride animal spirits such as goats, hares, cats, etc. Or they would ride atop objects such as brooms, spears, and arrows.

Spirit Wars

Central to much of European witchcraft was the notion that there was a limited amount of the energy of life. Because of this, there was only so much 'fat of the land,' so much rain, so much inspiration, so much luck, and wealth to go around. Because the energy which gave life was limited, a village or county could only survive if its witches stole these from their neighbors, while preventing its neighbors from stealing the life (often in the form of dew which they would collect with cloths) from their own land. Further, fairies, the devil, or other creatures would often try to steal this life energy from a village's farms as well. Thus, witches from different communities would often battle each other to bring the rain, improve their harvest, etc. Many people, therefore, believed they lived in a zero-sum world, in which someone must die, and supernatural wars are the only means of survival. From this, it's easy to understand why the witches of one community would attack the people in another with disease and pain.

Not all the enemies witches warred with were the witches of other communities, however, for there were always other dark forces from the other world which would seek to destroy crops and devour people, or which would steal the crop seeds and bring them to the underworld for themselves. There were also beasts such as dragons who would bring hail or tornados to a village.

Frequently, the shamans who went out to do battle would take the form of some animal spirit, with wolves being among the most common, if not the most common of these. The Irish would raid their neighbors by sending their souls out in the form of wolves, the Lithuanians would battle the devil, and the people of Central Europe frequently battled serpent witches and dragons in wolf form. In each of these cases, it was the person's soul which left their body behind that would do battle, not the person themselves.

> At times when there was a storm or approaching hail, they fell in into trances, and their souls, leaving their bodies, took the form of the animal corresponding to their fathers and their birthmarks. They were said to fight battles with the leadership of fiery, heavenly, and lightning and spirits against underworld "watery" dragons and other hostile demons who brought hail. In this watery-fiery battle, the antagonists shot lightning and ice at each other, and this exchange was followed by a storm with powerful noise. Their animal souls often fought along with them as alter egos (Pocs).

It was common in Indo-European lore for a fiery being of magic to defeat water dragons. From Zeus battling Typhon to Indra all the way in India. There were also some people who had serpents as familiar's villages with dragons as guardians, and even witches who would turn into dragons, thus showing that while there were many similar ideas, each location had its own

130

traditions. In general, black shamans in the Slavic tradition learned their powers in the underworld among the snakes and a goddess figure. This goddess figure would steal the crops from the world, forcing the shaman witches to retrieve it.

European beliefs were varied from one region to another, or even village to village, so one can't make absolute statements about the whole place. So, while many European witches battled serpents, there were some shaman warriors who had a dragon helping the spirit that helped her protect her town from hail and lightning, and kept the crops safe. It was more common, however, for people to battle the dragon and serpents in Central Europe. Other shaman's learned agricultural powers from serpents, which allowed them to become better farmers or perform other great deeds. So, while serpents were often the foils of good witches, they were also the teachers of many others.

One of the most interesting of the folk religions of Europe, with shamans who would send their souls from their bodies in order to fight evil forces was the

Perhaps the most famous of the shamans who would send their soul from their bodies were benandanti of Italy. A few hundred years ago, a man named Moduco stated:

> I am benandante because I go with the others to fight four times a year, that is during the Ember Days, at night; I go invisibly in spirit, and the body remains behind; we go forth in the service of Christ, and the witches of the devil; we fight each other, we with bundles of fennel and they with sorghum stalks... one time we fight over the wheat and all the other greats, another time over the livestock, and at other times over the vineyards. And so on four occasions, we fight over all the fruits of the earth and for those things won by the benandanti that year there is abundance (Ginzburg).

Others told how the bendantati would ride spirit animals out to battle, especially hares and cats, but other creatures as well. The benandanti not only fought to protect the harvest, but also to protect people's food stores, wine, and children from the witches. They could stop the witches from carrying children off or fight them away from people's homes. If the witches entered a person's home and found no clean water, they would enter the basement and spoil the wine, unless the benandanti were there to oppose them.

131

Two things are interesting to note at this point; the first is that clean water was a means of keeping the fairies from causing trouble it one's home in Ireland and Britain as well. The second thing to note was that the benandanti joined a precession of the dead, who were in many ways similar to the fairies of Ireland and Britain. It wasn't atypical for certain people's in Britain to invisibly join the fairies on their journeys into people's homes to steal the wine either.

This isn't to say that the benandnati were really fairies, or that the fairies, at least sometimes, were really benandanti. Rather, I point out the similarities to the benandanti who go on spirit journeys and the fairies who dwell within the spirit world to indicate the close connection between shaman figures and the spirits they worked with, and to show that, although Europe's folk religions had similar ideas, they were at their different core beliefs.

Fairy Wars

Just as shaman figures and spirits fought wars in Central and Eastern Europe, so too did the fairies go to battle with each other, often with the help of humans, in Western Europe. The wars between different fairy groups were often bloody affairs.

> 'There is an old abbey on the river, in County Mayo, and people say the fairies had a great battle near it, and that the slaughter was tremendous. At that time, the fairies appeared as swarms of flies coming from every direction to that spot. Some came from Knock Ma, and some from South Ireland, the opinion being that fairies can assume any form they like. The battle lasted a day and a night, and when it was over, one could have filled baskets with the dead flies which floated down the river".
>
> -Wentz

Fairy wars were extremely bloody and devastating events because they were embroiled in medieval politics long after humans had left it behind. In many ways, one can see their fairy courts, their wild parties as being similar to the parties of knights, of soldiers unwinding between or during wars. They had their own codes of honor which they were willing to kill and die for. Indeed, it can be argued that honor was more important to fairies than it was to humans. Their emotions as a general rule seem to be much stronger than ours.

132

Worse still because fairies were fertility spirits which gave life to the land; their wars and deaths would reshape the very land and throw the country off balance. The potato famine in Ireland that killed millions of people was said to be caused by a fairy war which disrupted nature and the fertility of the land. In this case, people could see the fairies flying over the land going to war with each other. Another fairy war left the land awash with so much blood that the moss where the battle took place turned red.

Fairies fought wars over the same things that humans fought wars over — land, food, honor, a desire for power, to kidnap women or men, etc. Fairies also fight wars to protect and help humanities'. "The War of the Trees" was a war between fairy beings in the other world (including Arthur) who wished to obtain a golden hind and a magical dog for humanities'. What purpose the hind and dog served humans isn't clear given that the poem is a fragment meant to remind people of something they already knew when it was written. What's important to understand is that the magical beings in this story lead an army of trees into the underworld in order to win treasure for humanity'. Fairies often fought for humans, certainly, the people Munster likely viewed their fairies as good beings who protected them and the fertility of their land, while viewing other fairies as enemies who would seek to take it. By the same token fairies needed humans to fight for them. Indeed it has been suggested time and time again that when two fairies fight a war, the side with humans will win over the one without them.

Joseph Jacobs collected a fairy tale about a man named Paddy O'Kelly who finds himself in fairyland where he encountered a lesser fairy court. This court of fairies eventually took him to see the higher court of King Finvara and Queen Nuala, where he was greeted warmly. King Finvara then told him; "We are going to play a hurling match tonight against the fairy host of Munster, and unless we beat them, our fame is gone forever. The match is to be fought out on Moytura, under Slieve Belgadaun." The story goes on to point out that:

> "it is necessary for the fairy host to have two live men beside them when they are fighting or are at a hurling match; this was the reason that little Donal took Paddy O'Kelly with him. There was a man they called the

133

"Yellow Stongirya" with the fairy host of Munster, from Ennis, in the County Clare.

They were hurling away, and the pipers continued to play until Paddy O'Kelly saw the host of Munster getting the strong hand, and he began helping the fairy host of Connacht.

The Stongirya came up and he made at Paddy O'Kelly, but Paddy turned him head over heels. From hurling, the two hosts began fighting, but it was not long until the host of Connacht beat the other host.

Then, the host of Munster made flying beetles of themselves, and began eating every green thing that they came up to. They were destroying the country before them until they came as far as Cong. Then there rose up thousands of doves out of the hole, and they swallowed down the beetles.

That hole has no other name until this day but Pull-na-gullam, the dove's hole.

When the fairy host of Connacht won their battle, they came back to Cnoc Matha joyous enough, and then King Finvara gave Paddy O'Kelly a purse of gold, and the little piper brought him home, and put him into bed beside his wife, and left him sleeping there (Hyde, 1890)

There are two key things to take away from this story. First, because fairies had such strong emotions, what began in this story as a sporting event quickly escalated into a serious battle in which hundreds or possibly thousands of fairies died. Yet in this case, neither of these fairy clans was evil per say, each fought to protect their land, while hindering another. The second thing to notice is that the fairies explicitly state that they need human aid in this conflict. Many Celtic witch-shaman figures who entered the other world did so in order to aid the fairies in their wars and sporting events, for the outcomes of these events was important to humans and fairies alike.

Fairies also concerned themselves with the outcome of human wars, choosing the side they wanted to win and aiding them in victory. Thus, it was important for humans to have treaties with

134

fairies if they wished to survive wars with other humans. In this way, the fairies were able to rebuild their power base from behind the scenes. Wentz states that:

> It is in the form of birds that the Tuatha De Danann appear as war-goddesses and directors of battle and we learn from one of our witnesses that the 'gentry' or modern Sidhe-folk take sides even now in a great war, like that between Japan and Russia. It is in their relation to the hero Cuchulainn that one can best study the People of the Goddess Dana in their role as controllers of human war. In the greatest of the Irish epics, the Tam Bó Cuailnge where Cuchulainn is under their influence, these war-goddesses are called Badb (or Bodb) which here seems to be a collective term for Neman, Macha, and Morrigu (or Morrigan) each of whom exercises a particular supernatural power. Neman appears as the confounder of armies, so that friendly bands bereft of their senses by her, slaughter one another; Macha is a fury that riots and revels among the slain; while Morrigu, the greatest of the three, by her presence infuses superhuman valor into Cuchulainn, nerves him for the cast, and guides the course of his unerring spear. And the Tuatha De Danann in infusing this valor into the great hero show themselves."

The Wild Hunt

> The modern concept of the Hunt is primarily a conflation of two different kinds of nocturnal procession or cavalcade. One was composed mainly of female spirits and travelled about, often visiting human homes to bless them if the inhabitants were clean and hospitable. Living people frequently claimed to have joined it, sometimes explicitly in spirit form while their bodies remained in their beds. In many areas it was believed to be led by a supernatural female, whom clerical writers tended to call Diana or Herodias, but who was also known as Holda, Abundia, Satia, Percht, and by other local names. The other sort of procession was mostly or wholly made up of dead human beings, and was rarely regarded as attractive or benevolent.
> "The Wild Hunt and the Witches' Sabbath", by Ronald Hutton

Similar to the notion of sending one's soul out to battle witches and fairies was the notion of joining deities and fairies in a massive wild hunt. However, as the above quote indicates, there were in fact two separate types of spirit journeys which have both come to be called wild hunts, and often confused for each other. The first of these is the trooping journey, in which witches would join chthonic goddess figures in trooping around the countryside. These goddesses were not usually connected with fertility, but were instead connected with the spirits of the dead, and household chores such as spinning. In Scotland this figure was Nicnevin, the queen of the fairies, on the borders between England and Scotland she was Gyre Carling, in Tyrol she was Perchta, and in Northern Germany Holda. She was also known by numerous other names in numerous other regions. In essence she was the queen of the witches, leading them along with troops of the dead and unborn children on hunts through the sky on holidays. She was in the habit of punishing lazy women who did not complete their spinning fast enough, while rewarding hardworking ones. This goddess, and by extension the wild hunt she led was ambivalent;

> she possessed the same ambivalence seen so clearly in the tribal dark shaman and the spirits he emulates, with a witch from Val di Fiemme claiming, for example, that when her mistress "journeys through the air she has two patches around her eyes, one on each side, so that she cannot see anything: and if she were able to see everything she would do great harm to the world." Similarly, however beneficent the fairy-procession nexus, when scholars have attempted to separate it—at the level of myth and legend—from that of the Wild Hunt, they have been ultimately frustrated, finding the two matrices of belief "hard to distinguish" or "indistinguishable." Also relevant (and under-researched) in this context is the fact that the act of killing and consuming both humans and animals emerges as a core rite in several classic accounts of the "Good Game," including those from Milan, Bressanone, and the Dolomite Valleys (Wilby).

In the modern day we often want to talk about these fairies and goddess as being either good or bad, separating them into clear cut categories. Odder still is the attempt to state that any bad people believed about deities and fairies was a later invention, tagged on by Christianity. The reality is that good and evil, kind and cruel were bound up in the same beings. A good example of this is the women in Corsica who were;

> "called" by an irresistible force to go out in dreams in order to hunt down, kill, and consume animals. As they killed their prey, for a brief moment they glimpsed the human face of an individual known to them, revealing the animal to be another person traveling in subtle-body form. Having been killed on the visionary plane this individual would then physically die within a short space of time (Wilby).

Those who engaged in these hunts were feared but tolerated because they had no choice, the urge to hunt was impossible to fight. The women involved in these hunts were good, but they performed evil acts.

In 1066 Buchard recorded a similar idea, discussing how some women believed that; " in the silence of the night when you have gone to bed and your husband lies in your bosom, that while you are in bodily form you can go out closed doors and able to cross the spaces of the world with others..." He of course continues to discuss how these women would kill and eat people, placing pieces of wood or straw in place of their hearts in order to reanimate them.

In 1280 Jean de Meung stated that one in three children would go forth three nights a week, and enter houses, for locks nor bars could stop them. While in 1468, the Thesaurus Pauperum stated; "Those who leave out vessels filled with food and drink at night intended for the ladies expected to visit." The hope in this case was that the ladies traveling with the goddess Fraw Percht would provide abundance to the households that left food for them. This hope, that the troop would provide abundance was the troops primary purpose. To travel at night, bringing blessings to the villages, households, and people. While at the same time these troops would punish the lazy. Those who left their homes dirty, who didn't respect tradition, and who didn't finish their spinning. These witches were in essence the matrons of the town, who along with the fairies and goddess figures, worked to ensure that traditions were adhered to by sending their souls into people's homes at night, where they would feast on offerings left for them, gossip by the fire, and determine which houses should be blessed and which punished.

137

Witches, both men and women, claimed that they gained their magical knowledge from traveling with these troops of 'good ladies.' The good ladies in this case were fairies, in the broad sense of the term. Such journeys to learn magic with the trooping ladies are recorded in the French Pyrenees, in 1319. As well as Milan in 1370. In both these cases the witches (one man and two women) focused on the houses they'd bless while on their spirit journey.

The hunt

The second form of the wild hunt, is actually the wild hunt or the spirit army. This was often lead by figures such as Odin, Freya, Gwyn ap Nudd, or anyone who had an army of the dead. Such hunts could also be lead by the cursed spirits of the dead themselves, with stories often stating that a man was punished for hunting on Sunday or breaking some other social norm, by being forced to lead or take part in a wild hunt. The focus of these journeys was the actual hunting of sinners, travelers, and fairies.

These spirit journeys are more story oriented. Often acting as horror stories, similar to the tale of the "Headless Horseman," in which people are chased by evil spirits. Another story common to Germany and Southern Scandinavia, is that of a huntsman chasing down a fairy woman, usually killing her, and hauling her home like a slain rabbit. In this case, it is interesting to note, that the fairies would sometimes ask the humans to help them escape the huntsman, for humans could draw magical symbols that would keep the huntsman away.

Both versions of what we now call the wild hunt, that is the spirit troop and the wild hunt itself, have at least some connections with the idea of dark shamanism, or cannibal shamanism.

Dark Shamanism and the Cannibal Spirit Journey

An important part of the wild hunt is the notion of the cannibal spirit journey. Cannibalism and the consumption of blood have been associated with shamanism all over the world. This isn't to say that even the majority of shamanistic traditions include such ideas, rather, it's to point out they are common enough to show up in traditions in Europe, Asia, Africa, and the Americas.

One of the foremost experts on witch mythology and folk religion, Emma Wilby points out that indigenous cultures often associated shamanism with cannibalism. She goes on to quote Ste'panoff's encounter with Tuvans shaman's that would proudly clam to have eaten several people himself, yet not enough to be a "great shaman." Further:

> It has long been recognized that psychophysical compulsion is a feature of most shamanistic traditions, typically emerging in the context of possession and initiation (in the latter case, acceptance of the shamanic vocation often being likened to profound surrender to an overwhelming force). Anthropologists studying dark shamanic traditions have noted that similarly compulsive urges underpin the shaman's need to journey in subtle body to hunt down and consume human flesh. In this respect, with regard to his random killing sprees at least, the shaman is believed to be fundamentally innocent of the murders he commits.

It is telling then that hags, vampires, and werewolves all have connections to the shaman's spirit journey and are each pushed by sudden, uncontrollable urges to devour. This is not to say that all vampire, werewolf, and hag tales come from stories of dark shamans, but many clearly do, and even those that don't, likely took at least some of their elements from tales of witches.

Keep in mind that despite the danger posed by such shamans they were often tolerated within their communities, for their devouring of life gives them the power to help their community and protect it from the greater dangers of other shamans or human eating spirit sand deities. In order to do this latter job the shaman would need to befriend these cannibalistic spirits in order to steer them in specific directions. Further, such dark shamans would often leave their villages and only devour the enemies of their people, at least until they died at which point their spirit might no longer be able to tell friend from foe. Again, Wilby quotes Ste'panoff that:

> In Siberia, shamans' cannibal practices are not seen as a bad habit of a particular category of "evil" or "black" shamans, or as a lapse contradicting their benevolent mission of healing. Rather, it looks like an inevitable expression of what makes them shamans. Humans are

139

just one of the numerous objects of their appetite, besides hostile spirits and simple presents of meat and alcohol . . . the shaman's body is from birth (as opposed to by will) an active channel, and that is why, traditionally, "devouring" is not precisely understood as a "bad action" from an ethical point of view.

In this context, even when a shaman is lynched or ostracized the process may be strangely devoid of blame, with Ste´panoff, noting that in Siberia, "Cannibal shamans are killed or abandoned in order to preserve lay people rather than as a kind of punishment." From this perspective, dark shamanistic traditions are sustained by the profound fatalism that thrives in any preindustrial culture required to endure a high incidence of sickness and death.

Ste'panoff's and Wilby's observation is that societies that had to endure a high incidence of death and fear of their own destruction almost all developed dark shamanism is likely true. After all, the peoples of Siberia, South America, and South East Asia all suffered conquest by foreign armies and rampant plagues before anthropologists began recording their religious beliefs. It shouldn't be surprising than that stories of shamanism in Europe cropped up during the darkest days of the medieval eras. In Chipley Lavicek's book "The Black Death," he quotes a writer who lived through the plague;

In many places in Siena great pits were dug and piled deep with the multitude of dead. And they died by the hundreds, both day and night, and all were thrown in those ditches and covered with earth. And as soon as those ditches were filled, more were dug. And I, Agnolo di Tura, called the Fat, buried my five children with my own hands. And there were also those who were so sparsely covered with ear that the dogs dragged them forth and devoured many bodies throughout the city. There was no one who wept for any dead, for all awaited death. And so many died that all believed it was the end of the world.

Such a world produced fatalistic notions related to magic and witchcraft. Eramus as quoted by Niehoff (1966) stated that:

Life, in a sense, is cheaper among many of the underprivileged people of the world because they have a much higher expectation of death than we do. If no one is to be blamed or made the scapegoat for illness and death, as is the case in areas where witchcraft is greatly feared, fatalism will probably be common.

Witch hunts can be a survival mechanism by communities who feel powerless. Yet, it's interesting to note that the most famous witch hunts in history didn't occur during horrific plagues or other massive tragic events, but after them. The greatest growth Europe had experienced in over five hundred years occurred between 1400 and 1500, the very time when witch hunts began to rise and the "Malleus Maleficarum", the manual of witch persecutions was written. These events occurred a hundred years after the Black Death and after much of the violence of the medieval era had petered off (thus the reason for the explosion in population). McGowan (1994) similarly points out that Rome's witch hunt against Christians occurred during what was generally "a rather stable and successful period, that of the Antonine emperors." During this time of relative stability, the Roman's began accusing the Christians of learning to heal sickness using human blood, and of holding wild celebrations with orgies in the presence of donkey headed spirits, during which they would drink blood and eat human flesh. One can't help but notice the similarity between such tales and stories of later witch's sabots. This similarity exists because the idea that there were cannibalistic and dark witch figures is an ancient one in Europe. Christian's likely didn't engage in these activities any more than the people burned as witches did in later times. What's important to take from this is that during times of relative instability and suffering people started to believe that members of their community were engaged in dark shamanism, but they accepted this because they believed that these 'wicked witches' were necessary for their survival.
Again Wilby's article states that

Kieckhefer notes that in central Italian trials from the fifteenth-century women accused of being bloodsucking witches were "regularly if perhaps not professionally engaged in the mediation of supernatural powers"— mediations that could include love magic, assault sorcery, and healing.

141

As Briggs has argued, "the relative acceptance of witches who doubled as healers must be one partial explanation for the reluctance of families and individuals to press home what were effectively murder charges." For some, the witch's protective abilities may have been seen as a communal asset worth tolerating...

Here then we see a pattern in dark shamanism as it relates to cultural morality. First there is a calamity that causes people to embrace the darker aspects of religious experience, or at least accept them. Second, as the calamity wanes people continue to accept the darker morality of survival for a number of years. Finally, as society stabilizes a new morality is formed, one which frowns upon activities related to dark shamanism. Industrialization can lead to this stability, but other things might as well. This cultural cycle of the acceptance of the darkest aspects of magic can be especially important within a fantasy world. Within a fantasy world devils, demons, dragons, ogres, and the like are very tangible things. Because of this people might tolerate a vampire who occasionally gives into their blood thirsty urges because it is capable of keeping away something far worse. Yet when fear wanes this tolerance can end. Certainly, European fairy tales seem to bare this idea out. Human sacrifice to earth spirits such as dragons and troll like beings, was discussed repeatedly in stories about and from the Early Medieval era. As society stabilized and fear waned, such sacrifices became less acceptable and were eventually outlawed. Yet, in England at least, there are still stories that water spirits will drown people in place of these sacrifices, as they still demand death from the community on a schedule.

Magic has long been associated with death and cannibalism in Europe. According to Richard Sugg, in 25 A.D. an epileptic patient might drink blood from a wounded and dying gladiator. "He and other suffers, we are told, were wont to drink from gladiators' bodies." Sugg's book also points out that this history of drinking blood for its magical properties lasted into the modern era. "In Germany and Denmark, poorer citizens paid whatever they could afford to drink human blood at execution scaffolds. "Skulls too were powdered as a medicine, and these skulls needed to come from people who died a violent death. Such procedures weren't performed in back allies, but by the permanent doctors and chemists of the early modern and even Victorian eras."

The idea of deaths association with power goes back even further, certainly the Celts seem to have sacrificed people in order to obtain victory in war. Dr Horton in an interview with The Independent states that; the evidence for cannibalism (among British Celtic sacrificial victims) is irrefutable."
Interestingly enough the remains of these eaten sacrifices are mixed with the remains of dogs, who are grim reaper figures in Celtic tradition, leading people as they do to the land of the dead. It shouldn't be surprising then that later witch Sabbaths often included dogs in Britain or that these were the most common familiars of witches.

Iping-Petterson (2011) stated that violence was believed to create an energy by people performing sacrifices. Violence and torture were often part of sacrificial rituals. Such violence was community sanctioned because it benefited the community as a whole. It was believed that victory against enemies, safe buildings, and abatement of disease couldn't be obtained without such violence.

Blood especially was believed to have magical properties. Matteoni (2009) points out that;

> Blood penetrates and escapes from the flesh, either providing the vital force or taking it away. Drinking the bodily fluid, therefore, has a double function—that of consuming a living being to empower another...

> the witch was likened to a supernatural creature, the vampire, and was considered a bloodsucker... According to the Italian philosopher of the Renaissance, Marsilio Ficino, human blood naturally attracted human blood. The old women, called witches, were believed to drink the children's blood to have their youth back... Blood was, then, considered as a remedy for old age and decay...

> From the examination of European witch-beliefs blood emerges as the vehicle employed by witches to waste the course of life that the liquid should assure, and by the devil to establish his domain over the human soul. It follows that blood was a crucial element of division between the natural world and the supernatural one. Like the witch, otherworldly creatures could use the fluid essence to penetrate the sphere of human and physical life, altering its normal course.

Witches were essentially those who were thought to be using the power of such dark magic for personal, rather than community benefit. The likelihood that someone would be accused of this increased after the community felt less need to tolerate what they might normally see as immoral or when the communities fear that the witch might take them was greater than the fear that they might be killed by some other means that the witch might prevent. This means two things;

1: The idea that witches, sorcerers, shamans, etc. would become vampires, werewolves, and hags is an obvious extension of the notion that magic could come from violence and cannibalism.

2: Witches, hags, vampires, and werewolves can all be dualistic figures, they can both help and hurt the communities in which they live. Depending on the time and place, people could respect them, respect and fear them, or simply fear them. This is especially true given that not all cannibal witches or shamans went after people within their own community. There does seem to be evidence that instead they attacked and devoured people from rival communities, enemies, and evil shamans. It could be then, that the vampires, hags, and werewolves within your game do not devour the people they seek to protect, but instead run rampant among enemies. While certainly this wouldn't be seen as good in the modern day, history has different moral codes. Perhaps more importantly for your stories this fits with well with anti-heroes such as Venom.

The key take away is that stories of witches who serve the devil in performing evil may not have been entirely a Christian perversion of beliefs, but rather part of a long cycle of beliefs in dark shamanism and spirit journeys. Such spirit journeys included; a flight to the other world where witches would dance and celebrate with evil spirits in the form of animals, shared cannibalism and blood drinking with such evil spirits, orgies, inversions of the common morality, the creation of magical potions from human body parts, the spreading of disease, and the learning of spells. Often such journeys and the acts carried out during them were compulsions which the witch could not escape, at times they were forced upon the witch by spirits far more powerful than they.

The Nightmare witches

Mart were witches who would undertake spirit journeys in order to cause nightmares and torment sleepers.

> A cabinetmaker living in Buhl would sleep in his workshop. For many nights something had laid itself onto his chest, and crushed him so he could hardly breath. He told his friend about this,. The next night he lay awake in bed, midnight a cat slipped through a hole in his wall. The cabinetmaker quickly stopped up the hole, caught the cat and nailed one of it's paws down. He then when to sleep.

> The next morning the cat had chance into a beautiful naked woman. One of her hands was nailed down. She was so pleasing that he married her.

> They had three children together. One day when she was with him in his workshop he showed her the hole where she came int, and opened it. Suddenly the woman turned into a cat and ran out through the opening, and he never saw her again. (Baader, 1851)

There are a few similar stories, although most of the time the mare remains in the form of a human, rather than a cat, and sometimes they talk about being from foreign nations (like being from England when the story takes place in Germany). Unlike the act of stealing fertility from the land, appeasing evil powers, etc. There isn't a reason given for the mare to cause nightmares. Like cannibalism so often is, it seems to simply be a compulsion connected with certain types of spirit journeys.

Adventurous in the Spirit World

A lot of information on adventures in the spirit world can be gleaned from fairy tales and myths, for many of these stories are about spirit journeys or take some of their themes from these. In his book Theory and History of Folklore (1984) Propp stated that:

> shamanism took over a great deal from prehistoric epochs, and much of it has been preserved in the

wondertale. If we collect shamans' tales of their trances - how the shaman went to seek a soul in the other world, who helped him in his endeavor, how he was conveyed, and so forth - and compare these with the wanderings and flight of the wondertale hero, the correspondence will be obvious.

Think about the oddness of fairy tales, of people talking to buckets, lakes, trees, and other objects or animals. Think about the convoluted plots in which people fly, travel to distant places, discover kingdoms near their home they didn't know about and it does indeed start to become obvious that at least pieces of these stories started out as vision quests, spirit journeys, and dreams worlds. Jeri Studebaker and Wilby have both pointed out that "many fairy tales mirror the stories of shamans told about their spirit-world journeys." Both stories involve a protagonist who leaves their family and travels a spiritual plane, and must battle supernatural beings. As already discussed such spirit journeys and battles have real world consequences. Should the shaman loose to a dragon in the spirit world they will die, and the dragon will continue to prevent the rain or cause the hail that makes their village starve to death.

Presuming Propp, Wilby, and others are right and that fairy tales have remnants of shamanistic tales in them, one begin to learn about the spirit world, spirits, and deities from wonder tales such as the "Frog King" in which a frog who earlier helped a girl is now harassing her to the point that;

> she became bitterly angry and threw him against the wall with all her might. "Now you will have your peace, you disgusting frog!"

> But when he fell down, he was not a frog, but a prince with beautiful friendly eyes. And he was now, according to her father's will, her dear companion and husband.

Compare this to the idea among the Northeast Asian Nanai idea that;

> Shamanic spirits are dirty from having served a previous shaman; they drive their new shaman mad and so must be tamed. Thus, a shaman has to "win" against their own spirit-helpers (Bulgakova, 2013)

In other words, new familiar spirits will tend to drive their shaman crazy and will often need to be tamed, either through offerings, kindness, or violence. This could explain why many, if not most, stories of someone with a beastly groom must show kindness in order to transform this beast. Yes, the meaning of such stories would likely have changed to fit the notions that women would eventually marry a husband they didn't know, who could turn out to be beastly, but the meaning of this story may have started with ideas about the spirit world.

The descriptions of the protagonists journey itself can teach us a lot about travel through and the landscape of the spirit world. Eva Pocs states that many of the stories which involve "Travel on narrow paths, crossing bridges, and passing through small gaps are all universal symbols of entering the otherworld." To this list I would include things such as glass mountains, gathering helping spirits, traveling impossible distances, returning to life after being cut up, traversing into the sky or deep underground, and needing to receive a ride from a supernatural being such as giants and talking horses or ducks.

> In Slavic lore the bridge between the human world and the land of the dead is often depicted as a bridge that is thin as a hair so only the righteous can cross it to meet with deceased relatives....(Macedonian Healers)

Other times this bridge was depicted as a rainbow or the Milky way. This bridge is often given such names as "Mouse Path" as the mouse is a typical form for the human soul to take when it leaves the body. In other stories, the land of the dead was an underwater city, to which the soul had to swim. Still other times it was a steep hill made of glass or iron, which had to be climbed to reach paradise or those who were imprisoned in the Other World. (Ralston)

The stories of journeys into the spirit world often suggest long lonely journeys through vast wildernesses, with impossibly high mountains and bazar geological features such as mountains of glass. In fairy tales, people often have to cross vast wildernesses or travel seven times seven kingdoms over, journey along paths of pins and needles, etc. Such journeys are also likely indicative of traveling into the spirit world.

Even with such ideas in mind, it's often difficult to tell if a person has in fact stepped into the spirit world, because the boundary between the human and other worlds, wasn't always viewed as clear cut. This is because people could seemingly step into the fairy realm / spirit world by seeming accident. For fairies didn't always dwell in distant places. Often times fairies would dwell in hills, underground, in crystal palaces under lakes and rivers, in the sky directly overhead and more (Henderson). People could stumble upon these wilderness fairylands by accident, as easily as falling into a well. In the story of "Belly Beg, Tom Beg and Fairies," Tom Beg is taken into some mist and soon finds himself "in a green glen such as he'd never seen before, though he though he knew every glen within five miles of him." It was here that he encountered the fairy host who was riding in a parade, which was more splendid than anything Tom had ever seen before.

Even when a story obviously moves into fairyland, the seeming normalcy of the characters within it often throws people off. In the Russian Tale of "The Girl in the Well" a girl falls down a well to find herself in a spirit world filled with villages and cowherds who need her help with the simple task of cleaning up after herd animals. Watching cows was a typical job for those who found themselves in fairyland, but it seems so prosaic that it is often easy to ignore the fairyland-spirit world elements of the stories which involve it. That is, until those who perform these simple tasks receive a great reward for them, one which can at times be magical. From these and many other stories one gets the impression that the "Other World" often serves as a dream for the underemployed to finely get paid what they are worth, or to get the jobs they want. So, a modern-day person entering the "other world" might be able to become heroic and rich by being an accountant or garbage truck driver as no one in fairy land wants to do these two jobs but they all need help with them. In other cases, a person pulled into fairy land in the modern day might become a rock star, an actor, or gain success in some other art with which they were struggling to be discovered in our world.

Reading Fairy Tales

There is no way to be a hundred percent certain of the meaning of any fairy tale element, or even if such an element is symbolic of a visionary quest. Still, attempting to understand fairy tales in this context can teach us a lot about such spirit journeys and just as importantly for this book – stimulate creativity. These goals in mind I would like to examine a few pieces of some fairy tales.

The Norka

Think about a fairy tale like "The Norka" in which a prince goes
into the underworld to slay a beast that is ruining the crops:

> His brothers lowered him accordingly, and when he had
> reached the other world, underneath the earth, he went
> on his way. He walked and walked. Presently he espied a
> horse with rich trappings, and it said to him:

> "Hail, Prince Ivan! Long have I awaited thee!"

> He mounted the horse and rode on--rode and rode,
> until he
> saw standing before him, a palace made of copper. He
> entered
> the courtyard, tied up his horse, and went indoors. In
> one of
> the rooms a dinner was laid out. He sat down and
> dined, and
> then went into a bedroom. There he found a bed, on
> which he
> lay down to rest. Presently there came in a lady, more
> beautiful
> than can be imagined anywhere but in a skazka, who
> said:

> "Thou who art in my house, name thyself! If thou art an
> old man, thou shall be my father; if a middle-aged man,
> my
> brother; but if a young man, thou shalt be my husband
> dear.
> And if thou art a woman, and an old one, thou shalt be
> my grandmother;
> if middle-aged, my mother; and if a girl, thou shalt be
> my own sister."

This woman that was so quick to seek a relationship with him,
and married him is the sister of the Norka he seeks to slay, and
she helps him kill her brother by telling Prince Ivan that he is
with his sister. Ivan goes to the sister who falls instantly in love
with him and tells him the Norka is with her other sister, who in
turn falls in love with Ivan and gives him a sword to kill her

149

brother.

> After killing the Beast, the Prince went back again,
> picking up all the three sisters by the way, with the
> intention of taking them out into the upper world: for
> they all loved him and would not be separated from him.
> Each of them turned her palace into an egg--for they
> were all enchantresses--and they taught him how to turn
> the eggs into palaces, and back again, and they handed
> over the eggs to him.

Even in the context of literature this story is bizarre, but it does
make sense as a spirit journey. The Norka being a spirit that is
destroying the crops is obvious, given that's what he is doing.
The horse and the Norka's sisters are spirit-helpers. Such
fairylike beings often want to help people, at least specific
people. Such spirits are drawn to humans, after all. What's
more they can see the future, or at least the present. In other
words, despite the fact that they just met Ivan, they knew
enough about him to know he was the human they wanted to be
spiritually married to, or in the case of the horse the one for
whom they wanted to work. Of course, not all familiar – mortal
relations are so simple. As already stated sometimes the wild
familiar spirit needed to be captured or tamed through violence
or offerings. In the story of "The Princess on the Glass Hill" a
farmers crop keeps getting eaten. His eldest two sons wait for
the thing that's doing it one at a time, but a sound of thunder
and an earth quaking drives them off. Finally the youngest son
boots waits, and he is brave enough to sit through the quake.
After he does he seek a horse with full saddle and armor, which
he captures. This magical horse later helps boots get a princess
from the top of the Glass Mountain.

In the story of "The Blind Man and the Cripple" a Princess Anna
will marry anyone clever enough to create a riddle she can't
solve, but will cut the head off anyone else. After Prince Ivan
solves the riddle with the help of his advisor Princess Anna gives
Ivan more tasks, which is servant resolves. After this

> Princess Anna the Fair lived for some time with Prince
> Ivan as a wife ought to live with a god-given husband,
> flattered him in every way in words, but in reality never
> thought of anything except by what means she might get
> rid of Katoma. With the Prince, without the tutor, there'd

150

be no difficulty in settling matters! she said to herself

Here again the Princess is constantly trying to undermine her
husband and most especially his relationship with his teacher.
This story gets even stranger when she succeeds in having the
tutor banished. Her tutor makes friends with a blind man
Princess Anna banished and together they kidnap a girl:

The heroes brought the merchant's daughter into their
forest
    hut, and said to her:

"Be in the place of a sister to us, live here and keep
house
    for us; otherwise we poor sufferers will have no one to
cook
    our meals or wash our shirts. God won't desert you if
you do
    that!"

The merchant's daughter remained with them. The
heroes
    respected her, loved her, acknowledged her as a sister.
They
    used to be out hunting all day, but their adopted sister
was
    always at home. She looked after all the housekeeping,
prepared
    the meals, washed the linen.

But after a time a Baba Yaga took to haunting their hut
and
    sucking the breasts of the merchant's daughter. No
sooner
    have the heroes gone off to the chase, than the Baba
Yaga is there
    in a moment. Before long the fair maiden's face began
to fall
    away, and she grew weak and thin. The blind man
could see
    nothing, but Katoma remarked that things weren't
going well.
    He spoke about it to the blind man, and they went
together to

151

their adopted sister, and began questioning her. But the Baba
  Yaga had strictly forbidden her to tell the truth. For a long
  time she was afraid to acquaint them with her trouble, for a
  long time she held out, but at last her brothers talked her over
  and she told them everything without reserve.

Just then from under the bench crawled Uncle Katoma, fell
  upon her like a mountain of stone, took to strangling her until
  the heaven seemed to her to disappear. Then into the cottage
  bounded the blind man, crying to the cripple--

"Now we must heap up a great pile of wood, and consume
  this accursed one with fire, and fling her ashes to the wind!"

The Baba Yaga began imploring them:

"My fathers! my darlings! forgive me. I will do all that is right."

"Very good, old witch! Then show us the fountain of healing
  and life-giving water!" said the heroes.

"Only don't kill me, and I'll show it you directly!"

Well, Katoma sat on the blind man's back. The blind man
  took the Baba Yaga by her back hair, and she led them into the
  depths of the forest, brought them to a well...

152

Eventually Katoma uses the water of life to bring his feet back and then he returns to the Princess who asks him.

"Who are you? Where do you come from?"

"I am he whose feet you cut off and whom you set on a stump. My name is Katoma _dyadka_, oaken _shapka_."

"Well," thinks the Princess, "now that he's got his feet back again, I must act straight-forwardly with him for the future."

And she began to beseech him and the Prince to pardon her. She confessed all her sins, and swore an oath always to love Prince Ivan, and to obey him in all things. Prince Ivan forgave her, and began to live with her in peace and concord.
The hero who had been blind remained with them, but Katoma and his wife went to the house of [her father] the rich merchant, and took up their abode under his roof.

Such a story is difficult to piece together, which may be a result of it being pieces of multiple stories which each have different plots and meanings. The beginning of this folk tale resembles the idea among the Nanai of a weaker female shaman marrying a more powerful male one in order to create peace between their two families. Yet this marriage is simply meant to conceal the female shaman's intentions. In such a case the woman may attempt to steal or drive away the male shaman's helping spirit. Yet, typically such stories don't follow the helping-spirit rather than the shaman (Bulgakova, 2013). It could also be that the tutor in the above story is in fact the shaman teaching the prince to be a shaman as well. When the helping spirit the prince wins discovers that he did not win her fairly she grows angry and attempts to drive the other shaman off. In either case it was common for rivalries between shamans and helping-spirits to be depicted in fairy tales.

Nisan's Journey

Perhaps the best way to understand shamanism and spirit journeys is by examining one of the few fully intact stories of a shaman's journeys we have, that of Nisan. Although this story is from Manchuria (in Northeast Asia, it still can be worth reading for this book, and as with many tales across Eurasia it includes a vision of hell, a meeting with a female queen of unborn children in the land of the dead, and a boy spirited away by otherworldly creatures interested in adopting him.) When the powerful shaman Nisan went into the land of the dead to retrieve a soul, which had been stolen by dark spirits, she encountered the goddess Omosi-mama, who kept the souls of babies until it was time for them to enter the world. Anxious to show her respect, Nisan approached Omosi-mama and bowed three times three, for a total of nine times to her, at which point Omosi-mama says that it's right that Nisan should be a shaman because;

> When you were born, I became annoyed with you because you absolutely refused to go, and I placed a shaman's cap on your head, tied bells on your skirt, and put a tambourine in your hand, and causing you to act as a shaman, I playfully brought you to life. It is proper that you have become famous. I myself ordained that you would someday come to this place, and I have decided that after you are shown all the consequences of doing good and evil, you shall make them known to the world. (Nowak and Durant)

This is how a shaman's story truly begins. And while different Steppes and Siberian peoples had different beliefs about the lands of the dead, almost all of them believed that there was a deity who kept the souls of the dead until they were ready to be reincarnated (this being also exists in Germanic Lore as well). Nisan was made a shaman because of something her soul had done before she was born. Sadly, this story doesn't make it clear why she was chosen to be a shaman, though a number of possibilities present themselves. First, as mentioned in the story, she refused to go to earth at first, and perhaps she did so as a means of bargaining for a better life. Shamans, such as Nisan, after all, gained much of their power from their ability to bargain with the spirit world.

154

Perhaps Omosi-mama was impressed with Nisan's stubbornness and resolve, and her independence of mind. It's important, after all, for a shaman to have a firm resolve. Further, the story of Nisan makes it very clear that she is an independent-minded woman, for she also declares in the story "without a husband, I shall live happily... Without a family, I shall live lovingly, pursuing my own youth." This is not unusual for a shaman, for many of them seemed to be very independent minded. Even when a shaman got married and had a family, they tended to reject many of society's rules. In some societies, they cross-dressed, they acted wildly, they did not respect authority, etc. Alternatively, perhaps, Omosi-mama was impressed with Nisan's strength and power at being able to refuse to leave.

Strength is an important part of being a shaman. In the Mongolian "Epic of Geser" the most important shaman of the Buryat lore is born incredibly powerful and difficult for his parents to control. He snores so loudly it rattles the evil spirits that live within the marshes, steppes and other places around where he sleeps. These spirits send two giant rats the size of horses to kill the baby, but the baby kills them instead. Therefore, despite the trouble he causes, Geser is important because he can defeat the evil spirits and protect the humans the good spirits seek to aid. So perhaps it's this power, this strength that the spirits need. In many European tales, fools who worry their parents because they are always causing trouble, acting foolish, or not fitting in will tend to be the ones who succeed at undertaking a heroes journey that often resembles that of a shaman's journey. Certainly, among the Nanai shamans (hunter-gatherers from Manchuria) there was a belief that to become a shaman someone had to be fearless. They couldn't be frightened by evil spirits, by fire, or really anything. Even as children, these shamans often astounded people with their fearlessness. This makes sense given that shamans had to travel to the land of the dead and negotiate with some very scary creatures at times. Similarly in Europe, people who didn't know what fear was often go out and end up negotiating with, and driving evil spirits away from kingdoms.

There are many characteristics that might lead someone to become a shaman. Regardless, it may be useful to keep in mind that no story begins with the shaman encountering the spirit world for the first time, or even with the birth of the shaman, but rather the shaman's story begins before birth, and may even have no beginning.

After Nisan and Omosi-mama talk for a little while, the goddess shows Nisan around the afterlife, or more specifically – hell. Omosi-mama shows Nisan how the wicked are punished and what they are punished for so that she can warn people to be moral and good. Similar spirit journeys into hell (or the equivalent of hell) are common throughout Eurasia. Similarly, many other shamans had to cross a bridge to get in and out of the spirit world, below which they could see the torments of the sinners and hear their lamenting (Stone, Alby). The shaman's journey into the spirit world is almost never straightforward, even when their goal is, and can have many branches and episodes. This is because they have so many tasks, one of which is to help ensure that their societies understand the importance of the morality which the gods, faeries, and spirits dictate.

This particular saga of Nisan began with a very clear goal. This tale began when a lord of one of the cities of the dead (in the Underworld) sent his servant to kidnap the soul of a boy who had killed many animals. At first glance it might seem like Ilmun Han is punishing the boy for having killed so many animals. However, the boy 'Sergudai' was taken before Ilmun Han, the lord of the underworld, who gave him an archery test, and then a test in wrestling. With the boy's soul having passed both of these, Ilmun Han decided to make the boy one of his children. Even so, kidnapping the boy's soul isn't acceptable behavior. From the human perspective, the boy, after all, has many souls, which must grow through the life he was supposed to have. Without the soul Ilmun Han took, these other souls will be forced into the afterlife before they are ready to go. More than this, however, the boy's family is left behind to mourn, which is why shamans like Nisan are called in to recover the souls of those who've been kidnapped by an otherworldly entity.

Before entering the underworld, Nisan calls up her helping spirits, like the running animal spirits, flying bird spirits, and slithering snake spirits. It seems as if she moves like a whirlwind through the spirit world. She is very clearly a powerful shaman, so powerful that the boatman into the land of the dead, whom she offers bean paste and paper for passage across the river, knows who she is and says he will take her across because of her fame, but he wouldn't take a lesser shaman across.

Nisan's story demonstrates very well that a shaman's ability to accomplish their goals is based almost entirely on their relationship with the beings of the spirit world. When Nisan needs to get Serudai's soul out of Ilmun Han's fortress, she calls down an eagle spirit to grab it. After retrieving his soul, Nisan takes Serudai's hand and begins to guide him towards the world of the living.

Further, while getting Serudai to return with her to the land of the living was easy for Nisan, there are times when a person's soul doesn't want to return to the land of the living and so must be bribed by the shaman. You might, of course, ask why the shaman is so anxious to bring back a soul who doesn't want to return, and there are possibly three reasons for this. First, it's important to keep in mind that any soul in the land of the dead which the shaman is recovering is only a third or sometimes only a seventh of the souls which a person has, so by refusing to come back, this soul is not only making the living sad, he is killing these other souls as well. This means that the shaman might even have to force a soul to return with them to save all these other souls. Secondly, there are of course people in the world who might need the person to come back. Finally, some shamans are often paid good money (reindeer, furs, or other barter items) to retrieve someone's soul, and many shamans wouldn't want to give that up. In fact, some shamans even offer to steal the soul of another person for the lord of the dead to retrieve their client's souls and so are paid. This means that while most shamans were spiritual leaders and healers, some were mercenaries who only cared about their pay.

As Nisan returns to the land of the living, a boy in tow, she encounters the spirit of her dead husband who threatens to boil her in oil because she hasn't bothered to raise him from the dead yet. She tries to explain that his body is completely rotted away, but he refuses to listen to reason, so she calls a crane spirit down to carry him to a city of the dead from which there is no return. As her husband's attack on her indicates, the journey into the underworld is dangerous. The Tungus people believed the shaman is attacked on their way into the underworld by other shamans who will shoot arrows at them, or by the spirits of the dead. Similarly, even shamans must travel down the side of a mountain range fending off evil spirits, and then they must squeeze through a small hole which is surrounded by wicked shamans and evil spirits who all try to capture the shaman's soul. In Europe, as already discussed, the witches from neighboring villages, and aligned with different supernatural creatures often fought battles with each other. At times, the shaman must deal with all these dangers even as they have the spirit of the person they are rescuing in tow, which can sometimes be a small child. This is likely part of the reason shamans will often put the person's soul in their ear, to keep them safe as they return to the land of the living.

More than danger, however, one gets the impression from Nisan's story that traveling through the world of the dead is a series of bartering exchanges. There are many gates, rivers, and other passages throughout the world of the dead, and Nisan was only able to buy passage across the first river of the dead because of her fame. At other gates, Nisan has to pay multiple gate guards with bean paste and paper to let her through various entrances and exits. Finally, she negotiates with Monggoldai (the servant of Ilmun Han, who took the boys soul) to promise to allow the boy to live for another ninety years. Thus, every step of her journey Nisan must negotiate with spirits in order to be successful. Bribing one's way through the beings of the land of the dead was common practice for shamans and shaman-like figures. In one story a different woman going to find her husband in the realm of Erlik Khan (the lord of the dead) has to give a drink to a man of iron who only has molten metal to drink. She has to give cakes to two fighting goats; then she has to enter a black building surrounded by a moat filled with human blood and human skin for a banner. At the door were two erliks (guardians to the realm of the dead) to whom she had to offer blood to let her into the building.

Traveling to the realm of the dead and dealing with such wicked spirits requires a lot of boldness. Nisan has to steal a soul from the lord of the dead. Further, when she was searching for the soul, she went up to the house of a spirit of death (in essence, the Grimm Reaper) and began yelling at him. When he grew angry, she merely scolded him for taking the soul of an innocent child. Yet at the same time, she has to know when to be respectful as she was with Osomi-mama, to whom she bowed.

158

Further Journeys into the Land of the Dead
While Nisan traveled through the spirit world in human form,
many other shamans will journey through the spirit world in
various animal forms. In such cases, these animal symbols
would often be present in their clothing, clothing they could take
on or off in the spirit world to change form. If they lost these
clothes, they would no longer be able to transform. The shaman
might start as an elk, searching for the right path to take
through the spirit realm. Then they might change into a bear
and still search, looking to the left and the right, change back
into an elk again who sniffs at the path. (Hoppal)

Similarly, the powerful shaman Tubyaku became a polar bear to
swim across the sea of the dead, in part to help the souls of
people escape this sea, so that they could be reincarnated.
Other shamans will turn into birds in order to ascend to heaven
or into diving birds in order to descend through water from the
sky. In a Kalmyk tale, a shamanistic figure must cross a vast
desert in the form of a donkey.

Crossing water and or vast wildernesses is an important theme
for entering the land of the dead, as the oceans and rivers act as
a filter keeping the weaker and decrepit shamans out, for only
the strong may cross it. In one story, a young shaman
encounters an old shaman on the shores of a rapid river. The
older shaman is no longer able to cross the river, so the young
shaman must leave him standing on the shore. This then may
be how the story of a shaman 'ends,' with the shaman as an old
man standing on the shores, no longer able to enter the other
world, no longer able to see their friends in the spirit world or
help those around them. However, truth be told, this is not
exactly an end as shaman's souls are reincarnated into other
shamans, so the cycle will begin again. Nevertheless, this is a
tragic ending for someone who was likely once revered and
powerful.

Another common feature of entering the other world is
encountering the people, who live very much like people would
in the human world. This same young shaman comes to a chum
(teepee-like tent) with whom he speaks; enabling him to learn
that this family is poor and starving. He promises to sacrifice a
reindeer for them so that they may eat when he returns to the
human world. The key point to understand here is that those in
the other world often need aid from those in the human world,

159

for they have poor and a need for resources just as we do. One must always use caution when encountering these spirits of the other world, however, for any of them might be dangerous. Another young man on his spirit journey, for example, encounters the daughters of an underworld owner of the ice. These spirits comb his hair for him, and because they rendered him service instead of him giving them service, they gain power over him. There is an important lesson for a shaman to learn from this, and that is to always give something to the spirits of the other world so they will owe you a favor, rather than the other way around.

Spirit Journeys within the Mortal World

Spirit journeys didn't always take place in the spirit world, for many witches sought to learn about or accomplish things within the mortal world. When this was the case the witch would send their soul out across the world.

Witches would often send their spirit double from their body in order to spread evil, disease, and pain. In Scotland the elves would carry people into the sky, where they would travel about invisibly and shoot magical arrows at people and animals. Those these arrows struck would suffer disease, phantom pains, deformity, and death. The Mora of German and Slavic regions would leave their bodies in order to sit on sleeping people's chests and suck the life from them. Other sorcerers would leave their bodies in order to curse weddings so that the bride and groom would suffer unhappiness.

It's rarely ever stated outright why the witches should wish to do these evil deeds. Many if not most evil beings, from werewolves to witches, were often viewed as serial killers; they caused suffering because they enjoyed it. In this sense their motivations could be explained as one would attempt to explain those of a serial killer. Others, however, were doing what they did out of revenge, to hurt communities that were enemies of theirs, to steal life for power, etc. Perhaps the strangest motivation of all was to appease and befriend dark deities and wicked fairies. This could be done simply as a way to obtain power, but it could also be done to keep these beings from becoming even more destructive than they were. One man who was traveling with the fairies in Scotland killed a farmers prized cow, in order to keep the fairies from killing the farmers daughter. Others would take people to feed to the dark spirits so that these would be appeased, and would go on a rampage, devouring the entire village or even whole worlds.

Types of Fairy tale adventures

One might undertake a spirit journey for numerous regions, to obtain knowledge, to gain a philosophical understanding of the world, and more. Yet the most common reasons for undertaking a spirit journey included rescuing someone and obtaining wealth. Both these reasons are common in fairy tales themselves.

Recovering a Soul, Rescuing a Familiar Spirit, Rescuing a Nature Spirit

People often journeyed to the spirit world to rescue someone, with recovering the soul of a person from otherworldly beings being among the most common reasons why a shaman figure would enter the other world in Siberia. There are many fairy tales which have similar themes; "The Corpse Watchers" is an Irish fairy tale about a woman who gains the help of a fairy to travel through dangerous lands and bring back the soul of a man who has died. "The Drummer" is the story of a man who encounters a spirit woman who is trapped in a distant mountain. In the Russian fairy tale "The Terrible Dunk" a boy's father is taken into hell by the 'devil' or at least a figure who is called such. The boy has the opportunity to visit the devil in hell and perhaps rescue his father;

> Next day Petrusha set off on his visit to the Devil. He
>   walked and walked, for three whole days did he walk,
> and then he
>   reached a great forest, dark and dense--impossible even
> to see
>   the sky from within it! And in that forest there stood a
> rich
>   palace. Well, he entered the palace, and a fair maiden
> caught
>   sight of him. She had been stolen from a certain village
> by the
>   evil spirit. And when she caught sight of him she cried:
>
> "Whatever have you come here for, good youth? here
> devils abide, they will tear you to pieces."

Petrusha told her how and why he had made his appearance
  in that palace.

  "Well now, mind this," says the fair maiden; "the Devil will
    begin giving you silver and gold. Don't take any of it, but ask
    him to give you the very wretched horse which the evil spirits
    use for fetching wood and water. That horse is your father.
    When he came out of the kabak drunk, and fell into the water,
    the devils immediately seized him and made him their hack, and
    now they use him for fetching wood and water."

Doing as he is told Petrusha is able to lead the horse his father has become out of hell and turn him back into a human by hanging a cross around his neck. An even more arduous journey is found in the Norwegian story "East of the Sun, West of the Moon."

Not all journeys need to arduous or long, however, for the fairies and the spirits of the dead are often people's neighbors. Indeed, there are many tales when one only needs to go to a hill or a cross-roads to rescue the person they love. In the Scottish Ballad of Tam Lin

Even assuming such stories are related to spirit journeys its challenging to know there exact meaning. A shaman would go into the spirit world and need to rescue either a potential helping spirit, a nature spirit, or a person's soul, and it is often hard to tell the difference between these three beings, at least in the stories about them. In one Naini tale for example, a boy lives with his sister on the taiga, when his sister is kidnapped, and the boy must go and rescue her. According to the teller of this tale, the sister in this story was in fact the boys helping spirit. Thus, even when a story explicitly calls someone a princess, a lover, a husband, wife, brother, or sister, it still might be referring to a helping spirit, or nature spirit. This is demonstrated by a story from Kalmykia (in European Russia) in which a shaman figure has to rescue someone who is in truth a rain spirit, without whom the rain will not fall. Of course the people hearing the story aren't really supposed to understand it, or at the very least they need to tease the meaning out of it, for it was wrong to directly discuss spirit journeys and the sacred. Regardless of whether it was a soul or a familiar that the character in a fairy tale must rescue the stakes are again real. For those entering the spirit world can die if they fail, and if the soul isn't recovered the person will die, and if the familiar spirit isn't rescued it too may die. Further, should a shaman fail to obtain or rescue their familiar spirit they may not be able to support their village in war, obtaining food, or healing the sick. In essence, failure to rescue the helping spirit or nature spirit could result in catastrophe for a community, and sometimes an entire nation.

To Steal

Among the most common tales are those of people stealing from the fairy world. Northern Europe is filled with glass cups which were supposedly stolen from fairies, trolls, elle folk, etc. Even King Arthur traveled into the other world on a magical boat in order to steal things like a magical dog or magical cauldrons. These are the heist stories of the past, for n fairy tales, and even mythology deities and humans alike stole form the other world through trickery, more than through strength. In one story Loki would turn into a female horse in order to seduce a male horse, and in addition to aiding in the theft of magical objects would ultimately give birth to the horse that Odin rode. In other tales Zeus would turn into an eagle to fly over potential enemies and steal magical fruit. For the shamans in these stories, being clever, and unconventional was more important than being strong and following the norms of society.

Tricksters were important in these stories, because while they broke social morality, and often annoyed their neighbors, they were able to steal the things that humanity or their fellow deities needed from the otherworld.

Witches and Shamans

The terminology of magic users in the English language is confusing because words like sorcerer, magician, enchanter, warlock, witch, and more could all be used interchangeably or for different purposes from one writer to another. Because of this there is no agreed upon definition for most magical terms. Sometimes a witch could be any person who utilized folk religious ideas to work magic, other times it was strictly those who used magic to cause harm. I choose to be more specific when I use the term witch. For the purposes of this book, when I use the term witch I'm speaking of a European practitioner of shamanistic techniques.

To further clarify I name witches who specifically worked for the kindlier fairies as cunning folk and those which worked for those beings which were likely to be cruel as hexes (the German word for witch). While cunning folk has become fairly accepted as a term for those who practiced magic for the good of their community, hexe isn't typically used, I use it now because of the need for a term to refer to the more wicked beings and the words relation to fairy tale witches who ate children. All witches were human, however, for any cunning folk could perform cruel deeds and any hexe could perform good ones.

In lore witches were much more than simply humans, they often became supernatural beings and fairies in their own right. Indeed, much of the natural world could, at various times be attributed to them. Heyl collected a story in which a hunter was eating when a storm sweapt over him. Angry the hunter threw his knife into the storm, but couldn't find it after. Later the man discovered that his knife had struck a young girl who was a witch, for she had become the storm. In other cases the 'good ladies' of Central Europe who would visit people's homes and night, make certain they had cleaned, worked hard, had pure water, etc. were human women traveling with a goddess like being. Thus, these witches took on the same role as fairies did in Britain and Ireland.

Obviously transforming into storms and animals doesn't make one a fairy, but it is also interesting to note that witches could be kept at bay by garlic, hazel branches, and similar objects, just as if they were fairies and vampires. This isn't to say that such witches were exactly the same as most of the other members of fairydom, just that they were often no longer seen as entirely human (Kropej)

Becoming a Shaman

The Shaman's Sickness and the Initiatory Journey

Many shamans in Siberia, Asia, and the Americas would become violently ill and begin acting strangely when the spirits first came to them, for the spirits would often torment them during their first few days or even years as a shaman. There were multiple reasons for this, the first of which was that people often didn't want to become shamans. Being a shaman requires a lot of work, spirit journeys are often dangerous, the shaman becomes an outsider within their own village, and they run the risk of being accused of performing wicked magic – even in places like Siberia, Asia, and the Americas. Thus, people would resist the call of the spirits, who did not take no for an answer. The Spirits would torment and torture the shaman until they finally gave in and began to shamanize. The second reason people often suffered when they first encountered the spirits was as a form of initiation, the transformation from a normal human to a shaman.

Although this shaman's sickness isn't discussed as clearly in the record of European witches, there is evidence for it. Pocs, 2009 states of new witch shamans that;

> Such a person becomes weak or ill, either physically or mentally. If they survive, they have the power of healing, soothsaying, and the ability to contact the afterworld. This motif may be found in a number of tales of South Slavic and the Balkan peoples as well as those from Central Europe.

> South Slavic folktale "Stanko and the Fairy" narrates about a shepherd named Stanko, who played beautifully on his shepherd's flute. When the Angelus bell tolled he did not start to pray but instead played the melody on his flute, and was punished. A Fairy appeared before him, and from that moment on he could not find peace any more. The fairy was following him like a shadow, even when he ate or slept. Neither the priest nor the

165

witch doctor could help him. Totally deranged, he was finally found stabbed in a cave.

> People who had been lured to remote places by the fairies returned to their homes only with great difficulty, and were physically or mentally afflicted. Some of them returned only after three hundred years, thinking that only a day has passed. (Kropej)

European fairytales especially reflect the suffering of those who initially encounter the fairies. There are some stories of people running off into the woods after they overcome fairies, or acting strange after encountering fairies. Fairy tales are full of tales of sickly people and fools who manage to gain power with the help of animals or other denizens of the other world. In Georgia a forest goddess named Dali also causes madness in those she loves:

> Ms.Eter Oniani from the village of Sasashi, Lentekhi Region recollects that in her childhood, Dali fell in love with her neighbor and turned him into a lunatic. The man used to sleepwalk at nights, go to the forest and get back with his clothes torn and himself scratched all over, though he remembered nothing about it. When he died, terrible screaming and wailing was heard from the graveyard. The appalled villagers went to his grave number of times, but never found anybody there. Finally, they concluded that it was Dali, mourning over her deceased lover (Meskhia).

Here again, encountering an otherworld creature leaves a person with almost exactly the same symptoms as the Shaman's sickness further east. Of course, in Europe, where shamanizing and giving into the forest spirits and hags wasn't an option most would accept, it would make sense for more and more of these stories to end in death, or in torment until the person's dying day.

Consider the story of Yallery Brown, in which a man frees a little man named Yallery Brown, who continually begs the man to give him work, and tortures the man when he refuses. There are also similar tales of Puks in Germany who will torture those who don't give them work. Another woman in Russia picks up a rock

166

which is connected with a Leshey (king of the forest) who then torments her until she agrees to work with him.

The initiatory aspect of the illness is shown in Siberia by the immense pain those going on their first spirit journey's often suffer.

> "Then his two guides, the ermine and the mouse, led him to a high, rounded mountain. He saw an opening before him and entered a bright cave, covered with mirrors, in the middle of which there was something like a fire. He saw two women, naked but covered with hair, like a reindeer. Then he saw that there was no fire burning but that the light came from above, through an opening. One of the women told him that she was pregnant and would give birth to tow reindeer; one would be the sacrificial animal of the Dolgan and Evanki and the toher that of the Tavgi.

> Then the candidate came to a desert and saw a distant mountain. After three days' travel he reached it, entered an opening, and came upon a naked man working a bellows. On the fire was a caldron "as big as half the earth." The naked man saw him and caught him with a huge pair of tongs. The novice had time to thing, "I am dead!" the man cut off his head, chopped his body into bits, and put everything in the caldron. There he boiled his body for three days.

The naked man who cut apart this person and boiled him, later put him back together and taught him how to shamanize. There are also stories of people being eaten and regurgitated with new bodies, being burned in fires, being eaten by maggots, and more.

European stories about those entering the spirit world rarely feature characters who come back to life after being eaten or cut to pieces, although these are present to an extent European spirit journeys tend to feature the threat of being eaten and the need for the protagonist to be cunning, kind, or hard working in order to succeed. These stories of cunning, kindness, and hard work under threat of death are present outside of Europe of course, but the stories of rebirth are far less common within

167

Europe. This is one of the biggest differences I can see between European shamanistic traditions and those of other regions. That rather than remake the witch the magical beings of European fairytales want them to prove their worth.

Consider, for example, stories like those in which a girl is forced to live with Baba Yaga;

A farmer lived with his wife and daughter for some time when his wife suddenly died. So the farmer married another woman and had a second daughter. And while the woman loved her own daughter, she made the orphans life miserable for her step daughter. So the farmer thought and thought of how he might help his daughter and so he eventually brought her into the forest, driving on until he sees a hut with chicken legs. "Hut, hut, look into my face and turn your back to the woods," the farmer tells the hut which then turns around allowing the farmer to enter where he found Baba Yaga.

"It smells of Russians," Baba Yaga said.

The farmer bowed down to her and said: "Baba Yaga with the wooden leg, I bring you my daughter to be your servant."

"All Right," Baba Yaga agreed. "If you serve me well, I'll reward you."

So the girl's father took his leave and went home.

Baba Yaga then gave the girl a spindle to spin flax and ordered her to heat up the kitchen furnaces so that they would be ready for her return.

The girl was at the furnaces wondering how she could spin as she worked them when she began to weep bitterly. A mouse ran up to her.

"Girl, girl why are you crying? The mouse asked." If you give me some sweet, sweet porridge, we'll give you some good advice."

So the girl gave the mice some sweet porridge.

"Put a spider on the spindle to spin your thread," the mice advised the girl.

"Are you finished with everything?" Baba Yaga asked when she returned home some time later.

The girl had finished with everything so Baba Yaga praised the girl and gave their precious Aleid. When

168

Baba Yaga went out again she gave the girl even harder tasks. So once more the girl began crying and the mice ran up.
"Beautiful girl, why are you crying? Give us sweet porridge and then we'll give you good advice," the mice promised.

Other's are imprisoned within fairyland for a long time, such as in the Mari-El fairy tale of "The Serpent and the Shepherd;"

A man had lived as a shepherd all his life. One day as he brought his flock out to feed he fell into a giant dungeon like snake hole which was inhabited by a giant snake who was the queen of the snakes. All summer the shepherd was held in the dungeon, but when autumn came the snakes began to gather in the hole with each licking a giant stone.
Hoping that licking the stone would help him in some way the man licked the stone as well and so gained the ability to understand the snake language. So as winter passed he was able to understand what the snakes were saying among themselves.
Then after three years the leader of the snakes released him warning him not to tell anyone he could speak the language of the beasts or he would die.

Although different from stories about people being cooked, eaten, sliced up, etc. the above story does show the terror which a person often experiences when they go on their first spirit journey. It also illustrates very well the importance of kindness to even the tiniest of beings in the spirit world, for survival in the spirit world almost requires the help of magical beings.

The Life of Witches

Although there were some witch-shamans who could obtain great fame and power, most were by in large very ordinary people, who were chosen by the fairies to learn magic and about the spiritual world. In fairy tales, these people are very often depicted as fools whom people make fun of, the youngest sibling who is completely unaware of the world. Or they are depicted as

169

the kindest and most gentle of people. Records of witch trials and memorates of them indicate that they were often the most desperate of people within a community, or that they had very ordinary jobs.

A person might be chosen by the fairies at any time; some chosen were middle-aged, or older, others were in their younger teens. These people could be chosen for many jobs, ranging from herding the fairy's cattle to fighting in wars or playing sports for the fairies. Others would act as mediators with the fairy world in order to help their village, or would heal the sick and find thieves within their community. The variety of people and jobs which people involved in the fairy world could engage in makes it difficult to make hard and fast statements about them. A few interesting points of note include;

Most, but not all, witches continued to hold normal jobs. They were housewives, farmers, blacksmiths, henwives, masons, laborers, etc. Although certain professions were more likely to be associated with magic and witchcraft, specifically blacksmithing, begging, and the care of animals, especially in wilderness areas.

Since fairies needed humans to perform normal jobs, such as herd their cattle, act as nursemaids, babysit their children, etc. Many people were taken or hired by the fairies to work normal jobs.

Fairies often wanted to help the poor and communities through witches, which meant witches weren't necessarily supposed to become rich off of the work they did to help others.

Shamanism becomes less socially acceptable the more stratified a society is. That is, within societies with large cities and powerful kings, people tend to start to view shamans in a more negative light. This is in part because shamans can threaten the status quo, the rich, and the powerful. This is why nations like Japan outlawed shamanistic activities because such people could cause revolutions. After all, the shaman can, at any time, state that the deities do not like the current king or some other person of power and so cause them to be overthrown. Even in Christian Europe, those communicating with angels, saints, or god often did so in order to ferment revolution. The France Joan of Arc lived in was being contested by three different potential kings. Under the guidance of angels, she chose to support the king that the lord of her region of France opposed. Thus, the reason her lord turned her over to the English and that they executed her.

What this means is that the larger and more stratified the society of a fantasy world you create, the more likely they are to frown on shamanism in general. Thus, the reason Rome and Greek city states were quick to condemn witches. Of course, any society might execute witches for fear that they were working for the darker fairies such as the Unseelie Court, or engaged in cannibalistic spirit journeys. Yet even when people feared and burned witches, "The cunning folk were both feared and admired. They could measure, bless, and show again, cure illness and, through reading, prevent injuries or make them better. In addition, they could stop blood, calm runaway horses and a lot more... The cunning folk did both good and bad" (Kristensen 1934).

Tangherlini (2000) points out that;

> given the fact that so few cunning folks were brought to court on charges of witchcraft, even in spite of the very thin line that separated the cunning arts from witchcraft, one must conclude that the benefit to the local community of having the cunning person as a local resource to help with curing illness and reversing misfortune outweighed any potential liability associated with their continued presence. In addition, the possibility for community censure -perhaps in the form of seeking out another cunning person -coupled to the strong corrective factor represented by the threat of execution for crossing the line over to deliberately malicious acts were apparently sufficient to keep most cunning folk on the straight and narrow.

Even during the middle ages, and other times when witchcraft itself was illegal, there were many who still operated openly as cunning folk. Such people could of course still be arrested, and even charged with using magic, though often for them the punishment was banishment rather than death. Russia is especially known for rarely ever executing those who performed magic, recognizing that they were most likely to work for nature spirits rather than 'devils.'
The benandanti of Italy managed to survive for generations, escaping the notice of authorities who might punish them, until such time as they accused someone of crimes that

Here again, we see that those engaged in shamanistic activities walked a thin line within a stratified society. For they could quickly be punished for angering the wrong person. What's more, society itself became better able to punish such people by ending their support for them.

> Competition among cunning folk was certainly a well-known aspect of the rural economic landscape as attested by records from this period. A clear example of such competition may be found in the case of Birthe Jensen. Although her practice developed quite quickly after her purchase of "den kloge mands bog" [the cunning man's book] she soon encountered difficulties because many felt that she had cheated them out of their money. A neighboring cunning man saw Jensen's plummeting popularity as an opportunity to eliminate a competitor and began suggesting that Jensen was, in fact, a witch. Soon, Jensen found herself the subject of a latter-day witch hunt, that in fact was "a well thought out conspiracy against the unsuspecting Birthe, which was set in motion by another local cunning woman who had less success with her business and was therefor envious and hateful towards her. She schemed to have Birthe chased away and thus get her out of the way." While not always as intense as in this case, the competition among cunning folk and debates among their customers concerning who had the better cunning person apparently acted as an impetus for the perpetuation of stories about witches and witchcraft (Tangherlini).

The precarious situation in which cunning folk found themselves in stratified societies meant that they lived with constant anxiety that they might be accused by another cunning folk or someone else who didn't like them. Yet at the same time, at least in many societies, most of them were never accused of anything, and so were able to ply their magical trade through their whole lives.

Folk Religions & Magic

People of the past believed that their world was steeped in magic, or perhaps it would be more accurate to say that they

172

didn't separate the world into magical and non-magical as much as we do in the modern day. Nearly every activity had some magico-religious tradition associated with it. There were certain days that were better for spinning thread, for farming, for gathering herds. Songs were sung while churning milk to ensure that it formed into better butter. Thus, in the past, nearly everyone performed a constant series of rituals to improve their odds of success and to see the future, rituals that we might consider magical, but which they didn't. Even the simple act of hanging a horseshoe in order to keep out evil spirits could in some ways be thought of as magical. Magic was something that everyone did without thinking about it. Shaman Witches were often the preservers of the knowledge of this magic, often learning it from the fairies themselves. In general, folk religious magic was such a big part of daily life that understanding it is important to understanding a person of the past's daily activities. One could almost think of using magic in the past as being somewhat akin to using computers in the modern day. Almost everyone uses them to the point that you can't talk about life today without talking about computers and cell phones. Even so, there are only a few people who have truly mastered their use.

Defining the term magic is more challenging than one might think because there is a lot of debate about the definition of this term and doing so, a minefield filled with scholarly criticism and disdain. Many scholars believe that we shouldn't use the term magic at all, for ancient peoples didn't use it in the way we would think. Take the medieval era for example. During this time, there were believed to be two forms of what we might think of as magic, neither of which they thought of as magic in the same way we would. These two forms of magic were demonic magic which involved summing magical beings to perform certain tasks or drawing on the power of demonic beings, and natural magic – using the laws of nature to get things to happen.

Natural magic is tricky because, at that time, it wasn't exactly thought of as magic. Natural magic; "were properties which could not be explained by medieval scientific knowledge but were nonetheless believed to be a part of the natural world, and not reliant on demons to make them work: one classic example was the power of the magnet to attract iron." (Rider)

In other words, people didn't believe that natural magic wasn't really magic; it was just science that people hadn't yet grasped. All matter was believed to be connected by spiritual and sympathetic relationships. In other words, a person could stab a nail from a coffin into a horse's footprint and hurt the horse, not because they were performing magic but because there was some force connected with death, and a force connecting the horse's footprint and the horse. Thus, people believed that there was simply some force connecting things that people didn't understand. Of course, such a force, assuming it exists, could be said to be no more magical than turning on a light, it's just the way things work. Within a Fantasy story, a good example of this comes from the anime "Full Metal Alchemist Brotherhood." In this show, the protagonist repairs a shattered radio by drawing a circle and clapping his hands. The people around him think that this must surely be magic, an idea he scuffs at. In his mind, he's a scientist, and the amazing feat he performed with the help of a circle of energy was science, not magic. Many Medieval Magicians would have understood this concept. Turning lead into gold, curing someone with a few words and a circle wasn't magic, it was simply tapping into the rules of nature. Magic to their minds was something that supernatural beings such as demons (or fairies) performed. Of course, they defined what god did as different from this as well, even if a person used rituals in order to get god to do it. So, to their mind, a voodoo doll would not have been magical, but calling on a demon to curse someone would have been.

Such distinctions are important because they explain how and why people act and react to different supernatural elements the way they did. For example, the medieval notion of magic as something performed by supernatural beings explains why alchemists often worked openly, and Queen Elizabeth had Nostradamus working in her court, while people burnt witches. Today, we might view this as hypocritical, but as magical as the things Nostradamus did might seem, some people considered them more akin to science.

The Romans had a different but similar view of magic. Magic to their mind was prayers and religious formulas which were done for selfish purposes. Thus, a prayer to help you win a competition was magic. Yet, a similar prayer to help your city win in a competition was religion. The Romans, in this case, frowned on the use of magic for selfish ends. Despite this disapproval, people would constantly pray for their own success and hire priests and others to do it as well. It was even believed that one could act as a divine lawyer through rituals, and essentially manipulate deities into doing something against their will using divine rules and laws.

The Greeks defined magic as the use of a tool with special powers, such as a wand and potions, or the use of secrets which were taught to a person by a deity. Similarly, the Yupik people believed that magic was a song or ritual a person learned from supernatural beings, which only one person could perform. Once the owner of a magical ritual taught this magic to someone else, they could no longer use it, for it now belonged to the person they'd taught. This made their magical researchers far more secretive than they were in much of Europe (although the cunning folk of England had similar ideas which explain why they were so secretive). Defining how magic works, and what it is not only helps to define what your characters can do, it helps to explain society's reaction to wizards and magic.

Of course, given the primary purpose of this book, I define magic a little more loosely than many would find acceptable for more scholarly journals. For the purposes of this book, magic is defined as "a means of taking control using forces which aren't well understood, and wouldn't be viewed as possible today." This would mean that stabbing a nail into a horse's footprint would be magical but magnetism. This would also mean that while summoning fairies and demons might have certain religious connotations, it's still magic, because people believed that they could control these things. On the other hand, praying would not be magical because it wasn't a matter of taking control but of asking for help and often giving oneself over to a higher power which a person trusted in.

Magical rituals of many sorts were historically used as tools for economic and social gain. Because of this, magic was tied closely to a society's economy. It's the ability to actually control outcomes that made magic extremely appealing for ancient peoples. So, appealing that Christian priests had to perform what amounts to magical rituals to heal the sick, bring luck, drive off evil spirits, help the crops to grow, etc. in order to compete with and eventually replace the previous pagan rituals. Nearly all ancient religions included a system of obtaining supernatural power in order to help people combat sickness, famine, and other dangerous forces. "The claim to supernatural power was an essential element of the Anglo-Saxon Church's fight against paganism." (Thomas)

Sacred things, in general, were often associated with magical energy. Thus, everything associated with the church, from the key for the door to the soil around the building was believed to have some magical power. Coins taken out of the offertory were

175

believed to act "as a cure for illness or a lucky charm against danger."

Magic wasn't just about survival; however, it was also a way to interact with the metaphysical, to connect with the divine. Many of the spells within folk religions were about controlling spiritual matters such as the afterlife. For example, in Ireland, people would sprinkle holy water on the clothes of a person who had died and give these clothes to poor people who would wear them for three Sundays in a row, sprinkling holy water on them each Sunday. This allowed the deceased person to have access to the spiritual version of these clothes (Curtin). Cunning folk would also often avoid swallowing sacramental wafers so that they could sneak them home to use in potions to cure sickness and drive off evil spirits. People believed that once something was imbued with religious powers, the 'magic' could be used for other purposes.

In the past, many people didn't consider such activities as magic, exactly.

What's important to understand is that all people had the power to influence supernatural forces. A person could prevent a leprechaun from using their magic by looking at them, for example. In a German tale, a man was able to thwart a powerful magical being by drawing a simple circle of chalk.

The Stolen Sheets
A Butcher from Lake Constance was returning from buying cattle when he saw three fine white sheets drying in a field. He couldn't figure out how they got so far from anyone, and so, he picked them up and brought them home with him.

That night he heard someone knocking at his window. He thought it was boys playing a prank, so he ignored it at first, but the knocking continued, again and again. Finally, he got up and went to the window to see who it was. He found outside three zwerg who told him that he'd taken their sheets and that he needed to return them to the hedge the next night or else he would die. The man was afraid of going out to the hedge at night where the zwerg were, so; he went to the minister who told him that after he'd finished hanging the sheets, he needed to draw a circle of chalk around himself so that the zwerg could not get him. That night he did exactly as the minister had told him, then, when the clock struck twelve; he saw the three zwerg come for their sheets.

One of the zwerg told him that he was lucky he was standing in his circle of chalk; otherwise, they surely would have killed him.

The person in this story wasn't a wizard, but he was able to use magic against a powerful being effectively. As already mentioned, magic was something that nearly everyone did. To cure whooping cough, they would hold a frog over a child's mouth three times at a holy well and finally put the frog in the water. The frog would swim away, taking the child's disease with it. To get a better grasp of this, I'm going to zero in on the Irish concept of piseogs.

Piseog is a difficult concept to understand. As with many ancient magical terms, it has no similar word in modern English. At its most simplistic level, Piseogs can be thought of as superstitions surrounding supernatural events. This meant that it could be anything from the fairy's theft of milk to spells to steal the fertility of a neighbor's fields. An event from a little over a hundred years ago will give some idea regarding one particular piseog based concept that could be useful for writers.

> A cattle drover named William Murphy, of Rahill, near Cahir, was brought forward in the custody of the constabulary on a charge of having unlawfully entered the lands of John Russell of Coolapoorawn, Ballyporeen, for the purpose of performing an act of witchcraft on the latter's cattle. Old tradition affirms that May morning was the one particular morning of the year on which sorceries of this kind - called Piseogs - could be practiced with the most success. Those who dread such evil influences on their cattle and property frequently remain up all night on guard. (Journal of the Cork Historical and Archaeological Society)

In modern times, people often make the mistake of focusing only on the dark aspects of piseogs, for example. "The Intendent" stated that;

> Piseogs were a kind of pagan curse, applied mainly by women that could wreak havoc on the unsuspecting farmer. They caused hens not to lay, crops to fail or butter not to keep. By putting rotten meat or eggs on a neighbors' land, it was ensured he had no produce. Putting them in the barn resulted in dry cows. Eddie

177

Lenihan described them as the Irish equivalent of Caribbean voodoo. "People used to believe that there was only a certain amount of luck to go around." Piseogs are evil magic, the working of badness on your neighbors or the taking away of his luck to add to your own luck," he explained. He revealed that on May Eve between midnight and dawn, the women would creep on to the neighbor's land and use a cloth to skim the dew from the grass, which she would use to do her bad work. Placing raw eggs on the neighbor's land was said to reduce his crop and increase your own. Placing raw meat on another man's crop would ruin his crop.

The Independent

However, the Independent is both right and wrong in their depiction of piseogs.. On the one hand, piseogs can be used for evil purposes. However, they are not "evil magic." Piseogs are simply magic and magical ideas. Piseogs include the notion of carrying a rabbit's foot for luck or a badger's tooth to improve your chances of winning a competition. As the Irish Examiner points out;

> Piseogs, or superstitions, are an extension of folk medicine and the Doctrine of Signatures also applies to them. If an animal or plant resembles an organ of the body, then, according to the famous Doctrine, it offers a cure for ailments of that organ. Likewise, the special qualities of an object will be transferred to a person who carries it. Oaks live to a ripe old age; keep an acorn in your pocket, and some of that longevity will rub off on you.

The problem is that people typically only write about the darker aspects of piseogs, just like the news now focuses primarily on negative events. But as already stated, piseogs could be about medicine, about helping people, and perhaps most significantly, they were a way of making good food, a way of growing food, of helping cows and more. Often Piseogs were passed along from mother to daughter through generations as women were the ones who traditionally handled the milk and therefore controlled the magical knowledge of transforming it into great butter and cheese. Traditional Irish Butter is so much more than a chemical process; it's a magical one as well.

Perhaps, what's most interesting for fantasy writers is the hundreds of little things people did to ward off dark influences and gain luck. Tying a red ribbon around a cow's tail, dressing boys up as girls on May Day Eve to keep the fairies from harming them, putting shoes on the wrong feet to make wild fairies think you were one of them. Each of these things is more than a cultural antidote, these ideas tell us something about the fairies as well, from their relationship to the color red, to the fact that they were particularly likely to kidnap boys to be their children when they were free to roam the countryside tells us how much they needed to raise children to help them fight their wars, and the fact that putting on ones' shoes backward would make them think of a person in a better manner tells us that they lived in a world which was somewhat backward from our own.

Piseogs and other folk-religious magic weren't the only forms of magic people believed in. Yet, even the more complex forms of magic were open to nearly anyone who could understand how to perform them. Consider, for example, the story of one boy who became a werewolf:

> One day a boy noticed that an Austrian soldier passing through his town was a werewolf, so, the boy stole his magical book. The Austrian tried to find out where the book was, but no one could tell him anything, so he had to leave without it. The boy zealously read the book in order to learn the art of turning into a wolf. A few years later, he would turn into a wolf and creep into people's houses in order to steal their ham, butter, eggs, etc.
> At home, he told a maid that if a wolf came at her, she should throw her skirt at him and it would leave her alone. One day, a large grey and red wolf came running at her, and she threw her apron at him. The wolf fell on the apron. Later, she noticed that the boy had a bit of this same apron in his mouth. When the boy's mother found out about this, she grew enraged and threw his book into the fire.
> After this, the boy disappeared into the forest and wasn't seen again in his village. There was talk from a neighboring castle that a Baron had started to lose many sheep to a wolf which couldn't be killed as each bullet would fall harmlessly to the ground without hitting the animal. Finally, the Baron got a silver bullet which had

been blessed. At last, the Baron was able to shoot the wolf which turned into an injured man who begged for his life. (Gredt)

One should note that in this story, the boy first thought when he got this book of magic was essentially, "how can I steal delicious food." So, whether a person used simple folk magic or more complex forms of magic, the economy and protection were two of magic's primary functions. Another man would change into a werewolf in order to spy on his workers to make certain that they were working hard so that he could make the maximum amount of profit possible. As a result, this wizards understanding of magic made him rich. Indeed, as I already mentioned in "The Devil's Bargain" section of this book, many people used the supernatural world to become rich. Thus, magic could have a huge impact on society. Consider also the fact that many of the spells in expensive spell books from the Middle Ages included ways to overthrow the leaders at court. There was a group of Scottish nobles who were accused of trying to use one of these spells to murder the Queen. In China, it was common to use spells to try to overthrow the emperor, and in ancient Germany, magico-religious figures would use rituals to ensure their tribe won in war. Imagine what a society would look like where a king could be assassinated by his angry nobles using a magical ritual, where the lepers could use magical potions to conquer a nation as people once believed nearly happened, or where a neighbor could cause someone they hated to grow sick and die. The fact that people believed all these things were happening explains why nearly every society in history would execute or arrest people for committing murder with the use of magic.

Another pillar of magic were chants and charms which were essentially prayers to fairies, deities, saints, and other spirit world powers. Black, in his book on Shetland folklore, provides a good example of one such 'spell' to chase away nightmares.

Arthur Knight
He rade a' night,
Wi' open swird
An' candle light.
He sought da mare;
He fan' da mare;
He bund da mare
Wi' her ain hair.

180

And made da mare
Ta swear:
'At she should never
Bide a' night
Whar ever she heard
O' Arthur Knight.

In this case, the spell is basically a story about Arthur hunting
down one of the witches who causes nightmares in people. This
explains, in part, why chanting scripture verse became a
common form of magic, for stories of sacred beings could have
power within the world. Among the Saxons, the sun was
originally an important part of such spells as shown by the spell
to recover stolen items in which a person would worship and
bow three times towards the east (the sun) and say three times;

The cross of Christ will bring it back from the east.

(Godford Storms – Anglo Saxon Magic)

Obviously, Christian elements were often added to such spells,
but nevertheless, the elements related to the worship of the
requesting power from the sun remains. Opposing the ideas of
gaining good from the sun, moving against the sun in its
opposite direction could be done to call on dark forces, and
doing so accidentally round a certain hill might bring these dark
forces without one expecting it. In either case, spells were often
either a request from, or an attempt to manipulate otherworldly
forces. Here again, witches, with their closer connection to the
spirit world, are more skilled at these.
Most spells are for daily activities, to prevent being stung by
wasps and bees, to help butter churn properly, to aid in hunting
and farming. Indeed, spells were often as much a part of daily
life as turning on a light is today. There were, of course, spells to
stave off sickness, bring fortune, see the future, etc., which
might be done with more thought and concern. For many of
these, such as to cure a child sick with whooping cough, a
person might go to the hobhole, to seek help from the fairy
within. In Russia, a person might call on the fairies to help them
win a fight or perform any number of tasks. In "Sleeping
Beauty," the king and the queen traveled to the sacred wells,
where fairies had been believed to dwell, in order to get
pregnant. Thus, the magic people often worked the hardest to
seek was from fairies.

The Relationship with the Familiar Spirit

Not all witches had a familiar spirit. Many would go on spirit
journeys with fairies, or with a deity of some form, but didn't
have a specific spirit which helped and guided them. Yet for
many others, the familiar spirit was an important part of their
lives. There were a number of forms this relationship could take.
Often times the familiar spirit would be sent by the fairy king or
queen to act as a teacher and guide for the witch. In this case,
the familiar was, to a limited degree in charge of the
relationship, as a teacher with a student. Of course, as in the
case of Bessie Dunlop's familiar spirit Tom Reid, so long as the
fairies were kindly, they might not force the witch to do
something they weren't comfortable with. What's more, they
would form a sort of friendship.

Also common was the notion that the familiar spirits were
desperate to work for and with a human. In this case, the
familiar spirits acted a little like servants or the witch's unruly
children. However, they did demand that the witch give them
work. The witch couldn't simply send them away, or even be
tired when the fairies were ready to do something, for these were
unruly children with the power to torture the witch should the
witch make them unhappy.

There were also bad relationships, in which the familiars had
tormented the witch into submission, and would even force the
witch to do evil. Many witches would talk about pleading with
god to help them escape the influence of such evil spirits.

In all these cases the witch often relied on the familiar spirits for
their magic. Indeed, in some cases, it seems that the witch
themselves had very little or no magic, but was simply passing
the potions along that the fairies made. They would almost all
consult with the fairies on spells and illness.

> In the early fifteenth century, Agnes Hancock, for
> example, claimed that she 'freely consulted the
> subterranean people whenever she felt in need of advice
> or information' and yet her professional specialism was
> in the diagnosing and curing of sickness caused by fairy
> malevolence (Wilby).

It's important to keep in mind that the familiar spirit would often have many of the same traits and motivations that any fairy did. They would be shy, not wanting to interact with anyone but their witch, thus the reason they likely chose to work through a single person, rather than acting on their own. Second, just as some fairies could be spirits of the dead, so could familiars. The spirits of dead uncles, people who'd died in battle, and others have all become the familiar spirits of witches. Such familiar spirits, although ghosts, still worked for the Queen of the Fairies or some other powerful fairylike figure and so were essentially a type of fairy.

The familiar spirits connection to the fairy realm is an additional reason why understanding the nature of these beings is important to understanding spirit journeys. The familiar spirits, after all, were many of the witches guides on their spirit journeys. Even when not guiding the witch on spirit journeys, it was essentially the familiar spirit that made the witch magical. Yes, just as other people could learn magic from books or in other ways, the witch could as well, but those witches that had familiar spirits tended to receive diagnoses of illnesses and the cure from these same familiars. Indeed, frequently when the witch would need to perform some task, they would often call upon their familiar spirit for information on the spell, or even to perform the magical task for them.

The close working relationship between the familiar spirit and the witch meant that in most cases they appear to have become friends, with the pet and master relationship so often depicted in the modern day nowhere to be found. Indeed, the familiar didn't typically appear to live with the witch; rather, they tended to live nearby. They would come when the witch called for their help, or appear at various other times for a variety of reasons, but were otherwise more akin to a co-worker, and very occasionally a roommate who might live in a section of the witch's home but still had their own lives. Exactly what the familiar spirit did when they weren't with the witch is never stated in memorates or stories, which is again why it is a good idea to understand the fairies in general in order to get a better understanding of them. One can imagine the familiar spirit Tom Reid, who was skilled at potions and seemingly obsessed with knowledge and philosophy studying and debating these with other fairies. One can picture more mischievous seeming familiar spirits playing pranks on the witch's neighbors as fairies often did.

Familiar Spirits in Siberia

Another shaman on his first spirit journey was guided by a girl spirit to a woman whose face was hidden from him. She gave him a thin reindeer as his first helping spirit. Though he quickly gained others such as an eight-legged reindeer known as Hotarie. He went on further spirit journeys to get helping spirits and;

> He got an iron reindeer from the Tenth god, a hornless reindeer from the Frosty god, a water-girl from the Mistress of water, seven sun girls from the Mistress of sun, seven women with dogs from the Smallpox god and an iron horse from the Westerly god (Aado Lintrop)

> Buryat shamans formed a very intimate relationship with their spirits helpers, as we learn from R. Hamayon's interpretation they could even enter into sexual relationships. The whole shamanic session, with its increasing speed of drumming, consist of symbolic motions altogether comparable to sex (Hoppal)

A Kalmyk man encountered a swan maiden whom he married, and she clearly acted like a helper spirit giving him knowledge of how to search for things in the spirit world and gifts with which he could negotiate with the spirits in the spirit world. Indeed many of these spirits knew or were related to this man's spirit wife, making his quest much easier than it would have been for most shamans. The story of the swan maiden who marries a shamanistic figure illustrates an important point, which is that, in many ways, the story of how someone seeks out and marries an animal spirit, a bear, a tiger, a fish or the like can be one type of story of obtaining a spirit helper.

In other cases, the helping spirit is;

> The spirits of shamans-ancestors, who at first reveal themselves to the devotee and force him to shamanize. More frequently they are supernormal beings, who were in close relations with the former helping spirits of a shaman-ancestor. The Gilyak researcher Taksami wrote: "The boy named Koinyt, whose father - the shaman - died not long ago, fell asleep in the afternoon and began

184

suddenly to toss about and cry, repeating typical shouts of shamans. After waking, he looked pale and tired. In his dream, he saw two spirits - a man and a woman, who said: "Before we played with your father, now we would play with you." (Aado Lintrop)

This leads to an interesting point that on the one hand, helping spirits often had a natural affinity for the shaman. So much so that they would attach themselves to the shaman at random, driving the shaman crazy for a time. The spirits who did this demanded that the person become a shaman and were very persistent about this too, those people who refused to work with them, who refused to become shamans would be tormented until they did, or killed if they refused long enough. For example:

A Kirghiz shaman Suimenbai told: "My grandfather and grandmother were shamans like my father and mother. When my father died, spirits (jinn) chose my elder brother Keregebai to be their master. But Keregebai desired not to become a shaman. This cost him dearly - his dead body was found behind the winter house. The second brother Sarynzits did not want to become a shaman too. Someday, he rode on ambling horse and suddenly cried: "Jinn, jinn!" The horse carried him into the steppe. In their way, there was a well; brother tumbled off the horse and broke his neck. I was then 30 years old. Someday, I went to seek for camels. It was a time of sunset. I went into bushes. Suddenly I saw that there was a coming multitude of mullahs from one side; from the other side approached a herd of warriors. I was frightened and lost consciousness. It was over midnight when I awoke and went home. My hands trembled, and I felt giddy. At home, I lied down and heard how jinn spoke: "Let's take Suimenbai to be our master."

In another case, a man was traveling by reindeer pulled sleigh when he came to a brook that was known to be the home of many spirits. These spirits began to whistle and shout at him, causing him to shiver as if water had been spilled on him. At the sound of the spirits, his reindeer grew frightened and stopped short of the brook. Soon after his reindeer team takes him to some unknown place and nearly frozen, he lays down to fall asleep; he is in essence dying. Then there was the sound of a

185

thunderclap and a beautiful young man riding a white horse appears. His voice was like an arrow shot with great strength; he saved the shaman from freezing to death and in return demanded that he become a shaman (Pentikainen, Juha)

The Witch's Sabbath and the Journey to Fairyland

Many witches would go to celebrations with the fairies and the demons. In modern times, these celebrations have come to be called Witch's Sabbaths, although this is a relatively new term, one which is frequently used to describe the more demonic celebrations. Interestingly the wicked celebrations tended to occur in the woods, on hills, at crossroads, or in empty churches. In other words, the wicked beings were likely to celebrate within the mortal world, or at least in the more shallow parts of the otherworld connected to it. Good fairies, on the other hand, tended to celebrate under hills, within fairyland itself. The exact reason for this isn't exactly clear, and certainly, good fairies could be seen celebrating on hills at times, but the cunning folk weren't usually described as celebrating with them when they did. This might have to do with the devils general association with the forest and wilderness. Fairies that helped people did live in liminal spaces, but the wildest and cruelest of them lived in the deep woods, whereas the good fairies generally seem to have lived closer at hand.

The celebrations with otherworldly beings reflected many celebrations of the time, and earlier times – feasting, dancing, and music as a way to build social cohesion, a way to form friendship, create loyalty towards the host, and emotionally unwind. Yet there was often another purpose for these celebrations – to learn magic and plot. Hexes would, of course, receive evil potions, poisons, and curses from the devil and his kin, asking them to go forth to use these to cause suffering in the world. The hexes' celebrations would also involve the eating of human flesh, the kissing of the devil's anus, and orgies. Some of these symbols are far older than Christianity, and even the Christians were accused of holding similar celebrations at one time. In general, with such stories, the more horrifying the better. Of course, one would expect the darkest creatures to enjoy inverting decency.

Cunning folk would receive potions to heal, and lessons on doing so. Here, people might encounter the spirits of the dead, and it may be that the celebrations in fairyland have their start in shaman's going to commune with the spirits of the dead. Such communication can provide many advantages, both related to the shaman's emotions who may be able to once more speak with loved ones who have moved on, and in gaining advice. In either case, good or bad, the journey to celebrate with each other and magical beings was an important part of many witches lives, although there are some cunning folk who were afraid to enter fairyland to take part in these and could refuse to do so as their fairy allies would allow them some level of agency. Hexes, however, had to do as they were told.

Folklore Sources Consulted

Abbott, G. F. (1976) Macedonian Folklore. Folcroft, PA: Folcroft Libr. Ed

Abercromby, John (1898) Magic Songs of the West Finns.

Achilli, A., Rengo, C., Battaglia, V., Pala, M., Olivieri, A., Fornarino, S., ... Torroni, A. (2005). Saami and Berbers—An Unexpected Mitochondrial DNA Link. American Journal of Human Genetics, 76(5), 883–886.

Aldhouse-Green, Miranda and Aldhouse-Green, Stephen (2005) The Quest for the Shaman: Shape-Shifters, Sorcerers and Spirit Healers in Ancient Europe. New York, Thames & Hudson.

Africa, Thomas W. (1970) The One-Eyed Man against Rome: An Exercise in Euhemerism. Issue 19 pp. 528-538, Historia: Zeitschrift für Alte GeschichteBd.

Andrews, Alfred C. (1949) The Bean and Indo-European Totemism. American Anthropologist New Series, Vol. 51, No. 2 (Apr. - Jun., 1949), pp. 274-292

Andrews, Elizabeth (2011) Ulster Folklore. Gutenberg.org: http://www.gutenberg.org/files/37187/37187-h/37187-h.htm#Fairies_and_their_Dwelling-places3

Anthony, David W. (2007) The Horse, the Wheel, and Language: How Bronze-Age Riders from the Eurasian. Princeton University Press

Asbjørnsen, Peter Christen, Jørgen Engebretsen Moe, and George Webbe Dasent. (1900) Popular Tales from the Norse. London: G. Routledge

Atkinson, J. C. (1891) Forty Years in a Moreland Parish. London: Macmillan and CO.

Baader, Bernhard (1851) "Alp," Volkssagen aus dem Lande Baden und den angrenzenden Gegenden (Karlsruhe: Verlag der Herder'schen Buchhandlung

Bain, R. Nisbet (2009) Cossack Fairy Tales and Folk Tales. Gutenberg.org: http://www.gutenberg.org/files/29672/29672-h/29672-h.htm

Balfour, M. C. (1904) Examples of Printed Folk-lore Concerning Northumberland. London: David Nutt.

Balzer, Marjorie Mandelstam (2009) Flights of the Sacred Symbolism and Theory in Siberian Shamanism. American Anthropologist. Vol 98, Iss 2, p. 305-318

Bandellow, Joseph A. and Cohen, Doy Patterns of Individualism and Collectivism Across the United States, Journal of Personality and Social Psychology, 1999, Vol. 77, No. 2, 279-292

Barber, Richard (2004) Myths and Legends of the British Isles by Richard Barber. Rochester, NY: Boydell Press

Bartlett, Sarah (2009) The Mythology Bible: The Definitive Guide to Legendary Tales. Sterling

Baumeister, Roy F. and Bratslavsky, Ellen (2001) Bad Is Stronger Than Good. Review of General Psychology, 2001. Vol. 5. No. 4. 323-370

Behringer, Wolfgang (2000) Shaman of Oberstdorf: Chonrad Stoeckhlin and the Phantoms of the Night. University of Virginia Press

Berezkin, Yuri (2005) The Black Dog at the River of Tears': Some Amerindian Representations of the Passage to the Land of the Dead and their Eurasian Roots. Anthropological Forum 2. St. Petersburg: Peter the Great Museum of Anthropology and Etnography (Kunstkamera); European University at St. Petersburg, pp. 174-211.

Beza, Marcu (1928) Paganism In Roumanian Folklore.
https://archive.org/details/paganisminrouman009481mbp

Biti, Vladimir & Katusic, Bernarda & Lang, Peter (2010) Märchen in den südslawischen Literaturen

Black, George Fraser (1903) County Folklore Vol. III – Orkney & Shetland Islands. London, UK: David Nutt.

Blackburn, Barry (1991) Theios Anēr and the Markan Miracle Traditions. Tübingen : J.C.B. Mohr

Bloomfield, Maurice (1905) Cerberus, The Dog of Hades.
http://www.gutenberg.org/files/19119/19119-h/19119-h.htm

Blumenthals, Verra (1903) Folk Tales From the Russia. Rand, Mcnally & Company.

Bock, E Wilbur (1966) Symbols in Conflict: Official versus Folk Religion. Journal for the Scientific Study of Religion Vol. 5, No. 2 (Spring, 1966), pp. 204-212 Published by: Wiley

Bottigheimer, R. B. (1986) To Spin A Yarn: The Female Voice in Folklore and Fairy Tale. In Fairy Tales and Society. Philadelphia: Univ. of Pennsylvania Press, pp. 53–74.

Bottrell, William (1873) Traditions and Hearthisde Stories of West Cornwall.

Boyer, Pascal (2008) Bound To Believe. Nature Vol 455, 23 p. 138-1039

Breeze, Andrew (2007) Britannia, Volume 35, p 228-229.

Briggs, K. (1959). The Fairy Economy. As It May Be Deduced from a Group of Folk Tales. Folklore, 70(4), 533-542. Retrieved from http://www.jstor.org/stable/1258225

Briggs, Katharine Mary (1967) The Fairies in Tradition and Literature. London, UK: Routledge

Briggs, Katharine (1968) Folktales of England. Chicago: University of Chicago Press

Briggs, Katharine Mary (1976) An encyclopedia of fairies: hobgoblins, brownies, bogies, and other supernatural creatures. New York, NY: Pantheon Books.

Briggs, Katharine Mary (1978) The Vanishing People.: Fairy Lore and Legends. New York, NY: Pantheon Books.

Brodman, James (2009) Charity and Religion in Medieval Europe. The Catholic University of America Press

Brown, M. S. (1966) Buried Horse-Skulls in a Welsh House. Folklore Vol. 77, No. 1 (Spring, 1966), pp. 65-66 Published by: Folklore Enterprises, Ltd.

Brown, Norman Oliver (1947) Hermes the Thief; The Evolution of a Myth. Madison, WI: University of Wisconson

Bruchanov (1991) Грузинские народные сказки. Ростовское книжное издательство: http://skazki.yaxy.ru/52.html

Bryant, Adam (2013) A Boss's Challenge: Have Everyone Join the 'In' Group. The New York Times: http://www.nytimes.com/2013/03/24/business/neuroleaders hip-institutes-chief-on-shared-goals.html?pagewanted=1&_r=0

Bulbulia, Joseph and Slingerland, Edward (2012) Numen, Vol 59, Iss 5-6, 564-613

Bunce, John Thackray (2005) Fairy tales their orgin and meaning. Gutenberg. Org: http://www.gutenberg.org/files/8226/8226-h/8226-h.htm

Campbell, John Gregorson (1900) Superstitions of the Highlands and Islands of Scotland. Glasgow, England: James MacLehose and Sons.

Carey, John (1983) Irish Parallels to the Myth of Odin's Eye. Folklore, Volume 94, Issue 2, 1983

Carmichael, Alexander (1928) Carmina Gadelica Hymns and Incantations. Edinburgh, UK: Oliver and Boyd

Ceng, Joey T., Tracy, Jessica L., & Anderson, Cameron (2014) The Psychology of Social Status. Personality & Social Psychology

Chaucer, Geoffrey (2011) Caterbury Tales. Amazon Digital Services, Inc.

Collins, Richard (2006) Paws and the power of piseogs:. The Irish Examiner. https://www.irishexaminer.com/lifestyle/outdoors/richard-collins/paws-and-the-power-of-piseogs-16967.html

Conrad, Joseph L. (2001) Male Mythological Beings Among the South Slavs. Folklorica

Craigie, William Alexander (1896) Scandinavian Folk-lore: Illustrations of the Traditional Beliefs of the Northern Peoples. Detroit, Singing Tree Press

Crawford, John Martin (1888) The Kalevala.

Croker, Thomas (1834) Fairy Legends and Traditions of the South of Ireland. LONDON: John Murray.

Crossing, William (1890) Tales of the Dartmoor Pixies. Amazon Digital Services, Inc.

Curry, Andrew (2013) Archaeology: The milk revolution When a single genetic mutation first let ancient Europeans drink milk, it set the stage for a continental upheaval. Nature, 500

Curtin, Jeemiah (1895) Tales of the Fairies and of the Ghost World. Boston: Little Brown & Company.

Czaplicka, Mari Antoinette (2004) Shamanism in Siberia. Kessinger Publishing.

Dando, William (2012) Food and Famine in the 21st Century.

Daniels, Cora L. M. & Stevens, C. M. (1903) Encyclopaedia of Superstitions, Folklore, and the Occult Sciences of the World. Chicago: J. H. Yewdale & sons Company

Dasent, George Webbe (1906) Popular Tales from the Norse and North German. London: Norrcena Society

Davidson, Hilda Roderick Ellis and Chaudhri, Anna (2006) A Companion to the Fairy Tale. BOYE6

Deguignet, Jean-Marie (2004) Memoirs of a Breton Peasant. Seven Stories Press

Denning, Kathryn (2009) Ten Thousand Revolutions: Conjectures About Civilization. Acta Astronautica, Volume 68, Issue 3, p. 381-388.

Dequiqnet, Jean-Mari (2011) Memoirs of a Breton Peasant. New York: Seven Stories Press

Deusen, Kira Van (2001) The Flying Tiger: Women Shamans and Storytellers of the Amur. Mcgill-Queen's Native and Northern Series

Dewing, H. B. (1914) Procopius. https://archive.org/details/procopiuswitheng01procuoft

Djordjevic, Tihomir R. (1903) Die Zigeuner in Serbien: ethnologische Forschungen.

Dorcey, Peter F. (1989) The Role of Women in the Cult of Silvanus. Numen Vol. 36, Fasc. 2 (Dec., 1989), pp. 143-155

Douglas, George (1901) Scottish Fairy and Folk Tales. New York: A. L. Burt Company, Publishers

Eirik the Red's Saga. https://archive.org/details/eiriktheredssaga17946gut

Eller, Cynthia (2001) The Myth of Matriarchal Prehistory: Why an Invented Past Won't Give Women a Future. Beacon Press

Elliot AJ, Pazda AD (2012) Dressed for Sex: Red as a Female Sexual Signal in Humans. PLoS ONE 7(4): e34607. doi:10.1371/journal.pone.0034607

Ellis Davidson, H. R. & Ellis Davidson, Hilda Roderick (1989) Myths and Symbols in Pagan Europe: Early Scandinavian and Celtic Religion. Syracuse, NY: Syracuse University Press

Emerson, P. H. (2003) Welsh Fairy-tales and Other Stories. Gutenberg.org: http://www.gutenberg.org/files/8675/8675-h/8675-h.htm

Fairbanks, Arthur (1900) The Chthonic Gods of Greek Religion.

Fansler, Dean S. (1921) Filipino Popular Tales. http://www.gutenberg.org/files/8299/8299-h/8299-h.htm

Fee, Christopher R., & Leeming, David A. (2004) Gods, Heroes, & Kings : The Battle for Mythic Britain: The Battle for Mythic. New York: Oxford University Press

Fillmore, Parker (2010) Czechoslovak Fairy Tales. Gutenberg.org: http://www.gutenberg.org/files/32217/32217-h/32217-h.htm

Frater, Jamie (2014) Listverse.com's Epic Book of Mind-Boggling Lists: Unbelievable Facts and Astounding Trivia on Movies, Music, Crime, Celebrities, History, and More, Ulysses Press

Frazer, James George (2003) The Golden Bough : a study of magic and religion. Gutenberg.org: http://www.gutenberg.org/dirs/etext03/bough11h.htm

Gar, Azar (2000) The Human Motivational Complex: Evolutionary Theory and the Causes of Hunter-Gatherer Fighting. Part I. Pri-mary Somatic and Reproductive Causes. Anthropological Quarterly Vol. 73, No. 1, pp. 20-34

Gat, Azar (2000) The Human Motivational Complex: Evolutionary Theory and the Causes of Hunter-Gatherer Fighting, Part II. Proximate, Subordinate, and Derivative Causes. Anthropological Quarterly Vol. 73, No. 2 (Apr., 2000), pp. 74-88

Gathorne-Hardy, Jonathan () The Rise and Fall fo the British Nanny.

Ghirotto S, Tassi F, Fumagalli E, Colonna V, Sandionigi A, et al. (2013) Origins and Evolution of the Etruscans' mtDNA. PLoS ONE 8(2): e55519. doi:10.1371/journal.pone.0055519

Gianakoulis, Theodore P. & Macpherson, Georgia H. (1930) Fairy Tales of Modern Greece. Boston, MA: E. P. Dutton & CO

Ginzburg, Carlo (1966) The Night Battles: Witchcraft and Agrarian Cults in the Sixteenth and Seventeenth Centuries. Routledge.

Gibbings, W. W. (1889) Folk-Lore and Legends, Scotland. Gutenberg.org: http://www.gutenberg.org/files/17071/17071-h/17071-h.htm

Gimbutas, Marija (1974) Lithuanian God Velnias. Myth in Indo-European Antiquity

Gjorgjevic, Tihomi R. (1903) Die Zigeuner in Serbien: ethnologische Forschungen. Budapest: Thalia

Goodman, Katherine (1992) In the Shadow of Olympus: German Women Writers Around 1800. State Univ of New York P

Gorman, Marianne (1993) Influences from the Huns on Scandinavian Sacrificial Customs during 300-500 AD. The Problem of Ritual. Vol 15

Grautoff, Otto (1916) Die Baltischen Provinzen: Märchen und Sagen. Felix Lehmann Verla.

Graves, Robert (1992) The Greek Myths. Penguin Books

Gray, L. H. (1918) The Mythology of All Races Vol. III. Marshall Jones Company

Gredt, N. Sagenschatz des Luxemburger Landes, gesammelt

Green, Miranda (1996) The Celtic World. Routledge Worlds

Gregoricka LA, Betsinger TK, Scott AB, Polcyn M (2014) Apotropaic Practices and the Undead: A Biogeochemical Assessment of Deviant Burials in Post-Medieval Poland. PLoS ONE 9(11): e113564. doi:10.1371/journal.pone.0113564

Gregory, Lady (1920) Visions and beliefs in the west of Ireland. New York and London: G. P. Putnam's Sons.

Griffis, William Elliot (2005) Welsh Fairy Tales. Gutenberg.org: http://www.gutenberg.org/cache/epub/9368/pg9368.html

Grimberg, Carl (1924) Svenska Folkets Underbara Berättelser. Stockholm, Sweden: L. J. Hjerta.

Grimes, Heilan Yvette (2010) The Norse Myths. Boston, MA: Hollow Earth Publishing.

Grimm, Jacob (1882) Teutonic Mythology. Londan, UK: George Bell and Sons.

Grimm, Jacob and Grimm, Wilhelm (2008) Gutenberg.org: http://www.gutenberg.org/files/2591/2591-h/2591-h.htm

Griswold, De Witt (1991) The Religion of the Ṛigveda. Motilal Banarsidass Publishers Private Limited

Gross, JH (2012) Toward a Neurobiological Understanding of Religion: Examining Ritual and the Body.

Grossberg, Lawrence and Polloc, Della () Cultural Studies 11.3. Routledge

Grummond, Thomson de (2006) Etruscan Myth, Sacred History, and Legend.

Guerber, H. A. (1988) Myths and Legends of the Middle Ages. Crescent

Guidera, Anita (2012) http://www.independent.ie/irish-news/land-of-the-fairies-28815367.html.

Gyula Pap (1896) The Folk-Tales of the Magyars. Zeluna.net

Haas, Alfred (1903) Rügensche Sagen und Märchen: Gesammelt und Herausgegeben. J. Burmeister

Hart, Terese B. and Hart, John A. (1986) The Ecological Basis of Hunter-Gatherer Subsistence in African Rain Forests: The Mbuti of Eastern Zaire. Human Ecology, Vol 14, No 1

Hartnup, Karen (2004) On the Beliefs of the Greeks: Leo Allatios and Popular Orthodoxy. Leiden, The Netherlands: Brill Academic Pub

Hartland, Edwin Sidney (1890) English Fairy and Other Folk Tales. London: The Walter Scott Publishing Co.

Hartland, Edwin Sidney (1891) The science of fairy tales : an inquiry into fairy mythology.
https://archive.org/details/scienceoffairyta00hartiala

Headland, Thomas N. and Reid, Lawrence A. (1989) Hunter Gatherers and Their Neighbors from Prehistory to the Present. Current Anthropology, Vol 30, 1

Headland, Thomas (1999) Could 'Pure' Hunter-Gatherers Live in a Rain Forest? http://www-01.sil.org/~headlandt/wildyam.htm

Hedeagera, Lotte (2007) Scandinavia and the Huns: An Interdisciplinary Approach to the Migration Era Scandinavia and the Huns: An Interdisciplinary Approach to the Migration Era. Norwegian Archaeological Review Volume 40, Issue 1, p 42-58

Heesterman, J. C., Van Den Hoek, Albert W., Kolff, Dirk H. A., and Oort, M. S. (1992) Ritual, State, and History in South Asia: Essays in Honour of J.C. Heesterman. Brill

Heikkila, Mikko (2013) From Surging Waves to the Spirit of Waves – On the Germanic and Sami Origin of the Proper Names Ahti and Vellamo in Finnic Mythology. SKY Journal of Linguistics, Vol 26, p 71-86

Hellman, Roxanne and Hall, Derek (2011) Vampire Legends and Myths. New York: Rosen Publishing Group

Henderson, Lizanne & Cowan, Edward J. (2001) Scottish Fairy Belief. Google eBook

Henderson, William (1879) Notes on the Folk-Lore of the Northern Counties of England and the Borders. London: W. Satchell, Peyton and CO.

Hofberg, Herman (1890) Swedish Fairy Tales

Homer (1999) The Odyssey. (Samuel Butler. Trans) Gutenberg.org: http://www.gutenberg.org/ebooks/1727

Hori, Ichiro (1994) Folk Religion in Japan: Continuity and Change (The Haskell Lectures on History of Religions.

Horizon Research Foundation. http://www.horizonresearch.org/main_page.php?cat_id=275

Horsley, Richard A. (1979) Further Reflections on Witchcraft and European Folk Religion. History of Religions Vol. 19, No. 1 (Aug., 1979), pp. 71-95 Published by: The University of Chicago Press

Hultkrantz, Ake (1987) On Beliefs in Non-Shamanic Guardian Spirits among the Saamis; The Donner Institute

Hunt, Robert (1908) Popular Romances of the West of England; or, The Drolls, Traditions, and Superstitions of Old Cornwall. London: Chatto & Windus.

Hutton, Ronald (2001) The Triumph of the Moon: A History of Modern Pagan Witchcraft Paperback. Oxford University Press

Hyde, Douglas (1890) Beside the Fire : A Collection of Irish Gaelic Folk Stories. London: David Nutt.

Independent (2012) Land of Fairies:.
https://www.independent.ie/irish-news/land-of-the-fairies-28815367.html

Ivanits, Linda J. (1992) Russian Folk Belief. Armonk, NY: M.E. Sharpe.

Jackson, Georgina Frederica (1883) Shropshire Folk-lore: A Sheaf of Gleanings, Part 1. Trübner & co.

Jacobs, Joseph (2004) English Fairy Tales. Gutenberg.org: http://www.gutenberg.org/files/14241/14241-h/14241-h.htm

Jacobs, Joseph (2011) Folklore, Volume 13. Ulan Press

Jana, Reena (2009) Innovation Trickles in a New Direction. http://www.bloomberg.com/bw/magazine/content/09_12/b41 24038287365.htm

Jegerlehner, Johannes (1907) Was die Sennen erzählen: märchen und sagen aus dem Wallis. Budjdruckerel Buhler & Werder

Jettmar, K. (1986) The Religions of the Hindukush 1: The Religion of the Kaffirs. Aris & Phillips

Johns, Andreas (2004) Baba Yaga: The Ambiguous Mother and Witch of the Russian Folktale. International Folkloristics

Johnson, Walter (1912) Byways in British Archaeology. https://archive.org/details/bywaysinbritisha00johniala

Jolly, Karen Louise (1996) Popular Religion in Late Saxon England: Elf Charms in Context. The University of North Carolina Press

Kuhn, A. and Schwartz, W. (1846) Mahrt gefangen," Norddeutsche Sagen, Märchen und Gebräuche No. 16, p. 14-15

Kaplan, Robert (2006) The Neuropsychiatry of Shamanism. http://www.academia.edu/3549088/The_Neuropsychiatry_of_S hamanism

Keightley, Thomas (1892) The Fairy Mythology. London, UK: George Bell and Sons.

Kelly, Robert L. and Thomas, David Hurst (2012) Archaeology. Cengage Learning

Kelly, Walter Keating (1863) Curiosities of Indo-European Tradition and Folk-lore. Chapman & Hall

Kennedy, Patrick (1866) Legendary Fictions of the Irish Celts by Patrick Kennedy. London Macmillan and CO.

Keyser, Rudolph (1854) The Religion of the Northman. New York: Charles B. Norton.

Khachapuridze, Luiza (2015) Dali, Tkashmapa and Related Beliefs on the Basis of Present Day Materials Recorded in Upper Samegrelo Svaneti:. Book of Scientific Works of the Conference of Belief Narrative Network of ISFNR 1-4 October 2014, Zugdidi

Kieckhefer, Richard (1998) Forbidden Rites: A Necromancer's Manual of the Fifteenth Century.

Kirby, W. F. (1894) The Hero of Esthonia. London: John C. Nimmo

Kucharz, Christel (2009) The Real Story Behind van Gogh's Severed Ear. ABC News. http://abcnews.go.com/International/story?id=7506786&page=1

Kukharenko, Svitlana P. (2007) Animal Magic: Contemporary Beliefs and Practices in Ukrainian Villages. University of Alberta: https://journals.ku.edu/index.php/folklorica/article/viewFile/3784/3622

Lady Isabel and the Elf Knight: http://www.springthyme.co.uk/ballads/balladtexts/4_LadyIsabel.html

Laidoner, Triin. 2012. The Flying Noaidi of the North: Sámi Tradition Reflected in the Figure Loki Laufeyjarson in Old Norse Mythology. Scripta Islandica 63: 59–91.

Lang, Andrew (1897) The Pink Fairy Book. Gutenberg.org
http://www.gutenberg.org/files/5615/5615-h/5615-h.htm

Larson, Jennifer (2001) Greek Nymphs: Myth, Cult, Lore. New
York, NY: Oxford University Press

Lauder, Toofie (1881) Legends and Tales of the Harz Mountains.
London: Hodder and Stoughton.

Lawson, John Cuthbert (1910) Modern Greek folklore and
ancient Greek religion: a study in survivals. Cambridge
University Press

Lecouteux, Claude (2003) Lecouteux, Witches, Werewolves and
Fairies: Shapeshifters and Astral Doubles in the Middle Ages.
Rochester, Vermont: Inner Traditions – Bear & Company

Lecouteux, Claude (2013) The Tradition of Household Spirits:
Ancestral Lore and Practices.

Leland, Charles Godfrey (1892) Etruscan Roman Remains in
Popular Tradition. New York, NY: Scribner's Sons.

Leung, Ak; Maddux, WW, Galinsky AD, and Chlu Cy (2008)
Multicultural experience enhances creativity: the when and how.
NCBI, Vol 63(3) p. 168-181

Lewis, Jerome (2002)
http://discovery.ucl.ac.uk/18991/1/18991.pdf

Lincoln, Bruce (1976) The Indo-European Cattle-Raiding Myth.
History of Religions, Vol. 16, No. 1 (Aug., 1976), pp. 42-65

Linden (2007) The accidental mind: how brain evolution has
given us love, memory, dreams, and God. Cambridge, MA:
Belknap Press

Linnell, J; Odden, John; Kaczensky, Petra & Swenson, Jon
(2002) The fear of wolves: A review of wolf attacks on humans.
NINA NIKU Stiftelsen for naturforskning og
kulturminneforskning

Linton, E. Lynn (1861) Witch Stories. London: Chapman and
Hall

Lonnrot, Elias (2010) The Kalevala. Gutenberg.org:
http://www.gutenberg.org/cache/epub/5186/pg5186.html

Lorrits, Oskar (1998) The Stratification of Estonian Folk-
Religion. The Slavonic and East European Review, Vol. 35, No.
85, p. 360-378

Macculloch, J. A. (1911) The Religion of the Ancient Celts.
Edinburgh, UK: Morrison & Gibb.

MacDermott, Mercia (1998) Bulgarian Folk Customs:. Jessica
Kingsley Publishers Ltd

Mackenzie, Donald (1912) Teutonic Myth and Legend
https://archive.org/details/teutonicmythandl027797mbp

Maenchen-Helfen, Otto J. (1973) The World of the Huns: Studies
in Their History and Culture. University of California Press

Magliocco, Sabina (2009) Italian Cunning Craft: Some
Preliminary Observations. Journal for the Academic Study of
Magic. Vol 5

Mallarach, Josep-Maria; Papayannis, Thymio; and Vaisanen,
Rauno (2010) The Diversity of Sacred Lands in Europe.
Proceedings of the Third Workshop of the Delos Initiative.
http://cmsdata.iucn.org/downloads/delos3_publication_the_div
ersity_of_sacred_lands_in_europe_9mb.pdf

Mallory, J. P. and Adams, Douglas Q. (1997) Encyclopedia of
Indo-European Culture. Routledge

Maple, Eric ()Cunning Murrell. A Study of a Nineteenth Century
Cunning Man in Hadleigh, Essex. Folklore Vol. 71, No. 1 (Mar.,
1960), pp. 37-43

Masson, Elsie (1929) Folk Tales of Brittany. Philadlephia:
Macrae, Smith, Company.

Matteoni, Francesca (2008) The Jew, the Blood and the Body in
Late Medieval and Early Modern Europe:. Folklore issue 119 (2)

McCall, Andrew (1979) The Medieval Underworld. H. Hamilton

McGowan, Margaret (2000) The Vision of Rome in the French Renaissance. Yale University Press

McRobbie, Linda Rodriguez (2013) The History and Psychology of Clowns Being Scary You aren't alone in your fear of makeup-clad entertainers; people have been frightened by clowns for centuries. : http://www.smithsonianmag.com/arts-culture/the-history-and-psychology-of-clowns-being-scary-20394516/#lxerAcab4j5rVJVB.99

Melton, J. Gordon (1998) The Vampire Book: The encyclopedia of the Undead. Canton, MI: Visible Ink Press.

Meyer, Kuno (1895) The Voyage of Bran, Son of Febal. London: David Nutt.

Mikhailovskii, V. M. and Wardrop, Oliver (1895) Shamanism in Siberia and European Russia, Being the Second Part of "Shamanstvo". The Journal of the Anthropological Institute of Great Britain and Ireland Vol. 24, (1895), pp. 62-10

Miller, David Harry (1993) The Case of Frankish Origins. Journal of World History, Vol. 4, No. 2, pp. 277-285

Monaghan, Patricia (2008) The Encyclopedia of Celtic Mythology and Folklore. Checkmark Books

Morrison, Sophia (1911)Manx Fairy Tales. London: David Nutt

Mortimer, Ian (2008) The Time Traveler's Guide to Medieval England. London: Touchstone

Müllenhoff , Karl (1845) Sagen, Märchen und Lieder der Herzogthümer Schleswig, Holstein und Lauenburg

Murphy, Caitriona (2011) http://www.independent.ie/business/farming/land-blessing-tradition-survives-as-farmers-seek-to-ward-off-piseogs-26729121.html

Narvaez, Peter (1997) The Good People: New Fairylore Essays. University Press of Kentucky

Näsman, Ulf (2008) Scandinavia and the huns : a source-critical approach to an old question. Journal of Swedish Antiquarian Research, Vol 103, p. 111-119

NIEHOFF, A., & ANDERSON, J. (1966). Peasant Fatalism and Socio-economic Innovation. *Human Organization, 25*(4), 273-283. Retrieved from http://www.jstor.org/stable/44125490

Nilsson, Martin P. and Nock, Arthur Darby (1972) Greek Folk Religion. University of Pennsylvania Press

Norenzayan, A., Atran, S., Faulkner, J., & Schaller, M. (2006). Memory and mystery: The cultural selection of minimally counterintuitive narratives. Cognitive Science, 30, 531-553.

Ó Giolláin, Diarmuid (1994) The Image of the Vikings in Irish Folk Legends. Sounds from the Supernatural: Papers Presented at the Nordic-Celtic Legend Symposium, pp. 163-170 Published The Folklore of Ireland Society

Olcott, Frances J. (1928) Wonder Tales From Baltic Wizards.

Oliver, Mary Beth and Sanders, Meghan (2004) The Horror Film "The Appeal of Horror and Suspense." Rutgers UP

Oppenheimer, Stephen (2007) Origins of the British: The New Prehistory of Britain. Robinson Publishing

Ostry, Elaine (2013) Social Dreaming: Dickens and the Fairy Tale. Routledge

Page, John Lloyd Warden (1892) An Exploration of Dartmoor and Its Antiquities: With Some Account of Its Borders. Seeley and Co.

Parnia, Sam; Spearpoint, Ken; de Vos, Gabriele; et al (2014) AWARE—AWAreness during REsuscitation—A prospective study. Resuscitation, http://www.resuscitationjournal.com/article/S0300-9572(14)00739-4/abstract

Patch, Haward Rollin (1918) Some Elements in Medieval Descriptions of the Otherworld. Modern Language Association, Vol. 33, No. 4 (1918), pp. 601-643

Palsson, Hermann (1999) Sami People in Old Norse Literature. Nordlit : Tidsskrift i litteratur og kultur

Paulson, Ivar (1965) Outline of Permian Folk Religion. Journal of the Folklore Institute Vol. 2, No. 2 (Jun., 1965), pp. 148-179

Petreska, Vesna (2008) The Secret Knowledge of Folk Healers in Macedonian. Folklorica: Vol 13

Petrovic, Sreten: СРПСКА МИТОЛОГИЈА http://svevlad.org.rs/knjige_files/petrovic_mitologija.html#vampir

Petrov, Vlerv (1995) Vital Energy, Spirits, and Gods in Mari Folk Medicine. Folk Belief Today, Tartu

Pettersson, Olof (1987) Old Nordic and Christian Elements in Saami Ideas About the Realm of the Dead:. Scripta Instituti Donneriani Aboensis

Philips, Sarah D. (2004) Waxing Like the Moon: Women Folk Healers in Rural Western Ukraine. Folklorica, Journal of the Slavic and East European Folklore Association.

Phelps, David (2013) Worcestershire Folk Tales

Polimen, Joseph (2003) Evolutionary Perspectives on Schizophrenia. Can J Psychiatry - Vol. 48 - Issue 1

Porter, C. C. and Marlowe, F. W. (2007) How marginal are forager habitats? Journal of Archaeological Science.

Purkiss, Diane (2007) Fairies and Fairy Stories: A History. Stroud, Gloucestershire: Tempus

Ralph P, Coop G (2013) The Geography of Recent Genetic Ancestry across Europe. PLoS Biol 11(5): e1001555. doi:10.1371/journal.pbio.1001555

Ralston, W. R. S. (2007) Russian Fairy Tales. Gutenberg.org http://www.gutenberg.org/files/22373/22373-h/22373-h.htm

Rhys, John (1901) Celtic Folklore: Welsh and Manx. Oxford: Clarendon Press.

Richards, M. P. (2002) A brief review of the archaeological evidence for Palaeolithic and Neolithic. European Journal of Clinical Nutrition, Vol 56, N 12, p. 1270-1278

Richard, M. P.; Jacobi, R.; Cook, J.; Pettitt, P. B.; & Stringer, C. B. (2005) Isotope evidence for the intensive use of marine foods by Late Upper Palaeolithic humans. Journal of Human Evolution 49 p. 390-394

Richards, Michael P.; Pettitt, Paul B.; Stiner, Mary C.; & Trinkaus, Erik (2001) Stable isotope evidence for increasing dietary breadth in the European mid-Upper Paleolithic. PNAS vol. 98 no. 11

Riordan, James (1991) The Sun Maiden and the Crescent Moon: Siberian Folk Tales. Northampton, MA: Interlink Publishing Group

Rochholz, Ernst Ludwig (1856) Schweizersagen aus dem Aargau, vol. 1, no. 222, p. 312.

Rodgers, Charles (1884) Social Life in Scotland, From Early to Recent Times. Edinburgh, UK: William Patterson.

Sager, Sumatra Steven (2008) The Sky is our Roof, the Earth our Floor Orang Rimba Customs and Religion in the Bukit Duabelas region of Jambi. A thesis submitted for the degree of Doctor of Philosophy of The Australian National University

Savina, Magliocco (2009) Italain Cunning Craft: Some Preliminary Observations. Journal for the Academic Study of Magic.

Schaefer, Charles E. (2002) Play Therapy with Adults. Wiley

Schneller, Christian (1867) Das Rothhütchen," Märchen und Sagen aus Wälschtirol: Ein Beitrag zur deutschen Sagenkunde. Innsbruck: Verlag der Wagner'schen Universitäts-Buchhandlung, 1867), no. 6, pp. 9-10.

Sebeok, Thomas Albert (1956) Studies in Cheremis: The Supernatural. New York: Wenner-Gren Foundation for Anthropological Research

Sephton, Rev. J. (1889) Erik the Red's Saga. Literary and Philosophical Society of Liverpool.

Seymour, John D. (2013) Irish Witchcraft and Demonology. Gutenberg.org: http://www.gutenberg.org/files/43651/43651-h/43651-h.htm

Sikes, Wirt (1880) British Goblins Welsh Folk Lore, Fairy Mythology, Legends and Traditions. London: Sampsons Low Marston, Searle, & Rivington.

Sky, Jeanette (2002) Myths of Innocence and Imagination: The Case of the Fairy Tale. Literature and Theology, Vol. 16, Iss 4. 363-376

Spence, Lewis (2010) Legends & Romance of Brittany. Gutenberg.org: http://www.gutenberg.org/files/30871/30871-h/30871-h.htm

Spence, Lewis (2005) Hero Tales and Legends of the Rhine. Guternberg.org: http://www.gutenberg.org/files/16539/16539-h/16539-h.htm

Speranza, Francesca (1887) Ancient Legends, Mystic Charms, and Superstitions of Ireland.

Spigel, Lynn (2001) Seducing the Innocent. Childhood and Television in Postwar America. Welcome to the Dreamhouse: Popular Media and Postwar Suburbs.

Stafford, Tom (2014) Why is all the News Bad. BBC http://www.bbc.com/future/story/20140728-why-is-all-the-news-bad

Stramberg, Susan (2007) The Color Red: A History in Textiles. http://www.npr.org/templates/story/story.php?storyId=7366503

Storms, Godfrid (1948) Anglo-Saxon Magic:. Springer; Softcover reprint of the original 1st ed.

Stroheker, Heinz, Karl & Walser, Gerold (1975) Historia: Zeitschrift für Alte Geschichte. Franz Steiner Varlog

Strong, W. D. (2009) North American Indian Traditions Suggesting a Knowledge of the Mammoth. American Anthropologist, Vol 36, Iss 1.

Stuart, John (1843) Extracts from the Presbytery book of Strathbogie. Aberdeen, Printed for the Spalding Club

Sugiyama, Michelle Scalise (2004) Predation, Narration, and Adaptation: "Little Red Riding Hood". Interdisciplinary Literary Studies Vol. 5, No. 2 (Spring 2004), pp. 110-129

Summers, Montague (1934) The Werewolf:. New York: E. P. Dutton and Company

Tacitus, Cornelisus (2012) The Germania. Gutenberg.org http://www.gutenberg.org/files/39573/39573-h/39573-h.html

Talhelm, T., Zhang, X., Oishi, S., Shimin, C., Duan, D., Lan, X., and Kitayama, S. (2014) Large-Scale Psychological Differences Within China Explained by Rice Versus Wheat Agriculture. Science 9 May 2014: vol. 344 no. 6184 pp. 603-608 DOI: 10.1126/science.1246850

Tangherlini, Timothy R. (2000) "How Do You Know She's a Witch?": Witches, Cunning Folk, and Competition in Denmark: Western Folklore, Vol. 59, No. 3/4 (Summer - Autumn, 2000), pp. 279-303

Tarmo, Kulmar (2005) On Supreme Sky God from the Aspect of Religious History and in Prehistoric Estonian Material. Folklore

Tatar, Maria (1999) The Classic Fairy Tales. Norton Critical Editions

Tatar, Magdalena (1987) *Nordic Influence on Saami Folk Belief: the "Buttercat"*: Saami Religion.

Taylor, Timothy (2007) The Real Vampire Slayers. The Independent.

http://www.independent.co.uk/news/world/europe/the-real-vampire-slayers-397874.html

Tehrani JJ (2013) The Phylogeny of Little Red Riding Hood. PLoS ONE 8(11): e78871. doi:10.1371/journal.pone.0078871

Telban, Monika Kropej (2106) Symbolic Equivalences in Belief Tales about Female Nature Spirits; Traditiones 44 (3)

Templin, Thor Heidrek The Specter of Wotan: Evolution of Proto-Indo-European God of Death. Journal of Germanic Mythology and Folklore, Issue 1
Thomas, Keith (1971) Religion and the Decline of Magic: (New York and London, Weidenfeld & Nicolson)

Thompsongaug, Derek (2012) The Case for Vacation: Why Science Says Breaks Are Good for Productivity. http://www.theatlantic.com/business/archive/2012/08/the-case-for-vacation-why-science-says-breaks-are-good-for-productivity/260747/

Thorms, William John (1865) Tree Notelets on Shakespeare

Tian-Shanskaia, O. S., & Ransel, D. L. (1993) Village Life in Late Tsarist Russia. Indiana University Press

Till, Rupert (2010) Pop Cult: Religion and Popular Music. Bloomsbury Academic

Tomlinson, Sally (2007) Demons, Druids and Brigands on the Irish High Crosses: Rethinking the Images Identified as The Temptation of Saint Anthony:. University of North Carolina at Chapel Hill

Tučkova, Natal'a Anatol'evna, Vladimir Vladimirovič Napol'skih, Anna-Leena Siikala, Mihály Hoppál, Sergeĭ Viktorovič. Gluškov, and Clive Tolley (2010) Selkup Mythology. Budapest: Akadémiai Kiadó

Tugend, Alina (2012) March 23rd, Praise Is Fleeting, but Brickbats We Recall. The New York Times, http://www.nytimes.com/2012/03/24/your-money/why-people-remember-negative-events-more-than-positive-ones.html?pagewanted=all&_r=1&

Turi, Johan (2011) An Account of the Sámi. Nordic Studies Press

Tuzelmann, von Alex (2013) The Channel Islands' Surviving Lore. BBC. http://www.bbc.com/travel/story/20130501-the-channel-islands-surviving-lore

Vadeysha, Masha (2005) The Russian Bathhouse: The Old Russian Pert' and the Christian Bania in Traditional Culture. Folklorica, Journal of the Slavic and East European Folkore Association

Uppsala University. (2009, September 25). Scandinavians Are Descended From Stone Age Immigrants, Ancient DNA Reveals. ScienceDaily. Retrieved February 17, 2015 from www.sciencedaily.com/releases/2009/09/090924141049.htm

Vajda, Edward J. (2011) Siberian Landscapes In Ket Traditional Culture. Landscape & Culture in Northern Eurasia, ed. Peter Jordan, Walnut Creek, CA: Left Coast Press, 2011. Pp. 297-314.

Vaz Da Silva, Francisco (2000) Complex Entities in the Universe of Fairy Tales. Marvels and Tales, Vol. 14 No. 2 p. 219-243

Vajda, Edward J. (2011) Siberian landscapes in Ket Traditional Culture. Landscape and Culture in Northern Eurasia.

Vandello, Joseph A. and Cohen, Dov (199) Patterns of individualism and collectivism across the United States. Journal of Personality and Social Psychology, Vol 77(2), Aug 1999, 279-292.

Västrik , Ergo-Hart (1999) The Waters and Water Spirits in Votian Folk Belief. Folklore, Vol 12 http://www.folklore.ee/folklore/vol12/spirits.htm

Veckenstedt, Edmund (1880) Wendische Sagen, Märchen und abergläubische Gebräuche

Veselica, Lajla (2006) Croatian 'Dracula' Revived to Lure Tourists. http://www.mg.co.za/article/2006-04-24-croatian-dracula-revived-to-lure-tourists

Vivian, Herbert (1908) The Perchten Dancers of Salzburg. The Wide World Magazine: An Illustrated Monthly of True Narrative, Volume 21

Vorren, Ornulv (1987) Sacrificial Sites, Types and Function

Waites, Margaret C. (1920) The Nature of the Lares and Their Representation in Roman Art. American Journal of Archaeology, Vol. 24, No. 3 (Jul. - Sep., 1920), pp. 241-261

Waller, Steven J. and Kolar, Miriam A. (2014) Shamans and Other "Magico-Religious" Healers: A Cross-Cultural Study of Their Origins, Nature, and Social Transformations. Acoust. Soc. Am. 136, 2270 (2014); http://dx.doi.org/10.1121/1.4900201

Wang, Hao-Chuan; Russell, Susan R. & Cosley, Dan (2011) From Diversity to Creativity: Stimulating Group Brainstorming with Cultural Differences and Conversationally-Retrieved Pictures. Department of Information Science, Cornell University.

Warker, N. (1890) Wintergrün sagen, geschichten, legenden, und märchen aus der provinz Luxemburg

Warner, Marina (1995) From the Beast to the Blonde: On Fairy Tales and Their Tellers. Farrar Straus & Girou

Watt, Diane (2001) Secretaries of God: Women Prophets in Late Medieval and Early Modern England. D.S.Brewer

Wigzell, Faith (2003) The Ethical Values of Narodnoe Pravoslavie: Traditional Near-Death Experiences and Fedotov. Folklorica, Journal of the Slavic and East European Folkore Association.

Wentz, W. Y. Evans (2011) Fairy Faith in the Celtic Countries. Gutenberg.org: http://www.gutenberg.org/files/34853/34853-h/34853-h.htm

Wibly, Emma (2006) Cunning-Folk and Familiar Spirits: Shamanistic Visionary Traditions in Early Modern British Witchcraft and Magic. Sussex, UK: Sussex Academic Press.

Wibly, Emma (2010) The Visions of Isobel Gowdie: Magic, Witchcraft and Dark Shamanism in Seventeenth-Century Scotland. Sussex, UK: Sussex Academic Press.

Wiessner, Olly (2014) Firelight talk of the Kalahari Bushmen: Did tales told over fires aid our social and cultural evolution? PNAS, September 2014 DOI: 10.1073/pnas.1404212111

Wigström, Eva (1881) Folkdiktning : Visor, Folktro, Sägner, Och en Svartkonstbok.

Wilde, Jane F. E. (1902) Ancient Legends, Mystic Charms & Supersitions of Ireland. London, UK: Chatto & Windus.

Winlow, Clara Vostrovsky (2014) Our Little Czecho-Slovak Cousin. http://www.gutenberg.org/files/45616/45616-h/45616-h.htm

Wlislocki, Heinrich von (1891) Märchen und Sagen der Bukowinaer und Siebenbürger armenier. Google eBook: http://google.com/books?id=dk0TAAAAYAAJ

Winkelman, Michael (2002) Shamanism as Neurotheology and Evolutionary Psychology. American Behavioral Scientist, Vol 45 No 12

Winkelman, Michael James (1990) Shamans and Other "Magico-Religious" Healers: A Cross-Cultural Study of Their Origins, Nature, and Social Transformations. Ethos Vol. 18, No. 3 (Sep., 1990), pp. 308-352 Published by: Wiley

Wood-Martin, W. G. (1902) Traces of the Elder Faiths of Ireland; a Folklore Sketch; a Handbook of Irish Pre-Christian Tradition. London: Longmans, Green, and CO.

Wratislaw, A. H. (1890) Sixty Folk-Tales from Exclusively Slavonic Sources. London Ellion Stock.

Young, Ella (1910) Celtic Wonder Tales. Maunsel & Company.

Yeats, W. B. (1888) Fairy and Folk tales of the Irish Peasantry

Zillmann, Dolf and Vordere, Peter (2000) Media Entertainment: The Psychology of Its Appeal. Routledge

Zipes, Jack (2013) The Irresistible Fairy Tale: The Cultural and Social History of a Genre. Princeton University Press

Made in the USA
Monee, IL
28 January 2024

52074464R00125